THE ECONOMIC CONSEQUENCES

OF

WORLD INFLATION ON SEMI-DEPENDENT COUNTRIES

Robert E. Looney

University Press of America™

Library of Congress Catalog Card Number: 78−65351

For Anne

PREFACE

No subject of inquiry is older and yet fresher than that of inflation. It has bedeviled governments and their economic advisers ever since the invention of money. Despite all efforts to understand inflation, there are always surprises when a new period of price increases appears; so it has been with the upsurge of inflation in the 1970s. Its most striking characteristic was its virulence, as inflation rates reached a double digit range in an increasing number of countries. This inflation has been widespread; all advanced countries and most developing countries have suffered from it. Moreover, the price increases have occurred in all countries nearly simultaneously. Thus, there is reason enough to describe the inflation as worldwide, to try to find a common source for it, and to pay increased attention to the process by which it spread among countries.

The aim of this book is to provide a description and analysis of this recent inflation, and to examine its impact on several individual countries. The writing of it has taken me far longer than anticipated when I embarked on the task in 1973. The main reason is that, during the course of writing, the rate of inflation throughout the world constantly accelerated; there was no time between 1973 and 1976 when I could finish the book, confident that my description and analysis were reasonably current. Moreover, the character of inflation appeared to undergo a significant change, forcing me continually to reappraise my ideas about its causes and consequences. Even now, it is not clear whether the deceleration which has occurred since mid-1975 represents a return to the moderate inflation of the 1950s and 1960s, or whether it is no more than a lull in the general tendency toward ever higher inflation rates.

A number of books have been written on the subject of inflation.[1] It may, therefore, be pertinent to ask "Why another one?" The justification for yet another venture into this much explored jungle in this case springs from the fact that the advantages of comparative analysis of national experience have by no means been fully utilized; most of the attempts to date have been restricted to rather general efforts to correlate a number of variables over a large number of countries, generally in a somewhat aggregative fashion and with only cursory reference to historical or institutional dimensions that shape the patterns of inflation in individual countries. Moreover, most of the studies have not examined the recent inflation in the context of a worldwide phenomena. Those that have explicitly viewed inflation in an international context have limited their analysis to one aspect of inflation--for example, the increase in world liquidity of the oil price increases of 1973-1974, or the 'worldwide wage explosion' rather than established some more complex relationships relating the various causes of inflation.

Because of the diverse nature of inflation, one study could not, of course, cover the multitude of countries. Even within the developing world, the particular characteristics of each country make generalizations a superficial exercise. Two countries, South Africa and Mexico, have been selected here, and though not typical of all they are shown to belong to a group of countries that may be referred to as semi-dependent; i.e., they are countries which are capable through domestic monetary and fiscal policy of altering somewhat the impact of world price increases on their own domestic price levels.

The significance of a new study on world inflation is that interest in the subject has been suddenly forced upon us by a series of disasters in countries where development seemed to be vigorously under way. The political crisis in Mexico, the stagnation of growth in South Africa, and the impending default of a number of governments on their international obligations can be traced directly to the acceleration in their domestic rates of inflation.

In writing on inflation there are two pitfalls to be avoided--moralism and nihilism. Some writers tend to assume that inflation is of such an evil character that it will soon destroy our whole civilization. They may be perfectly right in their judgment, but the case nevertheless needs to be argued rather than assumed.

Economists have a tendency to fall into the other trap; they are often so absorbed with the subtleties of the subject, most of all masses of statistics, that they sometimes appear incapable of making statements

iv

that have a direct bearing on the affairs of the world.

It is hoped that these problems are avoided in the chapters that follow, and that ultimately the study will be of positive value to policymakers in their attempts at controlling inflation.

Notes

1. A partial list would include: Erik Lundberg, Inflation Theory and Anti-Inflation Policy (Boulder, Colorado: Westview Press, 1977); Randall Hinshaw, ed., Inflation as a Global Problem (Baltimore: Johns Hopkins Press, 1972); Irving S. Friedman, Inflation: A World-Wide Disaster (Boston: Houghton Mifflin, 1973); Harry Johnson and A. R. Nobay, eds., The Current Inflation (London: Macmillan, 1971); Gardiner Means et. al., The Roots of Inflation (New York: Burt Franklin, 1975); V. V. Bhanoji Rao, ed., Inflation and Growth (Singapore: Samford College Press, 1974); Michael Parkin and George Zis, eds., Inflation in the World Economy (Manchester: Manchester University Press, 1976); Geoffrey Maynard and W. van Ryckeghem, A World of Inflation (New York: Barnes and Nobel, 1975); Jacob Frenkel and Harry Johnson, The Monetary Approach to the Balance of Payments (Toronto: University of Toronto Press, 1976); Lawrence Krause and Walter Salant, eds., World Wide Inflation: Theory and Recent Experience (Washington: Brookings Institution, 1977); Michael Parkin and George Zis, eds., Inflation in Open Economies (Toronto: University of Toronto Press, 1976); and David Meisleman and Arthur Laffer, eds., The Problem of Worldwide Inflation (Washington: American Enterprise Institute for Public Policy Research, 1975).

ACKNOWLEDGEMENTS

The book could not have been written without the benefit of the countless people over the years with whom I have had a chance to examine and exchange views on the economic and social problems of their countries. I am deeply indebted to these friends.

I also wish to express my gratitude to the many scholars at the University of California at Davis and the Stanford Research Institute with whom I had the opportunity to discuss various aspects of inflation during my stays there. They included particularly Professors Tom Mayer, Frank Child, and Bruce Glassburner at Davis, and Drs. Robert Davenport and Robert Brown at Stanford Research Institute. Dr. Redvers Opie of Mexico City was particularly helpful in pointing out a number of subtleties concerning the Mexican economy.

My seminar in the fall of 1977 on economic policy at the Monterey Institute of Foreign Studies provided a chance to test an earlier version of the study in a classroom situation. At Monterey, Donna Leiber was particularly helpful in commenting on parts of the manuscript. Tracy Call provided valuable help in organizing the statistical analysis.

Lastly, I owe a considerable debt to my wife, Anne, not only for typing the manuscript but also for suggesting substantive improvements to the text.

Monterey Institute of Foreign Studies
Monterey, California
August 1978

CONTENTS

LIST OF TABLES AND FIGURES

CHAPTER 1

INTRODUCTION

Introduction

We live in an increasingly interdependent world, as reflected in the rise of multinational corporations and international banking institutions. This development has added significantly to the ability of the world economy to provide a better standard of living for all; at the same time, it has reduced the ability of individual national governments to control economic developments within their own borders.

In particular economic interdependence between countries, especially between Europe and the United States, has restricted the scope of national economic policymaking. Nowhere has this interdependence been more confining than in the sphere of monetary policy.[1] Monetary linkages between financial markets have reduced the ability of national monetary authorities to conduct an independent monetary policy, and thus control the rate of inflation in their respective countries.

In a world of increased specialization among countries, the influence of internationally traded goods on the domestic economy is also rapidly expanding. Thus, when a number of developments in the world economy led to an explosion in prices of these goods, the impact on individual countries was substantial. Since the latter part of the 1960s, we have been observing such an impact.

The Problem of Inflation

The problem of inflation is one of the great recurring questions of economic theory. One reason is that inflation as an empirically observable phenomenon appears to be very different in different periods. Until the early 1960s the discussion of inflation focused on cost-push and demand-pull factors--with creeping inflation as the center of attention. Towards the end of the decade, however, the problem of continued inflation required new perspectives and induced an enormous growth in the literature. The rapid increase in inflation experienced in 1973-1975 gave

1

rise to the current round of effort expended in attempting to understand the causes, consequences, and cures of the inflationary process.

Before discussing inflation at any great length, a terminological note concerning the definition of inflation is necessary. Unfortunately neither a satisfactory nor an exact definition of inflation exists as yet. For the purposes here a pragmatic definition of inflation is adopted, inflation being looked upon as a continuous increase in the price level as measured by the consumer price index (CPI) or the GNP deflator.

Because these two measures include different items, they usually do not give precisely the same measure of price increase. Still the two give more or less the same picture as regards to trends over time. For example, an examination of price increases in the United States, West Germany, and Japan (Table 1) clearly shows that while both indices vary somewhat they show for each country similar patterns in the acceleration of inflation in 1970-1974.

Consequences of Inflation

Inflation, however measured, has had a number of important consequences. Increasing prices in the late 1960s put great strain on the international payments system which led to the general abandonment in 1971 of the system of fixed exchange rates. This was followed in 1972 and 1973 by rapidly rising commodity prices, which preceded the sudden fourfold rise in oil prices following the Arab-Israeli war. The rise in commodity prices was followed in turn by an inflation in wage settlements which augmented the general rate of increase of prices. The result was an unprecedented increase in prices and the spreading of inflation for the first time to all of the world's major economies. In the three years 1973-1975, inflation averaged 10.36 percent for the industrialized countries, ranging (for the three year period) from 24.26 percent for the United Kingdom and 24.27 percent for Japan to nearly 16 percent for Denmark and almost 10 percent for Switzerland.[2]

A unique aspect of this latest period of inflation was that it was accompanied by a marked recession in

TABLE 1

RATE OF INFLATION

(Annual average percentage change)

	Years	GNP deflator	CPI
U.S.A.	1960-1964	1.4	1.3
	1965-1969	3.3	3.4
	1970-1974	5.9	6.1
Germany	1960-1964	3.4	2.4
	1965-1969	2.7	2.6
	1970-1974	6.6	5.6
Japan	1960-1964	4.9	5.6
	1965-1969	4.7	5.3
	1970-1974	9.7	10.3

Source: OECD, Main Economic Indicators, 1960-1975 (Paris: OECD, 1976).

3

industrial production. World industrial production, which had risen at a fairly steady rate of 6-7 percent a year throughout the 1960s and by 8 percent a year in 1971-1973, was stagnant in 1974 and fell by 10 percent in 1975, accompanied by unemployment levels which had not been encountered since the 1930s.

Purpose of the Study

These developments have prompted much broad-based research. Many economists have increasingly recognized that recent inflation has been a global and not merely a national disease. Most economic research, however, still tends to reflect a national approach and to prescribe temporary, and often self-defeating, remedies. The search for a more comprehensive diagnosis and for anti-inflationary policies that really work has suffered from the continued tendency to view inflation almost solely from national perspectives.

The result has been the proliferation of various 'theories of inflation.'[3] Each theory was originally designed to explain the inflationary process in a specific country and under a specific set of circumstances.

Because the assumptions underlying these theories are rarely spelled out in detail, they appear as a set of conflicting approaches to the problem of inflation.

This study seeks to provide a basis for constructive discussion and work on the major outstanding and unsettled questions concerning the causes, consequences, and appropriate policies for dealing with inflation. As the title of the book indicates, main focus will be on the consequences of inflation. At a time when the world continues to experience relatively high and variable inflation rates, and the various schools in the economics profession continue to hold such sharply conflicting and strongly held views, the most pressing need appears to be to narrow the scope of analysis to an identifiable group of countries, which because of certain common characteristics are likely to experience similar inflationary patterns, and find that the pursuit of anti-inflationary measures through monetary and fiscal policies suffer from a similar set of limitations.

As the title indicates, the group of countries chosen for examination are called semi-dependent. Their selection and the criteria by which that selection was made account for a significant portion of the work that follows.

Questions for Examination

In pursuing our study of the inflations experienced by semi-dependent countries, the following questions are examined:

1. If U.S. monetary growth is conceded to be the cause of the increase in worldwide prices, by which channels was this impulse transmitted?

2. Did patterns of causation differ among countries?

3. Were some countries better able than others to pursue countercyclical rather than procyclical monetary policies?

4. Did differences in the manner by which countries varied in the degree of accommodation to supply checks in 1974 correspond with the degree of accommodation to wage-push or reserve inflows in earlier periods?

5. Do episodes of wage-push identified by others appear to have been genuinely exogenous or were they preceded by episodes of monetary accommodation?

6. What were the main factors responsible for the differences between the inflationary patterns in the developing countries.

Answers to these questions are useful not only for an understanding of inflationary history, but for future policymaking. Is control of the money supply either necessary or sufficient for a nation to control its inflation rate? Is it likely that the monetary authorities will be able in the future to insulate the inflation rate from the tendencies to wage-push, or are income policies required as a cure? Do certain groups of countries differ significantly with regard to answers to the above questions? And if so, why?

5

Our objective is to help achieve a clarification of the many questions surrounding the problem of controlling inflation. In so, we try to provide an agenda for discussion by attempting to identify those aspects of the inflation problem which are critical to an understanding of the mechanism by which inflation is transmitted from one country to another. In addition we are particularly concerned with the policy responses initiated by countries once inflationary pressures developed and the reasons for the success or failure of these policies in controlling inflation.

Notes

1. Richard Herring and Richard Marston, National Monetary Policies and International Financial Markets (Amsterdam: North Holland, 1977), p. 1.

2. Unless otherwise specified all data used in this study comes from the International Monetary Fund, International Financial Statistics.

3. There are several excellent reviews of the now extensive literature on inflation. See especially: Helmut Frisch, "Inflation Theory 1963-1975: A Second Generation Survey," Journal of Economic Literature (December, 1977), pp. 1289-1317; and D. E. W. Laidler and J. M. Parkin, "Inflation--A Survey," The Economic Journal (December 1975), pp. 741-809.

CHAPTER 2

NATURE OF THE CURRENT INFLATION

Introduction

The accelerated rise of wage and price levels
dating from early 1970 onward has attracted much attention because it is commonly regarded as exceptional
and outside the domain of orthodox economic theory.
Certainly the recent inflationary experience of most
countries is unusual on any historical accounting,
with both the magnitude and the duration of recent
price increases in those countries revealing a sharp
break with previous trends. The simultaneous coincidence of such rates of price inflation with high
unemployment is also unprecedented. It seems in fact
that wage increases and expectations in many countries
have become detached from the forces of supply and
demand in the marketplace, thus removing a traditional
constraint to any further inflationary spiral. It is
this which has so perplexed economists and invited so
much comment: the modus operandi of the inflation
process seems to have altered fundamentally in the
last few years, with 1973 marking a watershed in the
recent price and employment history of these countries,
particularly the developing countries.

Problems in Selecting the Proper Time Period

In addition to the problem of selecting a proper
measure of inflation, the relevant time period and
frequency of observation for examining a country's
inflationary process is also open to debate.[1]

For the problems at hand in this study, monthly
analysis seems likely to be too narrow a time period,
and in any case one which would involve a large amount
of data of questionable quality. The same is also true
of quarterly variations. To measure changes in prices
at such frequencies, particularly for the developing
countries, would result in the inclusion of random
elements in the analysis. As a general rule, the
longer the period of time over which the rate of price
change is calculated, the less it becomes subject to
the almost indefinite number of small factors which

from time to time are very important, but which over time tend to cancel each other out.

Obviously the final selection of data will depend on the precise question under consideration. By the very nature of the problem, however, the choice will be somewhat arbitrary. Decade average rates of change are very important and interesting for long-run and historical analysis; however, they are too long for a wide class of political-economic problems. This is particularly true concerning inflation in modern societies, in which the typical life of parliament or of a democratically elected administration runs for only four to five years. As a compromise between detailed monthly data and broad brush decade figures, annual consumer price indices are used almost exclusively in the analysis that follows.

Past Inflation Trends

Focusing on only the past several generations, however, it is clear that prices have risen in most countries since World War II. Earlier inflationary periods include the sharp inflation during and after World War I, and the gradual inflation from 1896 to 1914.[2]

The post-World War II period, however, has been the most widespread and persistent episode of inflation. Not only has there been no important deflation in the postwar generation on the scale experienced from time to time within the past century, but prices have risen to one extent or another in almost every one of the world's major free market countries.

During the 1950s, the importance of inflation seemed to be declining, but later the trend was reversed. During the 1960s, national income deflators in the industrial countries rose, on the average, at an annual rate of 3.57 percent between 1960-1965, and 3.79 from 1965-1968. While the rate of increase fluctuated somewhat, there was a gradual tendency for inflation to gather speed toward the end of the decade, increasing at an annual rate of 4.80 percent from 1968-1970. For a year or two this tendency was checked by the recession of 1970 and 1971, but in the following years the acceleration was rapid indeed with price

8

increases over 7 percent in 1972, 8.29 percent in 1973, 12.71 percent in 1975, and 11.85 percent and 9.77 percent in 1975 and 1976, respectively (Table 2).

Developing countries have usually had higher rates of inflation than have industrial countries, but the same rising trend is visible among them: On the whole, their consumer price indices, which had risen at an average rate of 13 percent during the 1960-1965 period, accelerated to 15.23 percent between 1970-1973, and to 31.43 percent for 1973-1976.

According to the available data, considerable variation exists in the average inflation rate in different geographical groups (Tables 3-7) of the developing countries.

In a world of fixed exchange rates and unrestricted trade, the synchronization of price movements throughout the world is to be expected. In general, countries such as Brazil, whose domestic rates of inflation have far exceeded the world average, are precisely those whose exchange rates have been unstable or which have isolated their economies behind tariff barriers.

Interpreting Recent World Inflation

A close look at the data (Tables 2-7) reveals that the current inflation is worldwide. For nearly all countries, the pattern has been a gradual increase in prices throughout the late 1960s and then their rapid acceleration in the 1970s.

It is possible to compute a world index of inflation by constructing an unweighted average of prices given in the International Monetary Fund's International Financial Statistics. The countries included are: the United States, Canada, Japan, Austria, Belgium, Denmark, France, Germany, Italy, Luxembourg, The Netherlands, Norway, Sweden, Switzerland, and the United Kingdom (Table 8). The data indicate broad conformity between the trend of the three major indicators of world inflation (the world index, average inflation in industrialized countries, and the consumer price index) and confirm the typical pattern observed of the usually lower rate of inflation in the United States with a higher rate in the industrialized countries and a still

9

TABLE 2

INFLATION IN DEVELOPED COUNTRIES, 1952-1976

(Yearly Average Rate) Country	1952- 1955	1955- 1960	1960- 1965	1965- 1968	1968- 1970	1970- 1973	1973- 1976	1973	1974	1975	1976
Australia	2.28	3.13	5.01	2.94	3.36	7.12	14.59	9.34	15.13	15.05	13.57
Austria	0.75	2.31	3.87	3.00	3.70	6.18	8.43	7.55	9.52	8.47	7.31
Belgium	0.15	1.76	2.53	3.29	3.81	5.58	11.51	7.00	12.66	12.75	9.16
Canada	0.00	1.91	1.60	3.80	3.98	5.04	9.70	7.61	10.87	10.74	7.52
Denmark	2.08	2.47	5.08	7.71	5.06	7.23	11.26	9.31	15.25	9.64	8.99
France	-0.19	5.63	3.70	3.32	6.00	6.32	11.56	7.32	13.73	11.78	9.23
Germany	0.00	1.83	2.76	2.28	2.65	5.91	5.83	6.93	6.99	5.98	4.53
Italy	2.25	1.87	4.91	2.01	4.48	7.09	17.62	10.83	19.14	16.95	16.77
Japan	3.84	1.94	6.23	4.85	6.36	7.43	14.96	11.81	24.27	11.88	9.28
Netherlands	1.94	2.71	3.34	4.31	5.47	7.78	9.55	8.02	9.66	10.20	8.79
New Zealand	3.91	2.90	2.67	4.34	5.76	8.49	14.20	8.22	11.04	14.67	16.97
Norway	2.43	2.76	4.07	3.72	6.78	6.97	10.06	7.46	9.40	11.65	9.16
Sweden	1.85	3.65	3.61	4.39	4.83	6.91	9.85	7.19	8.84	9.77	10.96
Switzerland	0.35	1.18	3.25	3.65	3.09	7.32	6.02	8.71	9.79	6.71	1.73
United Kingdom	2.25	2.40	3.31	3.74	5.88	8.55	18.90	9.13	16.03	24.26	16.59
United States	0.29	2.03	1.25	3.34	5.64	5.59	8.47	6.22	11.01	9.13	5.77
(Average)	(1.51)	(2.53)	(3.57)	(3.79)	(4.80)	(6.84)	(11.39)	(8.29)	(12.71)	(11.85)	(9.77)

Source: Computed from International Monetary Fund, *International Financial Statistics*, May 1977, January 1978.

10

TABLE **3**

INFLATION IN MEDIUM DEVELOPED COUNTRIES, 1952-1976

(Yearly Average Rate)

Country	1952-1955	1955-1960	1960-1965	1965-1968	1968-1970	1970-1973	1973-1976	1973	1974	1975	1976
Finland	0.00	6.62	5.23	5.52	3.14	8.01	16.26	10.53	16.67	18.37	13.79
Greece	9.80	2.40	1.64	2.36	2.71	7.46	17.71	15.55	26.91	13.40	13.33
Iceland	1.43	7.21	10.49	8.94	17.53	12.24	41.48	20.65	42.72	49.41	32.80
Israel	15.18	4.55	7.12	3.87	4.26	14.88	36.74	19.94	39.78	39.31	31.30
Portugal	0.64	2.07	2.62	5.54	7.58	11.84	20.45	12.91	25.16	15.25	21.16
South Africa	2.84	2.22	2.24	3.04	3.70	7.20	12.07	9.51	11.61	13.45	11.15
Spain	2.29	7.64	7.30	5.84	3.94	9.31	16.76	11.43	15.70	16.94	17.66
(Average)	(4.60)	(4.67)	(5.23)	(5.02)	(6.12)	(10.13)	(23.07)	(14.36)	(25.51)	(23.73)	(20.17)

Source: Computed from International Monetary Fund, International Financial Statistics, May 1977, January 1978.

11

TABLE 4

INFLATION IN THE MIDDLE EAST, 1960-1976

(Yearly Average Rate)

Country	1955-1960	1960-1965	1965-1968	1968-1970	1970-1973	1973-1976	1973	1974	1975	1976
Cyprus	4.32	0.29	1.58	2.38	5.58	8.08	7.78	20.65	0.85	3.77
Turkey	-	3.55	9.46	6.36	16.13	20.81	14.06	23.88	21.19	17.44
Egypt	1.44	3.23	4.49	3.58	3.17	10.29	4.27	10.84	9.70	10.34
Iran	6.85	2.00	0.60	2.65	6.82	12.77	9.82	14.19	12.79	11.34
Iraq	2.03	1.13	2.51	5.00	4.56	9.36	4.86	8.31	9.45	10.33
Jordan	-	-	-	1.69	7.58	15.61	10.47	20.00	11.98	15.00
Syria	4.07	0.48	4.50	1.53	11.52	10.96	33.37	13.41	7.69	11.87
Saudi Arabia	-	-	1.62	1.75	8.29	29.07	16.51	21.42	34.63	32.12
(Average)	(3.74)	(1.78)	(2.89)	(3.12)	(7.96)	(14.61)	(12.64)	(16.58)	(13.54)	(10.01)

Source: Computed from International Monetary Fund, International Financial Statistics, May 1977, January 1978.

12

TABLE 5

INFLATION IN DEVELOPING WESTERN HEMISPHERE, 1952-1976

(Yearly Average Rate)

Country	1952-1955	1955-1960	1960-1965	1965-1968	1968-1970	1970-1973	1973-1976	1973	1974	1975	1976
Caribbean and Central America											
Costa Rica	2.27	1.53	2.12	1.78	3.70	7.49	16.48	15.21	30.11	17.39	3.48
El Salvador	5.82	0.34	0.21	0.94	0.51	2.76	14.25	6.37	16.87	19.16	7.08
Jamaica	0.44	3.08	2.94	3.54	8.02	10.63	17.72	19.93	26.37	16.89	10.45
Latin America											
Colombia	4.98	9.38	12.34	11.15	8.47	15.23	22.45	22.79	24.38	25.70	17.43
Ecuador	1.83	-0.15	3.89	4.03	5.76	9.75	16.33	12.99	23.30	15.34	10.69
Mexico	6.17	5.88	1.87	3.13	4.48	7.29	18.46	11.16	22.51	16.85	16.12
Paraguay	36.34	12.25	5.25	-.64	0.71	8.94	11.76	13.12	25.21	6.73	4.46
Venezuela	-0.53	2.39	0.35	1.00	2.49	3.42	6.07	4.14	8.23	10.28	7.58
(Average)	(7.17)	(4.34)	(3.62)	(3.40)	(4.27)	(11.95)	(15.44)	(13.21)	(22.12)	(16.04)	(9.66)

Source: Computed from International Monetary Fund, International Financial Statistics, May 1977, January 1978.

13

TABLE 6

INFLATION IN ASIA, 1952-1976.

(Yearly Average Rate)

Country	1952-1955	1955-1960	1960-1965	1965-1968	1968-1970	1970-1973	1973-1976	1973	1974	1975	1976
India	-2.27	5.15	5.92	9.29	3.14	8.58	7.50	17.43	27.34	6.13	-8.09
Indonesia	-	-	-	-	-	13.44	25.99	31.53	40.41	19.02	19.67
Korea	51.83	10.71	14.95	11.34	11.39	8.94	21.71	3.03	23.74	26.25	15.40
Malaysia	-4.04	0.33	0.50	1.75	0.76	5.04	7.98	10.59	17.34	4.56	2.60
Pakistan	-	-	1.94	5.33	2.98	12.21	17.96	23.08	26.68	20.89	7.16
Philippines	-1.92	2.19	4.72	4.64	8.02	11.95	15.47	11.08	34.28	7.96	6.19
Sri Lanka	-0.09	0.74	1.68	2.59	6.66	6.18	6.65	9.72	12.28	6.62	1.33
Thailand	4.88	2.36	1.49	3.30	1.48	5.79	10.12	11.70	23.31	4.11	4.00
(Average)	(8.07)	(3.58)	(4.46)	(5.46)	(4.92)	(9.02)	(14.17)	(14.39)	(25.67)	(11.94)	(6.03)

Source: Computed from International Monetary Fund, International Financial Statistics, May 1977, January 1978.

TABLE 7
INFLATION - AFRICA, 1960-1976

(Yearly Average Rate)

Country	1960-1965	1965-1968	1968-1970	1970-1973	1973-1976	1973	1974	1975	1976
Cameroon	6.11	2.52	2.17	5.49	13.71	6.63	16.78	15.10	9.38
Central Africa	9.72	3.14	2.12	7.23	11.97	5.66	9.49	16.07	10.47
Chad	5.20	3.41	6.06	4.83	9.99	5.40	11.28	15.68	3.37
Ethiopia	-	-	5.70	0.92	14.15	8.90	8.66	6.54	28.49
Gabon	4.28	2.67	3.42	4.53	19.87	6.23	12.00	28.30	-
Ivory Coast	2.52	4.40	6.90	3.13	13.60	11.03	17.41	11.41	12.06
Kenya	1.85	2.39	0.96	6.27	16.80	9.29	17.75	19.25	13.47
Malagassy	-	1.66	3.36	5.70	11.50	6.21	22.02	8.19	5.00
Malawi	-	-	5.12	5.61	12.04	20.82	5.83	15.38	-1.06
Morocco	4.00	-0.45	2.17	4.00	11.30	4.17	17.69	7.93	8.54
Niger	-	2.51	5.82	8.52	11.70	11.71	3.36	9.08	23.59
Senigal	2.44	1.49	4.26	5.97	14.15	6.25	15.13	21.90	5.99
Sierra Leone	3.98	3.83	4.89	3.13	17.13	5.68	14.40	19.92	17.14
Somallia	7.44	-0.07	5.53	0.89	17.22	6.42	18.21	19.44	14.07
Sudan	3.22	0.55	8.21	9.86	16.71	15.30	26.09	23.98	1.69
Tanzania	-	-	-	7.58	17.23	10.37	19.60	26.06	6.87
Togo	1.17	-0.26	5.18	5.97	14.13	3.57	12.61	18.28	11.61
(Average)	(4.33)	(1.99)	(4.49)	(5.27)	(14.31)	(8.45)	(14.61)	(16.62)	(10.67)

Source: Computed from International Monetary Fund, International Financial Statistics, May 1977, January 1978.

15

T A B L E   8
YEARLY RATES OF INFLATION, 1952-1976

YEAR	World INDEX	AVERAGE INFLATION INDUSTRIAL COUNTRIES	UNITED STATES CONSUMER PRICE INDEX	COEFFICIENT OF VARIATION	STANDARD DEVIATION
1952	4.0	3.6	2.2	81.28	4.10
1953	1.2	0.5	0.7	264.11	2.34
1954	1.3	0.9	0.4	87.35	1.83
1955	1.5	0.5	-0.3	133.05	1.85
1956	3.1	2.0	1.4	57.66	1.70
1957	3.6	2.9	3.4	55.85	1.58
1958	4.6	3.5	2.7	109.79	3.56
1959	3.4	1.2	1.0	122.51	1.47
1960	3.1	1.9	1.6	68.15	1.29
1961	2.7	1.8	1.0	57.57	1.28
1962	3.7	2.5	1.2	54.07	2.06
1963	4.1	2.6	1.3	56.27	2.06
1964	4.8	2.3	1.3	37.59	1.36
1965	4.9	2.8	1.6	33.97	1.38
1966	5.1	3.3	3.0	36.16	1.49
1967	4.3	2.9	2.8	41.11	1.49
1968	5.0	3.9	4.2	47.55	1.71
1969	5.2	4.8	5.4	41.12	1.65
1970	6.0	5.6	5.9	36.23	1.97
1971	5.9	5.1	4.3	28.69	1.64
1972	5.8	4.5	3.3	19.36	1.14
1973	9.4	7.5	6.2	20.03	1.62
1974	15.0	12.6	11.0	34.28	4.26
1975	13.3	10.7	9.2	38.54	4.41
1976	11.2	7.7	5.7	42.89	3.89

SOURCE: Computed from International Monetary Fund, International Financial Statistics(May 197

NOTE: Coefficient of Variation and Standard Deviation calculated from rates of inflation in the individual industrialized countries.

16

higher rate for the world figure.

An examination of the inflation figures confirms what most people perceive to be the pattern of price increases after the second world war. The Korean War boom led to a first surge in 1952, inflation rose again from 1956 to 1958, proceeded at a fairly steady pace of some 2.3 percent per annum in the first half of the 1960s, and started accelerating thereafter (with a slight downturn in 1972). It may be worth noting that contrary to much of the earlier period, the United States inflation rate was higher than the average of column (2), Table 8, for the 1968-1970 period.

Initiating Causes of World Inflation

Undoubtedly, the source of many of the current economic problems can be traced to the slowdown in economic activity which occurred in most industrialized countries during 1970-1971. Real output expanded rather sluggishly during these two years, averaging 2.7 and 3.7 percent in real terms for the industrialized countries as a group.

In responding to the recession, most governments pursued expansionary monetary and fiscal policies. With hindsight, it is possible to say that the fiscal and monetary policy actions taken were probably too stimulative. For instance, the average rate of monetary expansion in the industrialized countries increased from a relatively moderate rate of 8.27 percent during 1968-1970 to over 12 percent in 1971 and 1972 (Table 9). This high rate of monetary growth was accompanied by the pursuit of expansionary fiscal policy in many countries.

Developments in the Eurocurrency Markets

To the rapid growth in the money supply taking place in the various national economies, one must add the sharp increase in credit available through the Euro-currency market. The estimated size of the Eurocurrency market increased from $44 billion at the end of 1969 to $132 billion or almost 15 percent of the world monetary stock at the end of 1973. This must have contributed in no small measure to worldwide inflationary forces.

17

TABLE 9

MONEY SUPPLY EXPANSION

(Yearly Average Rate)

Area	1960-1965	1965-1968	1968-1970	1970-1973	1973-1976	1968	1969	1970	1971	1972	1973	1974	1975	1976
World	8.32	8.49	8.27	13.09	11.89	9.64	8.79	7.65	12.01	13.32	13.96	10.64	11.49	12.11
Industrialized Countries	6.50	6.62	6.44	10.93	7.84	7.84	6.93	5.95	11.33	11.14	10.02	6.69	7.92	7.67
Other Europe	15.36	9.45	12.12	20.56	22.30	10.37	13.60	10.66	14.36	19.60	28.11	21.25	21.53	16.05
Australia, New Zealand, South Africa	3.87	5.54	7.42	13.10	10.76	8.14	9.81	5.09	5.14	12.41	22.41	8.67	12.63	13.13
Oil Exporting Countries	8.96	30.10	20.59	22.69	37.66	31.61	22.85	18.36	15.92	23.66	28.84	31.66	43.94	13.94
Other Less Developed Areas	18.91	16.40	16.64	24.27	33.72	17.22	17.01	16.28	17.80	21.73	33.82	32.66	28.19	32.34
Other Western Hemisphere	30.18	25.07	21.84	33.13	53.86	26.98	22.59	21.09	23.72	28.64	48.24	49.92	44.62	71.07
Other Middle East	11.74	8.51	6.12	17.18	23.46	8.96	6.76	5.49	12.30	18.43	20.98	23.37	23.48	16.15
Other Asia	9.89	9.59	12.49	16.97	14.23	8.95	12.52	12.47	13.49	15.49	22.10	15.08	11.36	-1.12
Other Africa	6.30	9.60	12.74	13.27	22.88	12.61	12.85	12.63	8.81	12.88	18.34	25.14	20.97	19.68

Source: Computed from International Monetary Fund, International Financial Statistics, May 1977, January 1978.

18

As a consequence of the stimulative actions taken during 1971-1972, the world economy entered a phase of strong expansion in 1972-1973. During these two boom years, the rate of real GNP growth averaged 6 percent, a rate that was not sustainable on a long term basis. As bottlenecks and capacity constraints were reached, excess demand pressures built up quickly and contributed to the acceleration in price increases.

Influences in 1972-1975

Though the current inflation began and gathered strength under the stimulus of above normal demand pressure, there seems little doubt that in its latter stages, it has been aggravated and accelerated by a number of influences, some of which have arisen from particular features of the demand inflation. It is these cost-push factors which have been responsible for the coincidence of inflation and declining output.

The years 1972-1975 were also abnormal in several respects, each liable to cause a higher than usual rate of inflation:

1. The aftereffects of the turbulent wage developments in 1969-1970 including unusually marked disturbances in long established wage and salary differentials and pressure of profit margins.

2. The consequences of great changes in exchange rates at the end of 1971 and again in 1973.

3. The unusual coincidence of very strong recoveries in the United States and in the rest of the industrial world in 1972-1973.

4. Exceptionally large exogenous increases in world market prices for foodstuffs and petroleum in 1973.

The sharp increase in crude oil prices at the end of 1973 added a powerful impetus to world inflation. Petroleum is the single most important commodity in world trade, and its widespread use as an industrial output, as well as consumer good, affects wholesale and consumer price indices directly. It has been estimated

19

that the direct impact of the crude oil price increase added some 2 to 3 percent to world prices.

Analysis of Inflationary Patterns in Industrial Countries

In the preceding sketch of the historical record, we have spoken of worldwide inflation. By this index the average rate of inflation rose. One may question, however, the legitimacy of the averaging, or of the construction of an aggregate price index for a number of countries. The argument for the aggregation is both practical (inflation rates have moved together) and theoretical (under fixed exchange rates, we would expect them to do so). That they have moved together is brought out by the last column of Table 8 which lists the standard deviation of the industrialized countries yearly rate of inflation around their mean. With the exception of 1952-1953, 1958, 1962-1963, 1970, and 1974-1976, these standard deviations remain in the 0.7-1.9 range.

These results are consistent with the pattern one would expect to take place under the Bretton Woods system (provided there were no major hindrances to trade and controls on capital movement). Under that system, exchange rate margins were one percent (or 0.75 percent under the European Monetary Arrangement) of any individual currency in terms of the dollar. Given this pattern, the total range of fluctuations of any two non-United States currencies in terms of each other was 4 percent (or 3 percent under the E.M.A.). Theoretically, temporary deviations in inflation rates could occur within that range.

The standard deviations (Table 8) for most years are in fact compatible with this range (since they imply roughly that 95 percent of observed inflation rates fall within a band of 1.4 to 3.6 around the mean inflation rate). Furthermore, years where the fluctuations lie out of this range are easily explained; 1952-1953 was still a period of post-World War II reconstruction and of high but changing trade and capital transactions restrictions; in addition the Korean War and associated raw materials boom created some abrupt changes in relative prices.

20

The high standard deviation in 1958 is largely the result of the French devaluations (bringing about a 15 percent rate of inflation).

The 1962-1963 increase in dispersion, though not very substantial, is harder to explain. A close examination of country data however reveals the cause was mainly due to a sharp acceleration of inflation in only two of the countries--Italy and Japan.

Certainly the sharp increase in dispersion beginning in 1974 can be explained as the consequence of the added degree of freedom given by the initiation of more flexible exchange rates by most of the countries. The stability of the dispersion in 1971-1973 when flexibility was already beginning to increase was undoubtedly due to the lag in price increases behind changes in the unusually rapid expansion of the supply of money in most countries.

Conclusions

The patterns of inflation taking place during most of the 1950s, 1960s and even the 1970s are similar to those predicted by standard economic theory. According to that theory, countries trading under rigidly fixed exchange rates will find their rates of price increases converging toward a uniform rate. This is in fact what was happening. Inflation rates, at least until 1974, were converging at a noticeable rate.

To reduce, and ultimately stabilize at lower levels, the rate of price inflation is rapidly becoming the main economic objective of most countries. For policymakers in many developing countries inflation is currently a problem as serious as was the problem of low rates of capital formation in the 1950s and 1960s. Yet, individual governments' attempts to control inflation, particularly in the developing world, have not been wholly successful. This relative failure may well be attributed to a wrong diagnosis of the nature of the problem, leading to the application of inappropriate cures. While the convergence of inflationary patterns is easily explained by orthodox economic theory, its acceleration in the 1970s is not so easily accounted for. Another theory capable of explaining the recent rise in prices must be formulated before proper stabilization programs can be designed.

Notes

1. This and other problems surrounding the study of inflation are given in Michael Parkin and Alexander Swoboda, "Inflation: A Review of the Issues," The Graduate Institute of International Studies, Discussion Paper No. 10 (Geneva, June 1976).

2. Cf. A. J. Schwartz, "Secular Price Changes in Historical Perspective," Journal of Money Credit and Banking (February 1973).

CHAPTER 3

ALTERNATIVE THEORIES OF WORLD INFLATIONARY PATTERNS

Introduction

The successful conduct of economic policy is al-most always based on sound theoretical-empirical foot-ing. Many of the observed rates and patterns of infla-tion examined in the previous chapter could be explained by orthodox economic theory. There were (and continue to be) certain inflationary movements, particularly those taking place in many of the less developed coun-tries that are not as easily accounted for by the standard economic approaches.

Clearly, since the economic consequences of world inflation on individual nations will, in large part, be determined by the success these countries have in responding to changes in the international environment, it is important that the precise origins and trans-mission of these price movements are understood by policymakers.

The Need for Theory

Failures in responding to international inflation can be discussed under three headings: (1) failure of concept; (2) failure of policy; and (3) failure of circumstance.

Failure of concept occurs when the authorities lack a sound theoretical framework enabling them to understand at any particular time the basic nature of international inflation. With a failure of concept, policy is likely to be based on an inaccurate view of the world, and is thus almost always doomed to failure from the start.

Failure of policy arises when a wrong policy was chosen by the authorities even though their understand-ing of the economic laws governing international price movements may have been correct.

Failure of circumstance[1] arises when policymakers are unable, because of the basic nature of internation-

23

al economic forces, to accompolish all they set out to do. This can arise because the structure of their economies may make it impossible to modify the impact of world inflation on their domestic economies.

More precisely, it is easy to conceive of one set of forces interacting in a manner that culminates in a pattern of world inflation amenable to control by individual countries. In this situation policymakers would be able through standard monetary, fiscal, and exchange rate policy to modify the impact world inflation had on their economies, while at the same time they were able to achieve a primary set of domestic economic objectives. It is just as easy to hypothesize a different set of forces and or causal mechanisms culminating in the same observed pattern of world inflation; in this case, however, the standard policy tools at the disposal of the authorities (because of the different nature of the inflation) might have no efficacy whatsoever in altering the impact of this inflation on their domestic economies. In this case the economic consequences of world inflation might be extremely serious, depending on the degree of incompatibility between the country's economic goals and the situation imposed upon it by forces outside of its control. This would be a case of failure of circumstance.

The difference in situations where policymakers have control over external price movements and those where they do not must originate from two sources: (1) differences in factors and mechanisms ultimately responsible for world inflation, and (2) differences in the manner in which this inflation is transmitted from one country to another. Since the underlying causes of inflation are never directly observable, theories must be designed capable of depicting the actual forces at work if policymakers are to ever be able to avoid failures of policy and concept. Obviously, the need for theory is just as great in situations where failure of circumstance exists, but policymakers are unaware of its presence.

To summarize, the proper conduct of policy is predicated on the existence of an economic theory capable of lending productive insights into national economic programs. If international inflation is present, the theory must also be able to explain the origin and patterns of these external price movements. The theory must also be capable of accounting for differences in the observed rates of inflation between countries. These criteria establish the basis for evaluating the ability of existing theories to lend insights into the economic consequences of world inflation on individual nations.

Overview of Existing Theories

Much of the research into the recent inflationary period has concentrated on explaining variations over time in the inflation rate. Inter-country differences in average inflation rates have attracted less attention, although their explanation is clearly as important.

That research which has been done on the transmission of inflation from one country to another (given a system of relatively fixed exchange rates) has identified four major channels of transmission:[2]

1. Price effects--direct transmission of inflation via internationally traded goods.

2. Demand effects--spill over of excess demand from one country to another.

3. Liquidity effects--changes in balance of payments affects the money supply and as a consequence money income.

4. International inflationary expectations and 'demonstration' effects.

The major theories of inflation that emphasize one or more of these factors are: (1) Keynesian; (2) Nordic (or Scandinavian); (3) Cost-push; (4) Structuralist; and (5) Monetary.

Transmission through Price Effects

Theories stressing the direct international price link usually argue that abritrage in internationally traded goods will equate domestic goods prices with foreign prices (multiplied by the exchange rates).

This hypothesis is used in the monetarist as well as the Scandinavian theories. Based on this hypothesis, the German Council of Economic Advisers argued that the direct international price link constituted a source of imported inflation even when the country's balance of payments exhibited a deficit.[3] For a system of fixed exchange rates it can be easily shown that the price effect mechanism of transmission implies that the domestic rate of inflation and the international rate of inflation will be equalized or, generally, that the inflation rates of different countries will eventually converge.[4]

According to this mechanism, inflation rates in the real world (also under fixed exchange rates) can differ because of the existence of non-traded goods.

Transmission through Demand Effects

In general, the Keynesian approach stresses the transmission of inflation through the spilling over of excess demand from one country to another (if they maintain a fixed exchange rate). The process is as follows: an increase in aggregate demand in one country increases the demand for the exports of other countries, initiating an expansionary income multiplier in those countries. The theory implies that if all countries are operating near full employment, they will try to divert demand to each others' goods. As a result, excess demand will be transmitted from one country to another, thereby sustaining the inflationary demand pressure being experienced by each.[5]

Transmission through Liquidity Effects

The monetarist approach to the transmission of inflation stresses the direct link between the balance of payments, the supply of money, and nominal income. In general, monetarist models must assume a stable demand for money and no major impediments to trade flows or capital movements.[6]

Transmission through Expectations and Demonstration Effects

Several versions of the structuralist and Keynesian

theories stress the role of international inflationary expectations in the transmission of inflation.[7] What happens to the international price level may influence the formation of domestic price expectations. Also a cross frontier wage bargaining demonstration effect may operate, whereby exceptional wage increases in one country may stimulate expectations in other countries, and eventually lead to anticipatory price and wage increases. The importance of this channel of transmission, however, is hard to judge and little rigorous research has been undertaken in this area.

The Keynesian Approach

There is no single all encompassing Keynesian theory of worldwide inflation.[8] Keynesian type theories are characterized by their emphasis on the role of expenditure on foreign goods. In these theories trade multipliers play a critical role in the transmission of economic disturbances from one country to another.

According to this approach,[8] external increases in aggregate demand are transmitted to the domestic economy (through increasing the demand for that country's exports). The resulting expansion of exports in turn stimulates increased output and employment. At or near full employment prices begin to increase as well. External pressures can, according to this theory, cause domestic prices to diverge (albeit temporarily) from world prices. This price structure is not stable, however, and adjustments in the balance of payments, capital markets, and the money supply will in the more sophisticated versions of this approach eventually lead to convergence of the domestic and world inflation rates. This result is similar in many regards to that obtained by the monetary theories. The two theories differ somewhat in the precise mechanisms used to transmit world inflation to the domestic economy. The generation of world inflation itself is usually not dealt with directly in the Keynesian writings.

Keynesian theory was originally presented as a theory to depict the workings of closed economies. Only recently has this theory been extended to open economies. In applying the theory to open economies, two basic problems have arisen.

First, the Keynesian theory (as originally formu-

27

lated) assumed that the level of money wages was fixed.[9] In adapting the theory to inflationary conditions, the theory must either assume that nominal wages rise at a rate arbitrarily determined by the collective bargaining process, or that their rate of increase follows some sort of Phillips curve pattern (a trade-off between wage increases and unemployment) caused by the pressure of excess demand for labor.[10] The precise nature of the Phillips curve is however extremely difficult to specify.

Second, because of its basic structure, the Keynesian theory when extended to analyze open economies must assume that the world price level is fixed. In this context a country's problem of equilibrating its balance of payments becomes one of adjusting domestic wages and prices to that fixed level. The approach's weakness in this regard is its neglect of the rate of inflation of domestic prices necessary to keep relative wages and prices constant when world prices are inflating.

These and other limitations of the Keynesian approach limit its usefulness in analyzing the impact of world inflation on individual countries. Even worse, those who use this approach often find themselves constrained by the theory to the search for simple empirical evidence on the transmission of world inflation from country to country (the propagation mechanism). Their failure to find any evidence supporting a propagation mechanism is then (wrongly) interpreted by Keynesians as an argument against the monetarist view and in favor of alternative cost-push, structural, or sociological hypotheses.[11]

The Nordic (or Scandinavian) Theory

In the Nordic theories of inflation,[12] the economy is divided into two sectors: one producing goods that are traded internationally, the other producing non-traded goods. The level and rate of change of the price of the traded goods are exogenously given, for the country is assumed to be a price taker in world markets. Regardless of the relative size of the traded goods industry, price developments in that industry are crucial for the economy as a whole, although prices in the non-traded goods industry are determined by interaction of domestic demand and supply. Price changes in the

28

traded goods industry combined with productivity changes determine wages.

In the Nordic framework, it is usually assumed that the percentage rate of change of the wage rate in the traded goods industry is equal to the rate of change of the price of the traded goods corrected for productivity growth. In notation form this is given by:[13]

(1) $\dot{W}_t = \dot{P}_t + \dot{Z}_t$

where $\dot{Z}_t$ is the percentage rate of productivity change in the traded goods sector. Equation (1) is sufficient to determine the percentage change in the wage rate since both $\dot{P}_t$ and $\dot{Z}_t$ are exogenously given. A similar relationship is postulated for the non-traded goods sector:

(2) $\dot{W}_n = \dot{P}_n + \dot{Z}_n$

Equation (2) however is used to determine $\dot{P}_n$. In order to do that one has to assume that wages are equalized between industries. There is adequate empirical verification of this assumption in several countries to give the model credibility. If one then accepts that wages are equalized between industries, the basic result follows immediately:

(3) $\dot{P}_n = \dot{P}_t + \dot{Z}_t - \dot{Z}_n$

Since the overall rate of inflation must be a weighted sum of $\dot{P}_t$ and $\dot{P}_n$:

(4) $\dot{P} = (1-x)\dot{P}_t + x\dot{P}_n = \dot{P}_t + x(\dot{Z}_t - \dot{Z}_n)$

follows where x and (1-x) are the weights in the overall price index.

According to equation (4) the domestic rate of inflation can be greater or less than the world rate of inflation depending on whether $\dot{Z}_t$ is greater or less than $\dot{Z}_n$. In reality one would expect that domestic inflation would proceed at a higher rate than the world rate because technological innovations (thus reducing cost pressures on their price) are generally concentrated in the traded goods sector.

The Scandinavian model is silent on the production structure of the economy and the underlying demand

29

conditions necessary for its predictions to hold. The
question arises then under what assumptions about
technology and preferences are its predictions valid.

In the present context, the Scandinavian model
suffers from two main defects. First, the path of inflation is entirely determined by supply considerations
to the neglect of aggregate demand and monetary and
fiscal policy (which are presumably accommodating); in
this respect it is inferior to the recently developed
general equilibrium macroeconomic models that distinguish between traded (exposed) and non-traded (sheltered)
goods while incorporating expenditure functions and a
monetary mechanism of adjustment. Second, the Nordic
model leaves open the mechanism of generation of the
world rate of inflation which is simply proxied by the
exogenously given rate of change of the prices of the
goods produced in the exposed sector.

The Cost-Push Theory

With regard to imported inflation, the cost-push[14]
approach is simple: increases in import prices raise
the cost of imports and hence domestic prices. Like
the Nordic and Keynesian theories, this approach has a
number of limitations.

First, by equating cost increases to the price increases, the cost-push approach like the Nordic model
focuses exclusively on supply, and thus ignores any
(domestic or foreign) adjustments in demand. Second,
because it fails to distinguish between individual price
increases and general price level increases, the approach cannot incorporate such important factors as the
aggregate budget constraint on market demand; i.e.,
rising import prices lead to a general price increase
only if permitted by central bank policy. As with the
Nordic theory the cost-push theory implicitly assumes
an accommodating monetary policy (which validates any
tendency for domestic prices to rise as a result of
import price increases).

For the purposes of designing policy, the cost-
push hypothesis does not have much to commend it--at
least as long as it makes no convincing arguments
(going beyond appeal to some vague international demonstration effect) as to why worldwide inflation should

occur when it does, why it should take the particular magnitude it does, and how it should spread throughout the world.

Those who advocate this theory usually cite the wage explosions that occurred in the second half of the 1960s as the major cost factors initiating the recent worldwide inflation. A careful examination of these wage increases, however, indicates that they occurred at quite different rates in different countries--and with some differences in timing. One would, therefore, expect national rates of inflation to vary considerably. The fact is they stayed within a fairly narrow band.

If anything is to be rescued from this theory, it is that disturbances in segments of the 'world' labor market may, to some extent, be transmitted to other segments through expectations, and so on. Why such disturbances should occur systematically remains, however, to be explained.

The Structuralist Theory

The structuralist approach to inflation attempts to identify specific rigidities, lags, and other characteristics of economies that affect economic adjustments and the choice of development policy.[15] The theory has in large part been applied to less developed countries.

The structuralists usually do not examine inflation by itself, but instead analyze it in a context which usually includes balance of payments disequilibrium, unemployment, and worsening income distribution. A common theme in most structuralist writings is the failure of the equilibrating mechanisms of the price system to produce steady non-inflationary growth and a desirable distribution of income.

The structuralist analysis looks at inflation as stemming from a number of alleged (structural) constraints which include: (1) an inelastic supply of foodstuffs; (2) lack of foreign exchange; and (3) insufficient tax revenues to finance government expenditures.

The structuralist theory of inflation stresses that these constraints together with inflexibility downward in prices and wages are the major cause of inflation. This position is in direct contrast to that of orthodox economic theory which is based on the assumption that there is no reason why an increase in the price of one commodity should raise the general price level (and thus initiate an inflationary spiral). According to orthodox theory, an increase in imports can, in a relatively open economy, keep prices constant. In a closed economy, orthodox theory would predict that a rise in the relative price of one type of goods (e.g., food) would lead to a shift in demand to other goods and a reallocation of the factors of production, leading to the restoration of an equilibrium position.

But if as the structuralists argue, the prices of manufactured goods are inflexible downward, a rise in food prices (with other prices constant) raises the average price level. In turn, if industrial wages are tied to consumer prices, they will rise, leading an upward movement in industrial prices. The change in relative prices may be insufficient to lead to a shift in demand and thus an inflationary spiral develops.

Structuralists often distinguish between a set of factors--budget deficits, devaluations, rising import prices, and so on--that start a price rise, and the spiral processes that keep prices rising. They usually maintain that the inflationary spiral may continue for reasons quite different from the initiating factors. In other words, the price increase stemming from the bottleneck is not a once-and-for-all change in relative prices, but instead may trigger an inflationary spiral.

Structuralists contend that once inflation begins, the budget deficit (the third major bottleneck referred to above) increases. This in turn leads to an increase in the supply of money. The increase in money stems from the fact that the government can only finance its deficits through obtaining loans from the banking system, issuing bonds to the social security institutions, and revaluation of monetary reserves. All of these measures expand the domestic monetary supply.

To the structuralist an increase in the supply of money is necessary (since the existing tax structure cannot expand revenues and essential government services cannot be eliminated). They also see increases in the money supply as a permissive factor which allows the

inflationary spiral to manifest itself and become cumu-
lative--it is a symptom of the structural rigidities
which give rise to the inflationary pressures rather
than the cause of the inflation itself. In other words
the increase in the supply of money is a necessary
condition for the rise in the overall level of prices,
but it is not regarded as a sufficient condition.

The success of a number of developing countries in
accelerating their rates of growth in the 1960s casts
some doubt on the importance of structural constraints.
However, in the past few years the existence of structural rigidities has been reemphasized by several new
phenomena: the limited ability of many developing
economies to absorb the growing labor force, the worsening of the income distribution in several developing
countries and, most recently, the disruption of world
trade caused by increased oil and food prices.

Structuralist arguments have been applied in large
part only to the Latin American countries. In terms of
explaining world inflation, its limitations are the
same as those of the cost-push theory. These will be
examined in detail in our analysis of the Mexican economy contained in Chapters 11 and 12 below.

The major criticisms of the structuralist theory
come from Latin American monetarists. As will be shown
in the Mexican case, monetarists contend that inflation
orginates in and is maintained by expansionist monetary
and fiscal policies, comprising government deficit
spending (coupled with the operation of inefficient
state enterprises and uneconomic pricing policies),
expansionist credit policies, and the expansionary exchange operations of central banks. It follows that
the rate of inflation can be reduced by curbing excess
demand via contractionary monetary and fiscal policies.
It should be noted that the Latin American monetarists
have little to say about world inflation and its consequences for developing countries. Although super-
fically similar, their approach should not be confused
with that of the monetary theory discussed below.

The Monetary Theory

The monetary approach to world inflation and its
impact on individual countries starts with a methodo-

logical stance that is rather different from that of
the other approaches.16   In particular, it views the
world rate of inflation as determined by the world
rate of monetary expansion. It thus starts from a
global point of view and then disaggregates down to
the national level.

A key assumption of the theory is that individual
countries maintain relatively fixed exchange rates.
This assumption allows analysis of the world economy to
proceed in a manner analogous to that of a closed
economy. Fixed exchange rates have two main implications. First, when coupled with the assumption of perfect arbitrage (the law of one price), they imply
equalization of the money price of traded goods expressed in a common national monetary unit (up to transport
cost and impediments to trade) and also equalization of
their rates of change (a feature incorporated in the
Nordic model). Second, the assumption of a fixed exchange rate assures that for each country the rate of
change of international reserves (in the short run)
and of the money stock (in the long run) becomes an
endogenous variable.

The rate of change in the price of traded goods
provides the world inflation peg toward which the rates
of change of non-traded goods prices (and hence national price levels) tend to adjust. The adjustment mechanism specified by this theory is dependent in part on
the substitution effects in both production and consumption brought about by a change in the relative price of
traded and non-traded goods. Associated changes in expenditure, liquidity, and balance of payments complete
the adjustment process, the result of which is that in
the long run, national rates of inflation can differ
only to the extent that productivity grows at different
rates in the traded and non-traded goods sectors across
countries (or that shares differ given similar productivity growth rates across countries).

If, as the monetary theory argues, the rate of
inflation is determined at the world level by the rate
of growth of the world money supply, what is the link
between the rate of price increase and domestic monetary policies? Suppose that the authorities in a
country which is on fixed exchange rate increases its
rate of monetary expansion. Assuming that the economy
is relatively small and that there is full employment,

34

then the theory predicts that individuals will now find themselves with an excess amount of money. They will attempt to exchange this for goods and or financial assets. In any case, aggregate demand will increase.

However, if the country is only a small part of the world economy, the increase in aggregate demand will not be large enough to have a significant impact on world aggregate demand (since the increase in the world money supply is not sufficient to affect the world rate of inflation). According to the monetary theory, individuals in this country will eliminate their excess money balances through the balance of payments, that is by exchanging money for foreign goods and securities. Thus, as a result of the increase in its relatively rapid rate of monetary expansion, the country will develop a balance of payments deficit. This in turn will lead to a reduction in foreign reserves. Because the country's money supply is small compared with the total world reserves, its rate of inflation will remain unchanged.

Thus under a system of fixed exchange rates, the monetary theory predicts that authorities will lose control over the rate of expansion of their nominal money supply if their economies are relatively small. The freedom of the authorities to conduct policy is limited to their ability to choose the level of foreign exchange reserves they desire. If they want to increase their holdings of reserves, the monetary theory predicts they will reduce the rate of monetary expansion. The reverse will occur if they find that their foreign exchange reserves are in excess of the desired level.

According to the monetary theory the world price level is determined in much the same way as it is for an individual country; i.e., it is a reflection of an adjustment of the price level to the supply of money in excess of the demand for money at the initial price level. Just as in the case of an individual country, it is the growth of the world money stock that determines the growth of the world price level.

Three interrelated and important questions remain: (1) over what time period should we expect the mechanisms outlined above to normally occur; (2) what

is the exact nature of the transmission mechanism; and
(3) what determines the growth of the world money stock.

The Process of Inflation Over Time

According to the monetarists, openness of the small
countries to trade and capital flows, together with their
relative fixed parity between local currencies and that
of their major trading partners, guarantees that world
inflation will eventually be transmitted in full measure
to their economies. Moreover, monetarists argue that
this proposition holds even though a minority (say less
than 40 percent) of the goods and services absorbed by
many of the small countries are imported.

The monetarists view further postulates that the
fact that not all goods are traded goods means only that
some internal prices will not be affected directly by
world inflation. In large part their theory is based on
a series of indirect effects which will take place over
time after an initial change in the world price level
occurs. Since it is well insulated from the world market (as no portion of the output is exported and only a
small part of the total costs are accounted for by imported inputs), the construction industry provides a good
example of this process. Assume that export prices in the
country increase by 100 percent due to world inflation.
The construction industry would be affected (albeit indirectly) since laborers would find wages to be lower
in that industry than in export and import competing
industries. Workers would soon be likely to demand
higher wages in the construction industry as well.

The monetarist mechanism would require that earnings in the construction industry, relative to those of
other countries, be restored to their initial level. A
considerable amount of time might be required, of course,
for this process to work itself out.

The monetarist proposition does not then specify a
precise time frame over which adjustment will take
place. In large part this simply stems from the fact
that the mechanism by which world inflation is transmitted to these economies is both highly complex and
subject to lags and disturbances. The inability to
specify or quantify a fairly precise time frame for
transmission is an obvious deficiency of the theory.

36

The Transmission Mechanism

In terms of the precise manner in which world inflation is transmitted to individual countries, monetarists usually assume at the outset that these countries have no influence over the world price for the goods they import. When world inflation occurs, prices of traded goods--both imports and exports--will then rise by the same amount in these countries' domestic markets.

The monetarist position stresses that those non-traded goods which are close substitutes for imports and exports will experience price increases resulting from substitution effects on the demand side; consumers will try to substitute the relatively cheaper domestic goods for imports and exportables. As the domestic consumption of exportables is, for most of these countries, unimportant, the substitution effect will be limited to substitution of domestic goods for imports. Since these goods are usually rather poor substitutes for imports, the induced rise in their prices through substitution will clearly be less than the increase in the prices of imports. Nevertheless, the immediate effect of world inflation will be to exert upward pressure on the non-traded as well as traded goods in these countries.

If no other effects were to come into play, the result would be a similar but smaller increase in the domestic price levels of these countries. Export proceeds, however, will rise in proportion to the world inflation (owing to the higher export prices) and will tend to rise even further due to the larger export volume induced by the increase in export relative to domestic prices.

The monetarists admit that this latter effect can be expected to be quantitatively weak in most of the small countries for two reasons. First, as an empirical matter, only a small fraction of exportables are usually consumed domestically (thus limiting the consumption-substitution effect; and second, many of these country's exports are of agricultural origin. Since the short run response of production in that sector to price changes is notoriously low (a point emphasized by the structuralists), it is unlikely that this sector could significantly increase its export proceeds.

Finally expenditures on imports will rise, according to the monetarist theory, due to the increase in the price of imports, but diminish to the extent of substitution of domestic goods for imports; the net effect could be either a rise or a fall in expenditure.

Based on the above assumptions and starting from a position of initially balanced trade, the monetarist transmission mechanism is easily traced. For example, an increase in the prices of all imports and exports by the same percentage would result in a trade surplus (as export proceeds would have to increase by more than would expenditures on imports). This surplus would in turn generate an inflow of money (and credit) that would have to be absorbed by the domestic economy. The increase in the domestic price level already experienced will cause part of that inflow to be readily absorbed (unless expectation of inflation reduced the demand for nominal cash balances at a more rapid rate than actual inflation is eroding real cash balances). Obviously, over time an excess stock of money and credit will emerge, particularly in the case of a once-and-for-all increase in world prices.

Ignoring the unlikely case in which each successive increment to the money stock is saved (thus affecting the savings gap), monetarists contend that these increments will no longer be desired and that they will be spent at least in part on importables and exportables-- thus directly diminishing the trade surplus--and on domestic goods driving up their prices and thus through further substitution effects indirectly diminishing the trade surplus.

The final equilibrium will again be one of balanced trade with the domestic price level increased by the same amount as world prices.

The monetarist transmission mechanism requires some modification before being applied. First, most relatively small countries are not in a position of balanced trade; but even more important, trade in goods is very unbalanced--imports of goods are often more than twice exports. In addition, the typical concentration of exports into a few basic commodities suggests that short run fluctuations in output and relative prices will blur the effect of world inflation on export proceeds. While it seems unlikely that these factors can cause the monetarist adjustment process to become unstable (i.e., that a rise in world prices will induce a trade deficit rather than a surplus), they do weaken the adjustment mechanism and introduce potentially long lags in the response of the domestic price level to world inflation.

Growth of the World Money Stock

Monetarists usually concede, therefore, that while it is neither correct nor sufficient to argue that the inflation in relatively small open countries is a mere reflection of world inflation, it remains true that external events are the prime determinant of their domestic price levels in the long run (meaning that these countries cannot long escape a world inflation in the context of fixed exchange rates). This is particularly true of the inflation beginning in the late 1960s as it is now quite generally accepted that the world inflation of the past few years has its roots in U.S. monetary and fiscal policy of the late 1960s.

In these years large increases in the U.S. money stock were transmitted to other countries, principally European, by the fixed exchange rate system in the form of U.S. balance of payments deficits, causing an accumulation of U.S. dollars in foreign central banks. The purchase of these dollars required domestic monetary expansion in the affected countries, with the result that by the early 1970s inflation had spread to virtually all currencies tied by fixed exchange rates to the U.S. dollar. These developments have affected the small countries directly owing to the openness of their economies to world trade and their policy of pegging their currency either to the U.S. dollar or to the currency of a major European country.

Conclusions

Economists have advanced a variety of diagnoses of the causes of inflation which have provided the basis for various policy prescriptions. Essentially, however, there are two schools of thought. First, there are those economists who regard inflation as an international monetary phenomenon, the causes of which are to be found at the world rather than at the individual economy level. This is essentially the monetarist position.

Second, there are those economists who view world inflation as the aggregate of national problems, the causes of which should be sought within the particular structure of each individual economy. This position is held by most non-monetarists. Depending on which view is adopted, alternative policy prescriptions follow. If inflation is a world problem, then its solution requires international policies. In addition small countries may have little or no control over this inflation being transmitted into their domestic economies. If, however, world inflation is a series of national problems, then each country should adopt such policies as are appropriate to contain its own special inflationary pressures. The need to discriminate between these alternative diagnoses, therefore, derives from the associated differences in policy recommendations.

A satisfactory theory of worldwide inflation should be able to explain both its generation and its transmission from country to country. Of the five approaches mentioned above, the monetarist model seems best at explaining both generation and transmission within a unified framework. As a starting point, this model is used as a framework within which to construct the empirical tests that follow. In large part, the empirical work is designed to test the validity of this theory.

Notes

1. The same type of problem but in a different context is discussed in Lance Taylor, "Short-Term Policy in Open Semi-Industrialized Economies--the Narrow Limits of the Possible," Journal of Development Economics (September 1974), pp. 85-104; and Subramanian Swamy, Indian Economic Planning (New York: Barnes and Nobel, 1971), p. 123.

2. Helmut Frisch, "Inflation Theory 1963-75: A Second Generation Survey," Journal of Economic Literature (December 1977), pp.1308-1309.

3. Discussed in Otmar Emminger, "The D-Mark in the Conflict Between Internal and External Equilibrium, 1948-75," Princeton Essays in International Finance (June 1977).

4. Michael Parkin and Alexander Swoboda, "Inflation: A Review of the Issues," in Erik Lundberg, Inflation Theory and Anti-Inflation Policy (Boulder, Colorado, Westview Press, 1977), pp. 7-10.

5. Basically the model developed by William Branson, "A Keynesian Approach to Worldwide Inflation," in Lawrence Krause and Walter Salant, eds., Worldwide Inflation: Theory and Recent Experience (Washington: Brookings Institution, 1977), pp. 65-81.

6. Elaborated at length by Harry Johnson in his Inflation and the Monetarist Controversy (Amsterdam: North Holland Publishing Company, 1972).

7. For example, Organization for Economic Cooperation and Development, "The International Transmission of Inflation," OECD Economic Outlook, Special Section (July 1973), pp. 81-96.

8. In addition to the Branson article cited above, Keynesian models of the type discussed here have been developed by: Akira Takayama, International Trade: An Approach to the Theory (New York: Holt, Rinehart, and Winston, 1972), Chapters 9-10; Alan Blinder and Robert Solow, "Analytical Foundations of Fiscal Policy," in Alan Blinder et. al., The Economics of Public Finance (Washington: The Brookings Institution, 1974), p. 3-115; and S. J. Turnovsky and Andre Kaspura, "An Analysis of Imported Inflation in a Short-Run Macroeconomic Model," Canadian Journal of Economics (August 1974), pp. 355-380. These models are the basis for the summary given in the text.

9. J. M. Keynes, The General Theory of Employment, Interest and Money (London: Macmillan, 1936).

10. Robert Gordon, "Recent Developments in the Theory of Inflation and Unemployment," Journal of Monetary Economics (April 1976), pp. 185-219.

11. Harry Johnson, "Secular Inflation and the International Monetary System," Journal of Money Credit and Banking (February 1973, Part II), p. 513.

12. The following summary is based on: Odd Aukrust, "PRIM I: A Model of the Price and Income Distribution Mechanism of an Open Economy," Review of Income and

Wealth (March 1970); G. Edgren, K. O. Flaxen and C. E. Odhner, Wage Formulation and the Economy (London: George Allen & Unwin, 1973); F. C. Holtem, "A Model of Estimating the Consequences of an Income Settlement," Economics of Planning (No. 1-2, 1968); and Odd Aukrust, "Inflation in the Open Economy: A Norwegian Model," in Krause and Salant, op. cit., pp. 107-176.

13. Cf. Henryk Kierzkowski, "Theoretical Foundations of the Scandinavian Model of Inflation," The Manchester School (September 1976) for a more elaborate exposition along these lines.

14. Elements of the cost-push approach developed here can be found in S. J. Turnovsky and Andre Kaspura, "An Analysis of Imported Inflation in a Short-Run Macroeconomic Model," op. cit.; and Sung Kwack, "Price Linkages in an Interdependent World Economy: Price Responses to Exchange Rate and Activity Changes," Paper Presented for the National Bureau of Economic Research Conference on Research in Income and Wealth, "Price Behavior: 1965-1974," November 21-23, 1974 in Washington D. C.; and Yoichi Shinkai, "A Model of Imported Inflation, Journal of Political Economy (July-Aug. 1973).

15. Structuralist writings summarized here include: D. Sears, "A Theory of Inflation and Growth Based on Latin American Experience," Oxford Economic Papers (June 1962); G. Maynard and W. van Ryckengham, "Argentina 1967-70: A Stabilization Attempt that Failed," Banca Nazionale del Lavoro, Quarterly Review (December 1972); and Marine Muller, "Structural Inflation and the Mexican Experience," Yale Economic Essays (Spring 1965).

16. In the last several years, excellent summaries of the monetarist theory have appeared. The following is based on: Jacob Frenkel and Harry Johnson, "The Monetary Approach to the Balance of Payments: Essential Concepts and Historical Origins," in Jacob Frenkel and Harry Johnson, The Monetary Approach to the Balance of Payments (Toronto, University of Toronto Press, 1976), pp. 21-45; Herbert Grubel, "Domestic Origins of the Monetary Approach to the Balance of Payments," Princeton Essays in International Finance (June 1976); and H. G. Grubel, "International Monetarism and the Expansion of World Inflation," Weltwirtschaftliches Archiv (No. 1 1978).

CHAPTER 4

INFLATION AND NATIONAL ECONOMIC CHARACTERISTICS

Introduction

One of the major problems encountered in examining
the recent world inflation with an aim toward identifying its underlying mechanisms and transmission from
country to country is that during this period rates of
price increases have varied somewhat between countries.

Alternative Solutions

This diversity conflicts with the (long run) monetarist view that national inflation rates should tend to
converge over time. Non-monetarists have contended that
this diversity indicates that there is an 'optimum' rate
of price and wage increases. Non-monetarists then attach a more or less significant 'propensity to inflate'
to every country. Allowing domestic wages and prices to
rise in accordance with this propensity will, according
to this approach, ceteris paribus maximize the possibili-
ties of that economy in attaining a relatively high rate
of real growth.[1]

Regardless of one's views as to the validity of the
last proposition, the fact remains that in large part
the existing theories have failed to adequately account
for the observed patterns of inflation because the:
(1) Keynesian-structuralist fails to examine the problem
in a sufficiently long term perspective, and (2) monetarist takes inadequate account of delays between causal
disturbances and inflationary consequences.

On the first point, many Keynesian writers on inflation have been preoccupied with ephemeral symptoms
or temporary disturbances. Events such as a rise in
the minimum wage, a poor wheat crop, the formation of
an international oil cartel, devaluation of the dollar
vis a vis other major currencies--the list could go on
and on--are capable of moving the inflation indicators
upward, at least temporarily.

Of course, such alleged causes of inflation operate
only sporadically; they cannot explain the sustained

rise in prices experienced by most countries between 1973 and 1976, nor the differential inflation rates between these countries. One could write a history of inflation that would explain it as a series of unrelated accidents.[2] In this case all the advantages derived from inductive generalization would be lost.

One way of avoiding this trap is, as the monetarists suggest, to focus on longer term price movements. However, while the emphasis on the monetary theory is useful in showing such things as the futility of lowering permanently unemployment in the long run, its very emphasis on the long run limits is useful for the analysis of short run phenomena and policies.

Besides, there is no particular reason to believe that the theory is just as applicable for many of the developing countries (because they usually lack the financial development needed to facilitate capital flows, a critical element in the monetarist adjustment) as it apparently is for the more industrialized countries.

A compromise approach would seem to be one which tries to identify similar patterns of inflation among countries and classify these countries into a limited number of groups based on a common set of environmental factors. Generalization would then be possible as theory could then be devised to explain inflation in each of these settings.

Empirical Evidence of Inflationary Patterns by Country Types

An initial test to determine what national characteristics might be associated with the varying propensities to inflate was made using per capita income. A regression of the rates of inflation of sixty developing countries against their respective per capita incomes yielded the following results:

$$P = 6.84 + 0.005043 \text{ PCY}$$
$$(1.59) \quad (0.003024)$$

where P is the inflation rate over the 1960-1975 period and PCY the per capita income in 1973 (figures in parentheses are the calculated standard errors of the

44

coefficients). The calculated t-statistic for the coefficient of GNP/P is 1.668, which means that we can reject the hypothesis of the true coefficient being zero or negative with a 95 percent confidence level. The coefficient of PCY indicates those developing countries with per capita incomes greater than the same average had a propensity to inflate greater than that of the average country by 0.5043 percentage points.[3]

When a similar regression was made on per capita income (1973) and the rates of inflation (1960-1975) for nineteen developed countries, the result was:

$$P = 11.260044 - 0.001343 \text{ PCY}$$
$$(2.266948) \quad (0.000728)$$

The calculated t-statistic for the coefficient of PCY is -1.845, which means that we can reject the hypothesis of the true coefficient being zero or positive with a 95 percent confidence level. The coefficient of PCY indicates that the more advanced countries (those whose per capita income is greater than that of the average per capita income for developed countries as a whole) had a propensity to inflate of 0.1343 percent less than that of the average country.

Although not shown here, a bell shaped scatter can be obtained by plotting the 1960-1975 inflation rates of the 79 countries against their 1973 per capita incomes.

The first cut at grouping countries according to their propensity to inflate was successful in that inflation rates appear to increase with per capita income up to a certain level, then decline as the per capita income range of the most advanced countries is reached. Similarly, the poorest countries also exhibit a relative degree of price stability. The highest propensity to inflate is found for those countries in the intermediate income range.

One can only speculate at this point as to the nature of the observed patterns. It appears that as per capita incomes increase, governments are more inclined after a certain level of development is reached to sacrifice price stability for other objectives, such as economic growth. As per capita income grows, another critical level is reached where an environment of relative price stability may, for one reason or another, be more desirable than say rapid economic expansion.

More precisely, Latin American countries appear to have a greater propensity to inflate than the nations of most other major geographical areas. As a whole these countries not only have on the average higher levels of per capita income than have the other main developing regions, but the richest (Brazil, Argentina, Chile, and Uruguay) countries in the area appear to be more inflation prone than do their poorer neighbors (with the notable exception of Venezuela).

The relatively rich developing semi-developed countries in Europe and the Middle East also have a relatively high propensity to inflate. The developing countries in Asia and Africa as a general rule have a relatively low propensity to inflate. The majority of countries in these two areas have very low per capita incomes. Some of the most advanced (but still relatively poor) nations in Asia and Africa (Korea, Taiwan, Philippines, and Ghana), however, appear to have relatively high propensities to inflate.

Other Factors Responsible for Differential Rates of Inflation

The grouping of countries into developed and underdeveloped while giving certain new insights into the inflationary process is undoubtedly still too broad a grouping for examining the mechanisms of international inflation and its consequences for individual countries. Many of the less developed countries for example are rather narrowly specialized open economies. On the other hand, a number of the larger less developed countries (e.g., India, Indonesia, Mexico, Brazil, Pakistan, Bangladesh, Nigeria, Egypt, Ethopia) are best described as 'closed' rather than open. In these countries the foreign trade sector is a relatively small proportion of the overall economy. Furthermore, exports of the large underdeveloped countries, even though composed mainly of primary products, are relatively diversified-- more diversified in any case at least in terms of the number of export lines than the exports of, say, the very small Central American countries. Even within the less developed group, it appears therefore that at this

stage of analysis, too much diversity exists for productive generalizations concerning inflation to be made.
It is quite likely in any case that a number of other
factors may, in addition to per capita income, influence
the rates of national inflation. On an a priori basis
a tentative list might include: (1) economic size,
(2) the degree of openness, (3) commodity diversification, (4) geographic diversification, (5) trade restrictions, (6) international financial integration, and
(7) the capacity to transform.

Economic Size

The actual economic size (per capita income times
population) of an economy either developed or developing may also have a bearing on that country's inflation
rate. In relatively small and homogeneous economies,
it may be possible to tailor macroeconomic policy much
more closely to the needs of the economy than in a diversified large economy where significant regional and
sectoral differences may exist. Also in very small
economies, it may be possible to obtain a social concensus on economic policies (such as for example the
need to accept a real wage reduction in response to a
deterioration in the terms of trade). In a larger
economy, such group concensus may be difficult to obtain. In such a situation reliance on the impersonal
market forces may be more practical and more commonly
found. Everything else equal, free market forces would
probably yield a higher rate of inflation than that
found where group pressures and national consciousness
might constrain cost-push inflationary tendencies. On
the other hand, increased size means that the possibility for increased specialization and diversity of activity exists. The larger countries would, in the case of
an increased import price, be more likely to be in a
situation where they could substitute cheaper domestic
products and thus minimize the inflationary impact of
increased world prices.

Openness

Open economies have large foreign trade sectors
(i.e., 40 percent or more of GNP inputs) and are clearly
more vulnerable to external economic events than countries importing a smaller proportion of their needs.
Other than this rather obvious observation, the litera-

ture on inflation contains little or nothing of the relationship between inflation and openness.[4] A notable exception is Triffin and Grubel's[5] study of this relationship. Their study however was limited to advanced countries. They examined the inflationary record (as of the early 1960s) of countries of the European economic community and found that the more open countries had experienced less price inflation than those countries having a smaller proportion of GNP as imports. They interpreted this finding as indicating that during this period, openness tended to serve as a kind of safety valve; domestic inflationary pressure spilled over into the balance of payments in these countries thus necessitating less domestic inflation.

A later study by Whitman[6] on a group of advanced countries produced similar results and further evidence in favor of this spill over effect. Unfortunately, little research along these lines has been done on the less developed countries.

A number of a priori arguments concerning inflation and openness in less developed countries can be made for the position that inflation is associated either positively or negatively with increased openness. This stems directly from the fact that in order to eliminate a trade deficit in the balance of payments (under fixed exchange rates) through contractionary monetary and fiscal policy, the authorities must deflate the economy by an amount which is inversely related to the economy's propensity to import.

It follows that relatively closed economies--characterized by a small foreign trade sector, such as India--may find it relatively costly to adjust to external imbalances via domestic inflation or deflation, and may therefore prefer the less costly option of exchange rate adjustment. Consequently, we might expect that relatively closed economies have an incentive to rely on flexible exchange rates and have a lower rate of inflation than relatively open economies.

An examination of several likely inflationary mechanisms shed some additional light on the relationship between openness and the propensity to inflate. Shifts in world market conditions obviously can have a direct and sizable impact on the economies of small, less developed countries. Changes in demand for ex-

48

ports may affect both their volume and price. For example, an increase in the demand for exports could raise incomes (both wages and profits) and thus consumption. If the boom in exports is strong enough, investment expenditure could also be stimulated.

There are, of course, leakages in the system which tend to moderate the size of the secondary multiplier effects. The important leakages are taxation which in many less developed countries tends to fall quite heavily on export incomes and spending on imports; but even so, a significant export boom will tend to raise the demand for labor and other factor and material inputs of a non-traded sort, producing an overall rise in the domestic price level. These forces will clearly be a good deal greater in an economy in which exports are 30 or 40 percent of national product than one in which they are only 10 percent. The rise in export demand may express itself solely in a rise in export prices rather than in volume (if for example the short run supply curve of exports has virtually zero elasticity), in which case the impact on the general price level may be direct rather than through the secondary effects associated with increases in income and expenditures over time.

Another possibility is that many goods normally exported are also consumed domestically. A rise in the external demand for these goods would result in a direct increase in the domestic price level and in incomes of its producers. The result could be the initiation of a wage-price spiral. Substitution away from a good could however cause a rise in the price level of non-traded goods.

Similarly, rising import prices stemming from events overseas may have corresponding effects on the domestic price level.

These considerations raise several questions: (1) how far can autonomous inflationary pressures arising abroad be offset, or at any rate, contained by a system of more flexible exchange rates; (2) is it necessary for the typical less developed country to import so much inflation from abroad; and (3) could a small, less developed country isolate its economy from a rise in prices abroad by altering its exchange rate. While issues are examined at length in later chapters, several observations are in order.

First, it is clear that a nation desiring to minimize price level fluctuations may find it advantageous
to keep its exchange rate fixed (to avoid the immediate
impact of any exchange rate fluctuation on the general
price level). Second, downward rigidity of prices and
wages may minimize any contribution devaluation might
make to the country's balance of payments. It follows
that open economies with a large foreign trade sector
(as found in many developing countries) will probably
prefer fixed exchange rates.

However, Giersch[7] holds the opposite view--namely
that open economies should have more exchange rate
flexibility than closed economies because: (1) a small
reduction in real wages is needed in an open economy to
currect a given amount of unemployment; (2) open
economies are more exposed to outside disturbances and
hence need exchange rate flexibility as a buffer; and
(3) open economies cannot readily use monetary policy
to fight inflation under fixed exchange rates (and
therefore exchange rate flexibility is needed).

Obviously a good case could be made either for or
against the use of exchange rate flexibility as a means
of countering world inflationary pressures. As a
practical matter, however, relatively closed economies
have tended to rely more heavily on flexible exchange
rates than have the relatively open economies (Table 10),
thus refuting Giersch's argument.

In general countries with imports smaller than 30
percent of GNP tend to adopt flexible rates, while those
with imports larger than 40 percent tend to maintain
fixed rates.

We may, therefore, conclude that the degree of
openness of the economy as measured by the percentage
of GNP exported or imported has a significant impact
on the domestic rate of inflation and on whether a
country adopts a flexible or fixed exchange rate policy.
Relatively closed economies tend to prefer floating
exchange rates, while relatively open economies tend to
peg. This tends to confirm the basic hypothesis that
relatively open economies prefer fixed exchange rates
in order to minimize changes in their price levels,
while running counter to the Giersch argument.

TABLE 10

PERCENTAGE OF GNP IMPORTED

VERSUS EXCHANGE RATE SYSTEM

Percentage of GNP Imported	Exchange Rate Practice (Number of Countries)	
	Flexible	Fixed
0 - 9.9	2 (8%)	0 (%)
10.0 - 19.9	7 (28%)	9 (16.7%)
20.0 - 29.9	6 (24%)	10 (18.5%)
30.0 - 39.9	4 (16%)	16 (29.6%)
40.0 - 49.9	2 (8%)	10 (18.5%)
50.0 - 59.9	3 (12%)	4 (17.4%)
60.0 - 69.9	1 (4%)	1 (1.9%)
80.0 - 89.9	0 (0%)	2 (3.7%)
≥ 100.0	0 (0%)	2 (3.7%)
Total	25 (100%)	54 (100.0%)

Source: Robert Heller, "The Choice of an Exchange Rate System," Mimeo, IMF (December 6, 1976), p. 7.

Note: Exchange rates of July 31, 1976.

Degree of Commodity Diversification

Countries with a high degree of commodity diversification should be expected to have lower rates of inflation than do countries that are narrowly specialized
in one or two products; a country with a highly diversified export sector is usually less subject to sharp
changes in its terms of trade and the exchange rate.
Shocks experienced in one or the other export sectors
are likely to be offset by opposite shocks in different
sectors. Diversified exports help to provide a cushion
against excessive fluctuations in total exports. It
follows that countries with a number of exports are less
likely to be forced to inflate their economies if a
sudden export shortfall should occur.

While commodity diversification is undoubtedly an
important explanatory variable in accounting for differential rates of inflation, it is conceptually difficult
to come up with an unambiguous measure of the relative
degrees of diversification. One possible index might
be based on the value of the largest export category
(according to the two-digit SITC classification) as a
percentage of total exports. Obviously, this is a
rather crude measure of the degree of commodity diversification, and a number of others would be just as conceptually satisfactory. As a result, commodity diversification was not explicitly introduced into the analysis
below.

Geographic Diversification

The degree of a country's geographical trade diversification is also likely to have an impact on the
economy's rate of inflation. As with exports, a country
that maintains a number of trading partners may be more
insulated against external shocks. Everything else
equal, a diversified country should be in a better position than a less diversified one to alter its markets in
the short run in order to avoid foreign exchange short
falls. It would be less likely therefore to maintain
full employment through deficit (inflationary) financing.
Unfortunately as in the case of export concentration,
there is no unambiguous index that can be used to
measure the degree of geographical diversification.

Despite the problem of specifying an index of

commodity concentration and geographic diversification that could be used for empirical testing, the effects of these factors on inflation can, for developing countries, at least be taken into account in a qualitative manner:

1. In the long run, many developing countries experience difficulties with their balance of payments due on the one hand to a rather low income elasticity of demand for their (limited number of) primary exports, and on the other to rather high income elasticity of demand for imports (mainly as a result of industrialization and development).

2. The long run deterioration in the balance of payments means that: (a) Imports have to be constrained. If imports are restricted through the use of direct controls, the result will be inflationary. (b) The usual strategy of import substitution used to reduce dependence on imports and strengthen the balance of payments almost always entails shifting demand away from lower priced imported goods to higher priced domestically produced goods.

A long term deterioration of the external position is, therefore, likely to be more inflationary than long term improvement. A long term improvement tends to result in demand-pull inflation which is controllable; on the other hand, a long term decline will most likely be cost-push inflation (which may be harder to avoid if output is to be maintained).

Trade Restrictions

Many medium sized developing countries are pursuing policies of import replacement. This process usually begins with the manufacture of consumer goods (for which a domestic market is already well established). Production usually takes place behind high protective tariff barriers. The result is usually a reduction of consumer good imports and a shift in the composition of imports changes toward raw materials, semi-finished imports and capital goods--imports that are used directly in the productive process.

Because most of the imports are now essential if

a decline in export proceeds is not counterbalanced by a net inflow of foreign capital, import curtailment will result in industrial recession. The process of import substitution therefore results in replacing non-essential consumer goods imports with essential raw material and intermediate and capital goods imports. These imports are needed to maintain domestic production and employment. While over time the country's import structure may not become completely inflexible, in general however the country becomes more dependent on foreign trade and thus more vulnerable to foreign influence and actions.

Increased dependence on imported goods increases the likelihood of inflation being imported through rising international prices of essential capital and intermediate goods.

Trade restrictions making import replacement possible, therefore, aggravate the inflationary tendencies already existing in many developing countries. By changing the structure of imports, these policies increase the economy's vulnerability to imported inflation.

International Financial Integration

As noted in the discussion of the monetary theory of inflation and the balance of payments, international capital movements may play an important role in the transmission of international inflation.[8] Countries, particularly those in Europe, with relatively free and large capital markets have in fact had considerable difficulties in maintaining their chosen optimal level of inflation. The monetarist mechanism centers around the role of interest rate differentials between countries, and the movement of money from one country to another to take advantage of these differentials. Since there is usually a close relationship between money and prices, international capital movements can be a major element in the transmission of international inflation.

Sophisticated financial markets facilitate capital mobility[9] and hence those countries possessing well developed capital markets should (everything else equal) be more integrated into the world economy and thus more

54

exposed to international inflationary forces.

Operationally there are several ways to derive proxy measures of relative financial integration. Each has its own particular limitations. The measure most commonly used is the ratio of commercial banks' foreign assets to the money supply. Presumably the higher this ratio, the greater the degree of financial integration and thus freedom for international capital movements (and thus the transmission of inflation). Appealing as this measure is, however, it has for our purposes only limited usefulness. For instance many developing countries place significant barriers to the convertibility of their currencies. They may nevertheless have, through favorable tax laws, attracted a large number of international banks whose transactions are carried out in foreign currency. The International Monetary Fund data for the country would in this case indicate a high ratio of foreign assets to the money supply, even though the country itself was not integrated into the world financial community. Because of this problem, capital mobility was not included (Chapter 5) in the empirical analysis used to identify those factors responsible for differential rates of inflation. It was however used as a means of determining the degree of monetary autonomy possessed by Mexico (Chapters 11 & 12).

Inflation and the Capacity to Transform

Some of the factors not amenable to quantification such as export diversification and concentration can be introduced in the quantitative analysis as simply reflections of a country's capacity to transform. Many developing economies cannot switch (at least in the short run) production from one type of activity to another, and thus lack the capacity to transform. The result is usually lost export markets and the economy's inability to shift resources into growing or out of declining markets.

Because of domestic rigidities in production (inability to transform), exports may in the short run reach a maximum amount over which they are not likely to grow. Similarly, because of difficulties in substituting domestic goods for foreign products, imports may grow as a function of domestic product or income, rising at a rate which is close to the rate of income

growth. This gives a maximum import requirement for a
given rate of economic growth.[10] If the export maximum
is not sufficiently high to cover the minimum import
requirements, then it necessarily follows that the
resulting foreign exchange gap will have to be pro-
jected into the future with a widening tendency over
time. If the gap is filled by foreign resources, the
domestic monetary expansion that is likely to follow
may be very inflationary.

Ordinarily, increased private savings might be
expected to diffuse some of these inflationary pressures. Given that much of the private savings that
takes place in developing countries is for direct investment in plant and equipment, increases in savings
will only take place if there is an increase in the
supply of investment goods.

Investment goods, however, must (because of the
inability to transform domestic consumption goods into
capital goods) be imported. If the increased level of
imports can not be financed (again because of the inability to transform production from the home market
to the export market) because of limited export earnings,
a good part of potential savings is likely to be frustra-
ted, and thus channeled into inflationary consumer
expenditures.

It also follows from the economy's rigidities that
shifts in the composition of demand, as distinct from
the generalized excess demand, will create an upward
bias in the price level--a higher bias than would be
the case in a more developed economy, or an economy
that had achieved a more flexible productive structure;
i.e., had a greater capacity to transform.

As seen from our examination of inflationary
patterns, price increases were lower in the very high
and very low per capita income groups (i.e., in those
countries that had finished or had not really begun
their industrialization process). Inflation rates were
highest in the intermediate income countries (i.e., in
those nations who had usually begun, but were still
some way from finishing their transformation from
agrarian to industrial economies).

The ideas on transformation developed above may
help (in conjunction with the other factors above) in

explaining these patterns. First, medium income countries tend to be involved in a process of industrialization which not only changes their productive structure but also indirectly contributes to demand-shifts by promoting changes in consumer tastes and in the distribution of income.

Second, to the extent that medium income developing countries tend to suffer long term declines in the performance of their exports of primary products (as a result of their industrialization policies), some change in the composition of production will be forced upon them. Third, to the extent that resources are less mobile in the medium income than the lower income and advanced countries, a given change in the output mix is for reasons discussed above likely to require or be associated with a relatively high rate of inflation.

If rigidities are present, then one would expect the average price level to rise:

1. the more sympathetic the money supply is to potential upward price movements,

2. the more rigid wages are in declining sectors (i.e., minimum wages, trade union strength),

3. the more immobile the factors of production (requiring in this case larger movements of returns to promote a given shift),

4. the greater the difference in skills required in the expanding and declining sectors, and

5. the greater the spread of wage movements from expanding to other sectors.

In this study we are primarily concerned with differences in inflation rates between countries. While the concept of the capacity to transform has only been used in the literature in conjunction with developing countries, the principle should logically hold for developed countries as well. The capacity to transform is not directly measurable. Since we have seen, however, that rigidities often manifest themselves in a low investment (and savings) rate and a large gap between exports and imports, it is depicted by the ratio of the deficit in the country's current account to its level of domestic investment.

Conclusions

Perhaps one reason for the diverse variety of theories on inflation stems from the fact that one theory may be quite adept in explaining the inflationary experience of a country or group of countries, but is deficient in terms of accounting for the observed price patterns in other countries. Evidence was presented indicating that inflation rates tend to vary with per capita income--with the lowest inflation rates experienced by high and very low income countries, and with the highest rates of inflation registered by intermediate countries.

Per capita income, however, only partially accounts for these inflationary patterns. It is worthwhile, therefore, to identify other factors that may play an important role in the inflationary process. On an a priori basis, a number of these factors were identified. These are used in the next two chapters to statistically place countries into a limited number of unique groups in terms of its member country's response to world inflation.

Notes

1. G. Magnifico, European Monetary Unification (New York: John Wiley Publishers, 1973), p. 69.

2. Richard Selden, "Monetary Growth and the Long-Run Rate of Inflation," American Economic Review (May 1975), p. 125.

3. A somewhat similar result using different time periods was obtained by Ovidio Cardozo. See his "Flexible Exchange Rates, Inflation and Economic Development," World Development (No. 7, 1976), pp. 613-626.

4. A recent contribution can be found in Milton Ame Iyoha, "Inflation and Openness in Less Developed Economies: A Cross-Country Analysis," Economic Development and Cultural Change (October 1973), pp. 31-37.

5. R. Triffin and H. Grubel, "The Adjustment Mechanism to Differential Rates of Monetary Expansion Among the Countries of the European Economic Community," Review of Economics and Statistics (November 1969), pp. 486-491.

6. Marina V. N. Whitman, "Economic Openness and International Financial Flows," Journal of Money, Credit and Banking (November 1969), pp. 727-749.

7. Herbert Giersch, "On the Desirable Degree of Flexibility of Exchange Rates," Weltwirtschaftliches Archiv (No. 2, 1973), pp. 191-213.

8. As spelled out by James C. Ingram. See his Regional Payments Mechanisms: The Case of Puerto Rico (Chapel Hill: University of North Carolina Press, 1962), and his "The Case for European Monetary Integration," Princeton Essays in International Finance (1973).

9. Cf. D. Sykes Wilford, Monetary Policy and the Open Economy: Mexico's Experience (New York: Praeger Publishers, 1977), pp. 104-106.

10. This analysis is based on the so-called 'two gap theory.' Cf. Hiroshi Kitamura, "Trade and Capital Needs of Developing Countries and Foreign Assistance," Weltwirtschaftliches Archiv (1966); Robin Maris, "Can We Measure the Need for Development Assistance?" Economic Journal (September 1970); and Susan Cochrane, "Structural Inflation and the Two-Gap Model of Economic Development," Oxford Economic Papers (1973).

CHAPTER 5

PATTERNS OF WORLD INFLATION: EMPIRICAL FINDINGS

Introduction

A sample of 60 countries was used to determine if
a limited number of country groupings could be identified on the basis of similarities in inflationary patterns and structural environmental factors. On an a
priori basis (see Chapter 4) the following structural
variables were chosen. Selection was made on the basis
of their potential to influence the inflationary pattern experienced by each country: (1) per capita income in 1973 $US: (2) the economic size of the country
as measured by its 1973 per capita income times its
1973 population; (3) the degree of openness as measured
by the average level of imports/GNP (in current prices)
over the 1968-1973 period; and (4) the relative ability
to transform as measured by the average current account
deficit/investment ratio (in current prices) over the
1968-1973 period[1] (Tables 11-14).

Initially the countries were placed in one of
three groups: (1) high income (as measured by per
capita income; (3) medium income; and (3) low income.
Regressions for each group were then run with inflation, the dependent variable, being explained by the
four independent variables above.

Results

The results for the high and low income countries
were fairly satisfactory (in terms of r^2) but not for
the medium group. Consequently, this group was divided
into two subgroups; one with a relatively high level of
per capita income, and a lower income group.

Regressions were then run for the four groups.
After each regression, that country with the largest
deviation from the estimated regression equation was
removed and placed in another group. This process was
repeated until it was impossible to reallocate countries between groups and improve the r^2 of each group.[2]

The final groups were arbitrarily referred to as:

61

TABLE 11

CHARACTERISTICS AND INFLATION RATES OF DEVELOPED COUNTRIES

Country	Per Capita Income (1973 US $) (Thousands)	Economic Size (1973 population X 1973 per capita income)	Imports/ GNP (%)	Deficit Current Account Investment (%)	Inflation Rate 1965- 1970	1970- 1973	1973- 1976	1970- 1976
Australia	4.35	57.1158	14.77	-4.7	3.11	7.12	14.59	10.24
Austria	3.51	26.3952	32.76	-2.0	3.28	6.18	8.43	7.30
Belgium	4.56	44.7336	41.93	9.4	3.50	5.58	11.51	8.51
Canada	5.45	120.6085	21.48	-2.7	3.87	5.04	9.70	7.35
Denmark	5.21	26.1542	32.05	-7.9	6.64	7.23	11.26	9.23
France	4.54	23.6806	15.56	1.8	4.38	6.32	11.56	8.91
Germany	5.32	32.9680	20.17	7.5	2.43	5.91	5.83	5.87
Italy	2.45	13.4481	19.09	5.6	2.98	7.09	17.62	12.23
Japan	3.63	393.3105	10.10	3.4	5.48	7.43	14.96	11.13
Netherlands	4.33	58.1519	46.75	3.4	4.77	7.78	9.55	8.66
New Zealand	3.68	10.8928	24.17	-1.0	4.91	11.84	14.20	10.21
Norway	4.66	18.4536	42.60	-2.1	4.93	16.97	10.06	8.51
Sweden	5.91	48.1074	24.09	1.9	4.56	6.91	9.85	8.37
Switzerland	6.10	38.6130	31.58	9.2	2.18	7.32	6.02	6.67
United Kingdom	3.06	17.1360	22.35	8.5	4.59	8.55	18.90	13.61
United States	3.68	1,304.4800	6.08	1.7	4.25	4.59	8.47	6.58
(Average)	(4.40)	(139.64)	(25.35)	(2.00)	(4.12)	(6.99)	(11.41)	(8.96)

Source: Calculated from: International Monetary Fund, International Financial Statistics, May 1977, December 1977; World Bank, World Tables 1976.

62

TABLE 12

CHARACTERISTICS AND INFLATION RATES OF MIDDLE INCOME I COUNTRIES

Country	Per Capita Income (1973 US $) (Thousands)	Economic Size (1973 population X 1973 per capita income)	Imports/ GNP (%)	Deficit Current Account Investment (%)	Inflation Rate			
					1965-1970	1970-1973	1973-1976	1970-1976
Greece	1.87	16.7739	20.05	-32.2	2.50	7.46	17.71	12.47
South Africa	1.05	25.4783	25.11	-9.2	3.30	7.20	12.01	9.61
Spain	1.71	59.4054	14.48	-8.9	5.07	9.31	16.76	12.97
Malaysia	0.57	6.6975	44.01	11.1	1.35	5.04	7.98	8.50
Mexico	0.89	46.8818	11.40	-12.5	3.67	7.29	18.46	12.74
Venezuela	1.63	18.7220	20.90	1.9	1.59	3.43	6.07	6.02
Egypt	0.25	8.9048	19.32	-38.8	4.13	3.17	10.29	6.67
Sri Lanka	0.12	16.2260	17.86	-18.6	4.20	6.18	6.65	6.14
Korea	0.40	13.1640	28.51	-31.8	11.36	8.94	21.71	15.15
Israel	3.01	9.5718	55.78	-66.1	4.02	14.88	36.74	25.33
Finland	3.66	16.7760	28.47	-5.3	4.56	8.01	16.26	12.06
(Average)	(1.38)	(21.69)	(25.99)	(-19.13)	(4.16)	(7.36)	(15.51)	(11.61)

Source: Calculated from: International Monetary Fund, International Financial Statistics, May 1977, December 1977; World Bank, World Tables 1976.

TABLE 13

CHARACTERISTICS AND INFLATION RATES OF MIDDLE INCOME II COUNTRIES

Country	Per Capita Income (1973 US $) (Thousands)	Economic Size (1973 population X) (1973 per capita income)	Imports/ GNP (%)	Deficit Current Account Investment (%)	Inflation Rate			
					1965- 1970	1970- 1973	1973- 1976	1970- 1976
Nigeria	0.21	14.9650	17.76	-16.7	5.46	7.92	22.63	15.04
Burma	0.08	2.2648	7.86	-23.4	3.52	11.25	26.33	18.55
India	0.12	69.0000	4.99	-11.2	6.79	8.58	7.50	8.04
Pakistan	0.12	8.2692	11.03	-26.6	4.38	12.21	17.96	15.05
Philippines	0.28	11.2613	19.30	-7.0	5.98	11.95	15.47	13.70
Thailand	0.27	10.6380	20.99	-10.8	2.57	5.79	10.12	7.93
Colombia	0.44	10.4619	15.35	-35.3	10.07	15.23	22.15	18.78
Algeria	0.57	8.3790	31.80	-15.7	2.00	4.13	6.48	5.06
Bangladesh	0.08	6.1360	12.50	-28.6	6.30	27.96	20.23	24.04
Morocco	0.32	5.1840	21.19	-7.6	0.59	4.00	11.30	7.59
Indonesia	0.13	16.2770	20.62	-36.6	-	13.44	25.99	19.55
(Average)	(0.24)	(14.80)	(16.67)	(-19.9)	(4.77)	(11.13)	(16.92)	(13.94)

Source: Calculated from: International Monetary Fund, International Financial Statistics, May 1977, December 1977; World Bank, World Tables 1976.

64

TABLE 14

CHARACTERISTICS AND INFLATION RATES OF SMALL COUNTRIES

Country	Per Capita Income (1973 US $) (Thousands)	Economic Size (1973 population X 1973 per capita income)	Imports/ GNP (%)	Deficit Current Account Investment (%)	Inflation Rate 1965-1970	Inflation Rate 1970-1973	Inflation Rate 1973-1976	Inflation Rate 1970-1976
Costa Rica	0.71	1.3292	37.55	-36.3	2.54	7.49	16.48	11.90
Ecuador	0.38	2.5563	21.71	-34.2	4.72	9.75	16.33	12.99
El Salvador	0.35	1.3302	15.52	-19.7	1.07	2.76	14.25	8.53
Paraguay	0.41	0.9906	15.36	-22.4	1.27	8.94	11.76	10.34
Ethiopia	0.09	2.3472	11.62	-10.9	1.80	0.92	14.13	7.33
Kenya	0.17	2.1216	31.61	-17.5	1.81	6.27	16.80	11.41
Sudan	0.13	2.2216	17.24	-16.0	3.55	9.86	16.71	13.23
Somallia	0.08	2.4336	39.40	-65.2	1.35	0.89	17.22	8.75
Malagassy	0.15	1.1415	21.63	-54.2	2.34	5.73	11.51	8.58
Cameroon	0.25	1.5515	23.58	-27.6	2.39	5.49	13.71	9.52
Iceland	5.03	1.0462	43.19	-12.2	12.30	12.24	41.48	26.01
Senegal	0.28	1.3960	29.06	-28.1	2.59	5.97	14.15	9.98
Malawi	0.11	0.5316	31.15	-74.4	5.70	2.77	11.62	8.57
Togo	0.18	0.3789	33.11	-45.4	1.88	5.79	14.15	9.97
Chad	0.08	0.3098	34.60	-100.1	4.46	4.83	9.99	7.38
Liberia	0.31	0.4500	50.45	-43.3	4.33	7.40	12.88	10.11
Sierra Leone	0.16	0.4459	30.48	-25.5	4.25	3.13	17.13	9.91
Tanzania	0.13	1.8166	30.16	-20.2	4.90	7.58	17.23	12.30
Jamaica	0.99	1.9470	40.33	-47.0	5.31	9.45	16.95	13.14
Nigeria	0.10	0.3870	21.70	-66.9	3.82	8.52	11.70	10.10
Central African Republic	0.16	0.2736	33.50	-53.6	2.73	7.23	11.97	9.58
Gabon	1.31	0.6810	58.30	-14.2	2.97	4.53	19.87	10.41
(Average)	(0.52)	(1.2585)	(30.51)	(37.95)	(3.55)	(6.25)	(15.82)	(10.91)

Source: Calculated from: International Monetary Fund, International Financial Statistics, May 1977, December 1977; World Bank, World Tables 1976.

65

(1) large countries; (2) Medium I; (3) Medium II; and (4) small countries.

For the four periods--1965-1970, 1970-1973, 1973-1976, and 1970-1976--the high income countries had lower rates of inflation than the Medium I countries. The Medium I countries had in turn lower rates of inflation for each period than the Medium II countries. The small countries had lower rates of inflation in each period than the Medium II countries, and in each period except 1973-1976 lower rates than those experienced (15.82 versus 15.51) for the Medium I countries.

The rates of inflation for the large country and small country groups were roughly comparable, with the small countries experiencing a lower rate of inflation for 1965-1970 and 1970-1973, and the large countries experiencing a lower rate of inflation for 1973-1976 and 1970-1976.

In terms of the relative importance of per capita income, economic size, degree of openness, and ability to transform in explaining each groups' inflationary patterns, several striking patterns emerge. Per capita income has for all time periods a negative impact on the inflation rate experienced in the large countries and in Medium II, but a positive impact for Medium I and small (the 1965-1970 coefficient for per capita income is not statistically significant for Medium I and Medium II countries). The deficit/I ratio was an important determinant for all four groups and was statistically significant (as determined by the "t" test in parentheses under the coefficients).

Economic size (S) does not seem to be an important factor in explaining inflation except in the 1970s for both Medium II countries (where it had a negative coefficient--larger the economic size the lower the rate of inflation) and small countries (where it had a positive impact).

The degree of openness was an important element in explaining Medium I country group's pattern of inflation (where it had a positive impact--the higher the percentage of imports in GNP, the higher the rate of inflation)(Table 15).

The reverse seems to be the case for Medium II

TABLE 15

PATTERNS OF WORLD INFLATION

INDEPENDENT VARIABLES

Country Group	Period	A	Y/P	S	1M/6NP	DEE/I	r^2	F
Large Countries	1965-1970	4.61	-0.23 (0.41)	0.001 (0.58)	0.03 (0.60)	-0.12 (2.12)	0.-3	1.35
	1970-1973	9.77	-0.55 (1.22)	-0.001 (1.55)	-0.002 (0.35)	-0.025 (0.30)	0.28	1.05
	1973-1976	25.94	-2.64 (4.10)	-0.0004 (0.89)	-0.09 (2.41)	-0.03 (0.24)	0.68	5.89
	1970-1976	17.12	-0.04 (2.02)	-0.007 (1.44)	01.49 (3.81)	-0.02 (0.21)	0.65	5.18
Medium I	1965-1970	3.49	-0.51 (0.41)	+0.02 (0.11)	-0.005 (0.14)	-0.05 (1.08)	0.19	0.34
	1970-1973	-1.88	0.56 (3.59)	-0.13 (0.73)	0.16 (3.66)	-0.08 (3.20)	0.86	9.28
	1973-1976	-6.67	1.60 (4.01)	0.27 (0.07)	0.34 (3.66)	-0.27 (4.89)	0.89	13.35
	1970-1976	-3.86	0.94 (4.43)	0.19 (0.07)	0.28 (4.60)	-0.15 (4.35)	0.91	14.93
Medium II	1965-1970	2.24	7.21 (0.40)	0.05 (1.06)	-0.17 (2.14)	0.15 (1.23)	0.59	7.60
	1970-1973	11.78	-9.59 (1.62)	0.07 (0.88)	-0.20 (0.79)	-3.02 (1.56)	0.52	1.62
	1973-1976	18.17	-15.21 (2.25)	-0.16 (2.45)	-0.14 (0.90)	-0.36 (2.36)	0.74	4.35
	1970-1976	14.96	-11.95 (2.95)	-0.11 (2.42)	-0.18 (1.36)	-0.33 (2.98)	0.80	6.32
Small	1965-1970	0.27	2.12 (6.26)	0.49 (0.24)	0.0004 (0.61)	0.38 (2.39)	0.73	11.35
	1970-1973	6.67	1.72 (2.33)	0.14 (0.31)	-0.06 (0.87)	-0.007 (0.20)	0.28	1.58
	1973-1976	10.08	5.62 (8.69)	2.37 (2.73)	-0.04 (0.57)	-0.006 (0.19)	0.84	20.85
	1970-1976	8.85	3.35 (9.34)	0.78 (1.84)	-0.02 (0.55)	0.004 (0.18)	0.85	22.75

Source: Computed by Author

countries, although the coefficients are not statistically significant. For 1970-1976 the more open large countries were, the higher their inflation rates.

The ability to transform was important in contributing to Medium I and Medium II countries' inflationary patterns. As one would expect, the greater the deficit on current account to investment, the higher was the rate of domestic inflation experienced by the members of each group.

The four variables did a particularly good job of explaining Medium I countries' patterns of inflation, with r^2 of .86, .89, and .91 for the 1970-1973, 1973-1976, and 1970-1976 periods, respectively. Results were also rewarding for the small countries, but somewhat disappointing for large countries. Medium 11 countries' inflation rates were adequately explained by the variables. In general the results were better (in terms of a higher r^2) for the 1970s than the 1960s. The analysis also confirms the bell shaped pattern of inflation rates in terms of per capita income, with rates of price increase being lower for the very high and very low (or small) income countries.

Interpretation

The data on inflation and the regression results are suggestive of several underlying factors which may influence the patterns of price increase in each group of countries. Clearly, however, much more work needs to be done before any definitive answer as to the precise nature of the inflationary mechanism in each case is known.

The following observations on the patterns of inflation experienced by the small and medium countries are to some degree conjectural. They are, however, entirely consistent with the empirical analysis.

The Small Countries

Many of the countries in the small country group are very low income African countries. For these countries, the subsistence sector is often large, with the monetary economy growing but still relatively small in many of the countries. In general these countries have had relatively low rates of inflation. There is a built in mechanism in most of these countries assuring such a result. During inflationary periods, agricultural workers in these areas may prefer to have their wages paid in kind (that is in the form of agricultural produce) rather than asking for money-wage increases. Reversion to a barter economy thus becomes an automatic stabilizer which can easily prevent the outgrowth of a wage and price spiral.

Similarly, a flow of resources into and out of the money economy may also help to maintain price stability.[3] When expenditure in the money sector of these economies increases beyond the amount that can be satisfied (at current prices) by growth within that sector, a small increment in demand may induce increases in production and resource inflows from the non-monetized sector. With augmented resources, the money economy can over time also expand output and thus tend to dampen the rate of price increases.

It is conceivable that if prices increase at a very fast rate, however, uncertainty and perhaps the inability of peasants to obtain expensive inputs would result in a reduction in the real quantum of marketed agricultural produce. A substitution effect (leisure for income) might develop. To the extent that there is a substantial withdrawal of the supply of farm produce from the money sector into the subsistence sector, the inflation would continue. In general, however, the monetary arrangements of these countries have assumed that excessive rates of inflation would not occur. Many of these countries had, until recently, the status of colonies rather than that of independent nations. The currency issued in most colonies was backed by the accumulation of an equivalent amount of reserves in the metropolitan country's currency. Thus there was a rigid control limiting excessive expansion of the money supply. Remanents of this practice still exist and undoubtedly continue to influence government policies.

In general many of these countries continue to give excessive backing to their money supply causing it to grow at a relatively slow rate. The chronic credit squeeze that has characterized many of these nations helps to explain their low inflation rates. In any case the tendency of all the smaller countries to peg their currencies rigidly to that of one of the major industrial countries (Table 16) assumes that the rate of inflation in the more advanced countries will sooner or later be transferred to their smaller partners.

The Medium Countries

Governments of the Medium I and II countries are, as a general rule, concerned with promoting high levels of employment and rapid economic growth. At the same time the associated urbanization and industrialization have substantially increased the demands placed on the authorities to provide a number of activities such as infrastructure (roads, hospitals, sewage systems) and welfare services which if not expanded may increase social tensions in the cities and hamper industrial growth.

Recent research[4] indicates that countries with relatively low per capita incomes (say $250) are in a phase of development where the capital-output ratio is rapidly increasing. Rising capital costs, therefore, absorb most of the nation's investment. The rate of growth of output remains low.

At a higher level of per capita income (say $500) the capital-output ratio reaches what is called Bicanic's[5] threshold. After this point the ratio begins to decrease and the rate of growth accelerates. Much of the reduction in the capital-output ratio is due to changes in the composition of industries; i.e., the share of capital intensive industries declines.

In a similar view Hovart[6] confirmed the hypothesis that countries pass through three successive phases of development: (1) an initial phase of stationary or slow growth; (2) a phase when the growth rate is increasing (accelerating) growth, and (3) finally, a phase of decreasing (decelerating) growth. One of the consequences of this pattern is that the gap is widening between the least developed and other countries, but the countries at the intermediate level of development are gaining on the most advanced countries. He concludes that the usual two-fold classification of countries will have to be replaced by a three-fold one: less developed, developing, and developed countries.

T A B L E 16

EXCHANGE RATE POLICY

Practices in Effect Mid 1976

LARGE GROUP	EXCHANGE RATE POLICY
AUSTRALIA	Dollar Pegger
AUSTRIA	Other Basket Pegger
BELGUIM	Snake
DENMARK	Snake
FRANCE	Floater
GERMANY	Snake
ITALY	Floater
JAPAN	Floater
NETHERLANDS	Snake
NEW ZEALAND	Dollar Pegger
NORWAY	Snake
SWEDEN	Snake
U.K.	Floater
U.S.	Floater

MEDIUM I GROUP	
GREECE	Floater
SOUTH AFRICA	Dollar Pegger
SPAIN	Floater
MALAYSIA	Other Basket Pegger
MEXICO	Dollar Pegger
VENEZUELA	Dollar Pegger
EGYPT	Dollar Pegger
SRI LANKA	Other Basket Pegger
KOREA	Dollar Pegger
ISRAEL	Dollar Pegger
FINLAND	Other Basket Pegger

MEDIUM II GROUP	
NIGERIA	Floater
BURMA	Dollar Pegger
INDIA	Dollar Pegger
PAKISTAN	Dollar Pegger

71

T A B L E **16** (Contd)

MEDIUM.II GROUP	EXCHANGE RATE POLICY
PHILIPPINES	Dollar Pegger
THAILAND	Dollar Pegger
COLOMBIA	Floater
ALGERIA	Other Basket Pegger
BANGLADESH	Dollar Pegger
MOROCCO	Other Basket Pegger
INDONESIA	Floater

SMALL GROUP	
COSTA RICA	Dollar Pegger
ECUADOR	Dollar Pegger
EL SALVADOR	Dollar Pegger
PARAGUAY	Dollar Pegger
EHTIOPIA	Dollar Pegger
KENYA	SDR Pegger
SUDAN	Dollar Pegger
SOMALIA	Dollar Pegger
MADAGASCAR	Franc Pegger
CAMEROON	Franc Pegger
ICELAND	Floater
SENEGAL	Franc Pegger
MALAWI	SDR Pegger
TOGO	Franc Pegger
CHAD	Franc Pegger
LIBERIA	Dollar Pegger
SIERRA LEONE	Dollar Pegger
TANZANIA	SDR Pegger
JAMAICA	Dollar Pegger
NIGER	Franc Pegger
CENTRAL AFRICAN REPUBLIC	Franc Pegger
GABON	Franc Pegger

SOURCE: H. Robert Heller, The Choice of an Exchange Rate System: Theory and Practice, Mimeo International Monetary Fund, December 6, 1976, P.29.

While the evidence is sketchy, there is sufficient reason to believe that the Medium I countries have for the most part (Sri Lanka and Egypt are probably exceptions) completed at least the first stages of their national infrastructure plans and are now experiencing a decline in their capital output ratios as growth accelerates. Medium II countries are in general still in the high capital-output and thus capital expenditure stage of development.

The Medium II countries are, therefore, much more likely than Medium I nations to be in situations where they must resort to emergency government expenditures to enhance economic growth and to avoid social turmoil. In general governments of the Medium II group seem to be inclined to go ahead with their expenditure projects, financing them through money creation and deficit budgets. This may explain the somewhat higher rates of inflation in the Medium II countries versus that found for the Medium I group.

Differential rates of inflation between Group I and Group II countries (and within each grouping) can also be thought to be a by-product of on-going domestic clashes between organized groups, some aiming at changing and others at retaining the existing distribution of wealth and income, the shares of private and public investment, and the shares of investment and consumption. Conflict between the aims of different groups may frequently mean that too many forceful, simultaneous claims are being made upon the real value of national production.

In the more advanced Medium II countries (e.g. Philippines, Colombia) there has been a greater degree of sophistication and organization by the urban proletariat. The result may mean that, in response to price increases, labor in these countries will press for more or less substantial wage increases. A cost-push inflationary spiral may, therefore, be a more likely feature in a Medium II country than in a small group country.

Differentials in the militancy of trade unions may perhaps be partially explained by differentials in real income levels. After a certain relatively high standard of living is attained, labor unions, as well as industrial management, may easily be willing to compromise for a 'fair' (that is for a non-inflationary)

wage bargain. Not so in poor countries, where union
leaders often aspire to realize a number of pressing,
legitimate goals (income redistribution, improvements
in the standard of living) by means of the imposition
of successive mark-ups in wages and salaries.

More generally, the excess of forceful claims by
the various sectors over the real value of national
production may diminish through time in mature, advanced societies where relatively high standards of
consumption make the desire for a greater share of the
national pie less and less pressing in every sector.

Conclusions

Causal observation indicates that individual countries have different propensities to inflate. In general these propensities are associated with different
stages of economic development. In an examination of
60 countries, those with a very high per capita income
have in general since 1960 experienced fairly significantly smaller inflation rates than have countries
in intermediate stages of development. Very backward,
primitive and small economies appear to have more price
stability as compared with more dynamic developing
economies. Several factors in addition to per capita
income--openness, economic size and capacity to trans-
form--were shown by regression analysis to play important roles in the inflationary process of one or more
of the four country groupings. A number of explanations
may account for these patterns, all of which at this
stage of the analysis must be considered rather tentative. The discriminant analysis performed on the countries and presented in the next chapter attempts to
quantify these relationships more precisely.

Notes

1. Data for these indices was taken from The
World Bank, World Tables 1976 (Baltimore: The Johns
Hopkins University Press, 1976).

2. For a somewhat similar procedure, but in a
different context Cf. Charles Frank and William Cline,
"Measurement of Debt Servicing Capacity: An Application of Discriminant Analysis," Journal of International

Economics (August 1971), pp. 327-344.

3. An idea advanced by Ovido Carsozo in his "Flexible Exchange Rates, Inflation and Economic Development," World Development (No. 7, 1976), pp. 613-626.

4. Willy J. Stevens, Capital Absorptive Capacity in Developing Countries (Leiden: A. W. Sijthoff, 1971); and Branko Horvat, "The Relation Between Rate of Growth and Level of Development," The Journal of Development Studies (April/July 1974), pp. 382-394.

5. Based on his conclusions contained in R. Bicanic, "The Threshold of Economic Growth," Kyklos (No. 1, 1962), pp. 7-28.

6. Hovart, op. cit., p. 382.

CHAPTER 6

MEASUREMENT OF INFLATION PROPENSITY: AN APPLICATION

OF DISCRIMINANT ANALYSIS

Introduction

The origin of economic development as a major
branch of economics was based on the conviction that a
number of economic settings are unique enough to warrant the construction of growth models capable of incorporating their distinguishing characteristics into
trailor made analytical frameworks.[1] Such ideal types
have been constructed for such tasks as examining the
impact of foreign aid,[2] determining the economic consequences of the size of nations,[3] and so on. However,
there has been no comprehensive attempt to identify
them with regard to particular sets that encounter the
same problems in combating world inflation or that
experience similar patterns of domestic price increases.
We cannot tell, therefore, whether the policy conclusions of a particular theory (monetarist, Keynesian,
and so on) are of wide applicability or are limited to
a few special cases.

An alternative approach to the analysis of inflation policy is developed below. Instead of trying to
define policy in an analytical vacuum, the regression
analysis of Chapter 5 is extended in an attempt to
classify the propensity of countries to inflate according to a set of structural differences in their economies. Using these differences as the basis for classifying countries, four country groupings are identified.

Countries within each group not only have experienced similar patterns of inflation but have, in addition, faced world inflation from the same basic environment.

An analysis of inflation based on a limited number
of environmental types enables us to determine whether
a government has chosen, for example, an anti-inflation
program that is best suited to its situation. From
this perspective, it is relatively easy to evaluate
the success or failure of individual country's stabili-

zation policies.

Methodology

Since this approach is essentially inductive rather than deductive, it requires an empirical basis for classifying countries according to the observable features of their economic environments. The regression analysis in the previous chapter was an initial attempt along these lines. Here a more complete explanation of inflationary relationships is attempted through the inclusion of additional variables.

The results should lead to the possibility of defining an optimal anti-inflationary strategy--and measuring its results--in relation to the results obtained by other countries in a similar environment (rather than in the more limited terms that have been used up to now). The analysis should also open up the prospect of associating optimal anti-inflationary strategies with the objective conditions of individual countries, enabling the design of policy to be placed on a sounder **footing** than has often been the case in recent years.

A general explanation of inflation in less developed economies seems especially called for because of the paucity of research in the field. Three recent papers-- Argy,[4] Conlisk[5] and Iyoha[6]--are exceptions. Each uses a large number of countries in their analysis, but in each case their aims were rather specific. Conlisk was interested in testing for the moneyness of time deposits; Argy attempted to verify some specific hypothesis of the structuralists; and Iyoha was primarily concerned with testing directly in the context of a cross-country regression analysis the hypothesis of a negative relationship between inflation and the degree of openness measured by the import-income ratio.

The analysis below is designed with the intent of creating a general framework for examining the economic consequences of world inflation.

Discriminant analysis is the main mathematical tool **used in establishing** this framework.

Discriminant Analysis

Discriminant analysis[7] is a nonparametric statistical technique used in the social sciences when it is necessary to classify population into certain groups according to various observable characteristics. Our problem is to find an answer to the question: what national characteristics such as openness, per capita income, size, and so on are associated with the patterns of inflation in broad types of economies. The objective of the analysis is to identify those characteristics that will permit us to discriminate most effectively between these broad country types. Having determined the discriminant function, it is then possible to predict the inflationary pattern (given an overall world rate) that an individual country not previously included in the analysis is likely to have.

Another use of the discriminant analysis lies in the fact that it allows us to see whether any countries analyzed in Chapter 5 through regression analysis were 'misclassified' in that they have an overall environment that could be better described by one of the other country groupings. In more technical terms, discriminant analysis will classify countries into groups so that the combined variance of the various structural characteristics selected for examination of all members placed in a group is minimized, while the combined variance of these factors between the different groups is maximized.

Purpose of Discriminant Analysis

More specifically with discriminant function analysis one attempts to identify clusters of the various categories into which the dependent variable is divided. These clusters are located in n-dimensional space, where n represents the number of independent variables. For example, if there were only two types of countries-- open and closed (or A and B)--and only two variables such as per capita income (x_1) and per capita debt (x_2) that were responsible for each country's inflationary pattern, a plotting of these patterns in two-dimensional space (Figures 1, 2, & 3) would show the degree to which the inflationary experience of each group of individual countries differed from that of the countries included in the other group.

79

Figure 1

Values for "A" and "B"
Countries X_1 and X_2

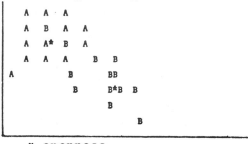

Per Capita
Income X

```
A    A   A
A    B   A   A
A    A*  B   A
A    A   A      B   B
A           B       BB
            B       B*B  B
                    B
                         B
```

x_2 openness

Figure 2

Clusters and Centroids for Two Classes

Per Capita
Income X_1

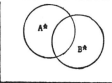

x_2 openness

Figure 3

Projection of Values of X_1 and X_2 to Discriminant
Function Z line

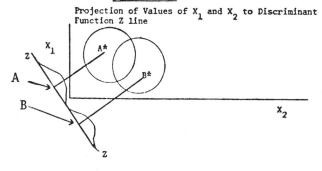

80

In our example there is a considerable overlap between the values (areas) associated with each group's inflationary pattern as determined by the experience of each of the member countries (A's and B's in Figure 1) for specific values of x_1 and x_2. Discriminant function analysis attempts to combine the information from the independent variables (x_1 and x_2) in such a manner as to discriminate as much as possible between the two groups of countries. As a first step, distinction is made between the members of the two groups. To accomplish this, a linear discriminant function of the form:

$$Z = aX_1 + bX_2$$

(where Z = discriminant function score, X_1, X_2 = values of the two variables , and a, b = the coefficients of the variables) is formed. The weights a and b are applied to the values of the two variables for each of the countries being examined. The result is a Z score for each country. By using the Z scores, one is able to project the values from the two dimensioned space to a single line and depict as frequency distributions (as shown in Figure 3).

The weights for the coefficients used in a discriminant function are calculated so as to maximize the F ratio of variances between group means for Z values to variance within groups for Z values.

Problems in Applying Discriminant Analysis

Discriminatory analysis is an extremely useful tool when several groups are defined a priori and for purposes of analysis must be distinguished as much as possible from one another. The approach's main weakness lies in a number of rather arbitrary assumptions as to:

1. Determining whether differences in score profiles for two or more groups are statistically significant.

2. The best way to maximize the discrimination among groups through combining variables.

3. Establishing rules for the placement of new individuals into one of the groups.

With regard to the first problem, statistical tests like the F test are often difficult to interpret. It is possible for two groups to have non-significant differences on each of the variables, but for the overall difference between profiles to be significant. Such tests combine all the information from the different variables in one overall test of significance. Unless there are significant differences on some of the variables, preferably on the majority of them, it is difficult to interpret the significance of differences in overall profiles. At best such tests provide rather meager information about the significance of differences.

With regard to the second and third limitations, discriminatory analysis suffers in that there are some logical difficulties involved in deciding the basis upon which to form initial groupings prior to performing discriminatory analysis. In many cases such as in comparing those countries that float their exchange rate and those that do not, or those countries that have defaulted on their international debt and those that have not, the groupings are rather obvious. With regard to situations such as inflation where all the variables are quantifiable numerically, the number of relevant groups to form and the initial country assignments to each become somewhat arbitrary and ambiguous. It is not clear for example whether 4 or 5 (or 3) groups should be used. The regression analysis was a helpful tool in this regard, but a certain amount of arbitrariness remains.

Discriminant Scores

To distinguish groups of countries whose members have, because of similar environments, experienced corresponding patterns of inflations, a number of discriminatory factors were selected. These included: (1) income per capita; (2) economic size; (3) imports as a percentage of GNP; (4) the ratio of the current account deficit to investment; (5) the percentage of agriculture in GNP; (6) the percentage of manufacturing in GNP; (7) savings as a percentage of GNP; and (8) the rate of inflation.

The discriminant analysis procedure used attempted to differentiate by forming one or more linear combinations of these variables. These 'discriminant functions'

82

are of the form:

$$Z_1 = a_{i1}X_1 + a_{i2}X_2 + \cdots a_{in}X_n$$

where Z_1 is the score of discriminate function i; the a's are weighting coefficients, and the X's are the standardized values of the discriminating variables. The functions are formed in such a way as to maximize the separation of the groups.

The eight values and their associated conical correlations denote the relative ability (Table 17) of each discriminant function to separate groups. Clearly the third function (Table 18) is marginal. Before any functions were removed, lambda was 0.0731. This indicates a considerable discriminating power exists in the variables being used (the larger lambda is, the less discriminating power is present). After some of this discriminating power has been removed (by placing it into the first discriminant function), lambda increases, but the chi square statistic indicates that a statistically significant amount of discriminating information still exists and is removed by the second and third functions. The large lambda value indicates that a fourth discriminant function would not significantly add to our ability to discriminate between the groups. Analysis, therefore, stopped at three functions.

The standardized discriminate function coefficients are of great analytical importance in and of themselves. When the sign is ignored, each function represents the relative contribution of its associated variable to that function. The sign merely denotes whether the variable is making a positive or negative contribution. The interpretation is analogous to the interpretation of beta weights in multiple regression. Interestingly enough, per capita income (Table 17) is over twice as important as the inflation rate in the first function, while imports, the agricultural sector, and savings all as a percentage of GNP are of little importance.

The import and agricultural percentages do, however, make a significant contribution to the second determinant. Economic size contributes very little to any of the functions.

Centroids were calculated (Table 19) and represent the average profile of each of the four groups. Since

83

T A B L E   17
THE DISCRIMINANT FUNCTION COEFFICIENTS IN STANDARDIZED FORM

VARIABLE	FUNCTION 1	FUNCTION 2	FUNCTION 3
Per Capita Income	-0.69920	1.09654	0.87869
Economic Size	-0.12324	0.17624	-0.05962
Imports/GNP	0.05815	0.37709	-0.73330
Deficit Current Account/Investment	-0.21883	-0.01239	0.33226
Agricultural Sector/GNP	-0.05716	0.79478	0.38192
Manufacturing Sector/GNP	-0.15551	-0.37748	-1.16399
Savings/GNP	-0.06251	-0.42875	0.41125
Inflation Rate	0.23539	-0.29536	-0.10569

NOTE: Deficit Current Account/Investment not statistically significant.

TABLE 18

STATISTICS FOR DISCRIMINANT FUNCTIONS

Discriminant Function	Eigenvalue	Relative Percentage	Canonical Correlation
1	7.36765	92.93	0.938
2	0.35126	4.43	0.510
3	0.20943	2.64	0.416

- -

Functions Derived	Wilks' Lambda	Chi-Square	DF	Significance
0	0.0731	125.547	24	0.000
1	0.6119	23.577	14	0.052
2	0.8268	9.127	6	0.167

TABLE 19

CENTROIDS OF GROUPS IN REDUCED SPACE

GROUP	Function 1	Function 2	Function 3
Large	-1.54641	0.13694	0.12290
Medium I	0.10975	-0.64678	0.63467
Medium II	0.66310	-0.56940	0.68014
Small	0.69056	0.54456	-0.07871

the centroid is the point about which the points for
individuals in a group balance in all directions, the
groups would be well discriminated if their centroids
(as in the case in Figures 4, 5, 6, & 7) are far apart,
and the members of each group fairly near their centroid
(Figure 5).

Classification of Countries

The next step in the analysis was to confirm the
correctness of the initial group classification given
to the sample countries.

Final groupings of the countries was achieved
through the use of a series of classification functions,
one for each of the groups. Under the assumption of a
multivariate normal distribution, the classification
scores were converted into probabilities of group
membership, and countries assigned to groups on the
basis of their highest probability.

Interestingly enough, a comparison of the final
classifications based on discriminant analysis and
those made initially using regression analysis indicate
that the preliminary results were largely satisfactory
and independently confirm those obtained by the more
sophisticated procedure. Discriminant analysis (Tables
20 & 21) indicates that only 20 percent of the countries
were misclassified by the regression procedures. This
is a rather small percentage given the number of additional variables introduced into the discriminant analysis.

The small group from the regression analysis had
the largest number of reclassifications undoubtedly due
to the relatively large economic size of several of
the countries--Paraguay, Ethiopia, the Sudan, and
Iceland.

Conclusions

In general the results obtained from cross-section
regression analysis and the discriminant analysis are
in agreement. The discriminant analysis has allowed
us to identify four distinct country groups, each of
which has a unique environment in which the recent

FIGURE 4

PLOT OF DISCRIMINANT SCORE 1 (HORIZONTAL) VS. DISCRIMINANT SCORE 2 (VERTICAL).   * INDICATES A GROUP CENTROID.
THE SYMBOL 1 DENOTES A CASE FROM GROUP 1 SUBFILE LARG

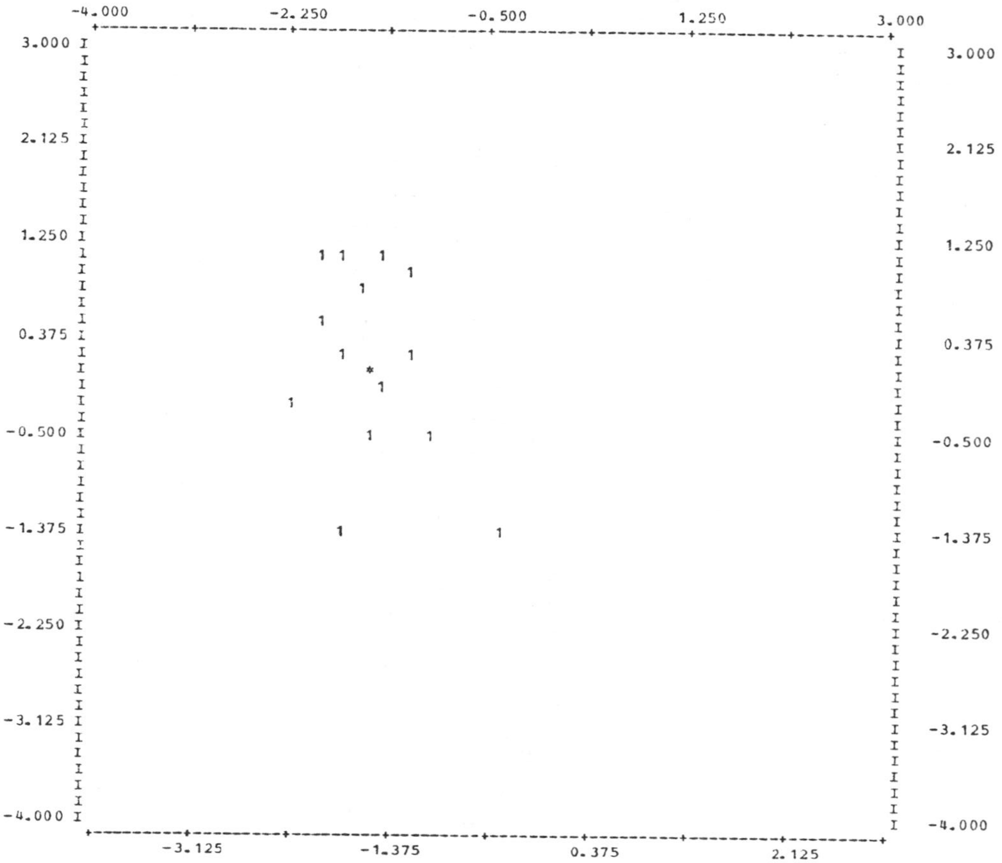

88

FIGURE 5

PLOT OF DISCRIMINANT SCORE 1 (HORIZONTAL) VS. DISCRIMINANT SCORE 2 (VERTICAL). * INDICATES A GROUP CENTROID.
THE SYMBOL 2 DENOTES A CASE FROM GROUP 2 SUBFILE MED1

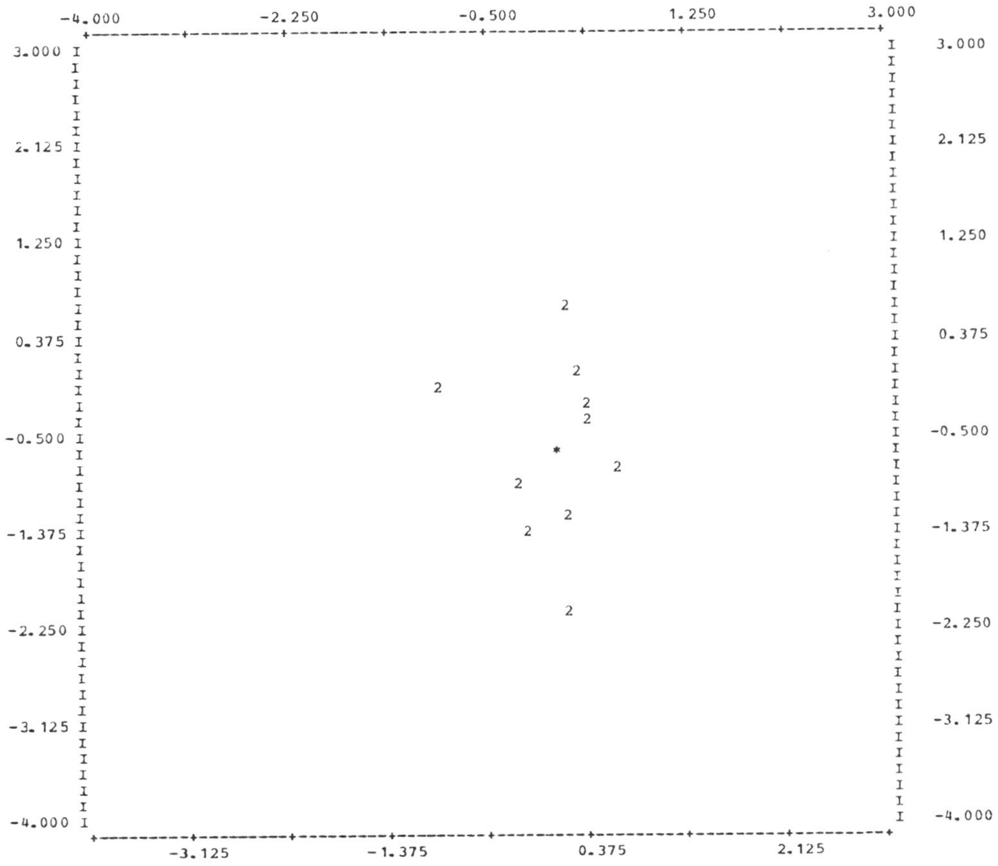

89

FIGURE 6

PLOT OF DISCRIMINANT SCORE 1 (HORIZONTAL) VS. DISCRIMINANT SCORE 2 (VERTICAL). * INDICATES A GROUP CENTROID.
THE SYMBOL 3 DENOTES A CASE FROM GROUP 3 SUBFILE MED2

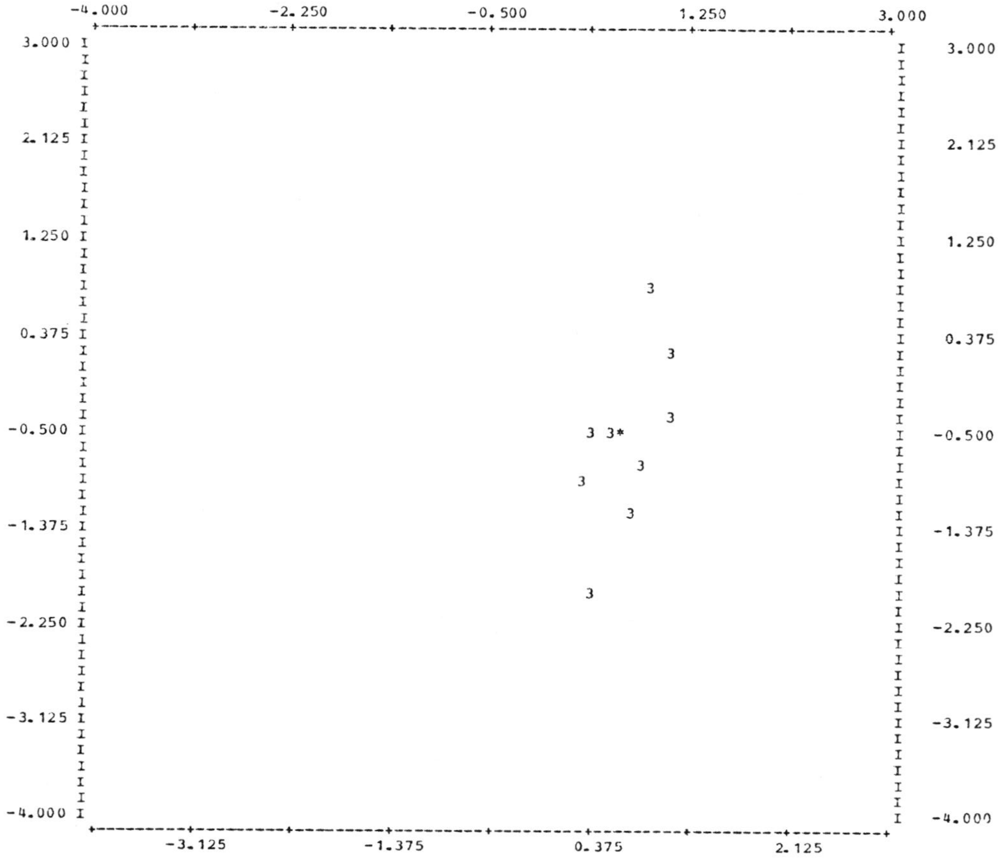

90

FIGURE 7

PLOT OF DISCRIMINANT SCORE 1 (HORIZONTAL) VS. DISCRIMINANT SCORE 2 (VERTICAL). * INDICATES A GROUP CENTROID.
THE SYMBOL 4 DENOTES A CASE FROM GROUP 4   SUBFILE   SMAL

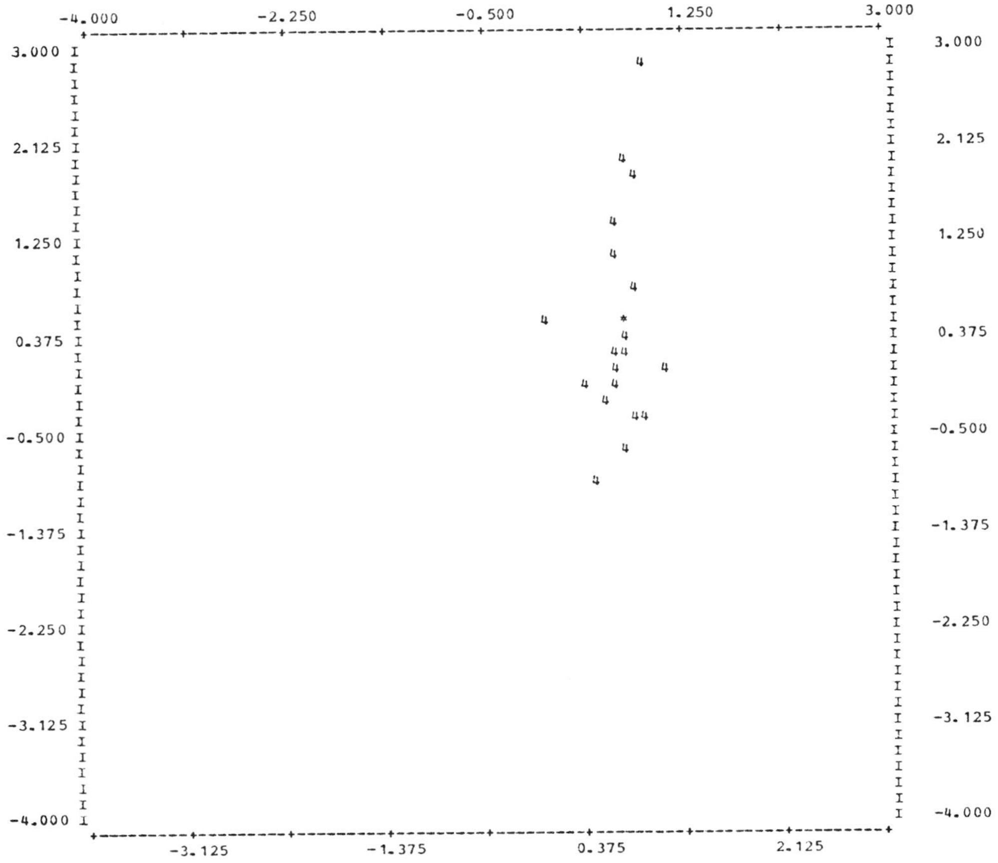

T A B L E 20
RESULTS DISCRIMINANT ANALYSIS

COUNTRY	INITIAL GROUPING	DISCRIMINANT ANALYSIS PLACEMENT	DISCRIMINANT SCORES FUNCTION 1	FUNCTION 2	FUNCTION 3
AUSTRALIA	Large	Large	-1.437	-0.090	-1.313
AUSTRIA	Large	Large	-1.164	0.207	-0.170
BELGUIM	Large	Large	1.819	0.219	-1.489
CANADA	Large	Large	-1.837	1.106	1.815
DENMARK	Large	Large	-1.486	1.069	-0.258
FRANCE	Large	Large	-1.581	-0.474	-0.393
GERMANY	Large	Large	-2.276	-0.159	-0.963
ITALY	Large	Medium I	-0.379	-1.386	-0.420
JAPAN	Large	Large	-1.061	-0.490	0.829
NETHERLANDS	Large	Large	-1.634	0.816	-0.807
NORWAY	Large	Large	-1.235	0.996	-0.938
SWEDEN	Large	Large	-1.955	1.048	1.136
UNITED KINGDOM	Large	Large	-1.825	-1.443	1.450
UNITED STATES	Large	Large	-1.962	0.497	0.616
GREECE	Medium I	Medium I	0.082	-0.697	0.340
SOUTH AFRICA	Medium I	Medium I	0.185	-1.271	-1.117
SPAIN	Medium I	Medium I	-0.110	-1.436	-0.548
MALAYSIA	Medium I	Medium I	0.320	0.061	-0.332
MEXICO	Medium I	Medium I	0.230	-2.114	-0.853
VENEZUELA	Medium I	Medium I	-0.212	-0.984	0.113
EGYPT	Medium I	Medium I	0.390	-0.316	-0.710
SRI LANKA	Medium I	Medium II	0.396	-0.181	0.732
KONEA	Medium I	Medium I	0.651	-0.764	-1.692
ISRAEL	Medium I	Medium I	0.195	0.705	-2.227
FINLAND	Medium I	Large	-0.919	-0.118	-0.654
NIGERIA	Medium II	Medium II	1.096	-0.417	1.581
INDIA	Medium II	Medium II	0.392	-1.952	0.954
PAKISTAN	Medium II	Medium II	0.785	-0.759	0.631
PHILIPPINES	Medium II	Medium II	0.294	-0.946	0.474
THAILAND	Medium II	Medium II	0.364	-0.436	0.227
COLOMBIA	Medium II	Medium II	0.768	-1.242	-0.095
ALGERIA	Medium II	Mediun I	0.390	-0.428	-0.346
BANGLADESH	Medium II	Medium II	0.905	0.742	2.156

TABLE (CONTD.)

COUNTRY	INITIAL GROUPING	DISCRIMINANT ANALYSIS PLACEMENT	DISCRIMINANT SCORES		
			FUNCTION 1	FUNCTION 2	FUNCTION 3
MOROCCO	Medium II	Medium II	0.563	-0.517	0.273
INDONESIA	Medium II	Medium II	1.074	0.261	0.947
COSTA RICA	Small	Medium I	0.553	-0.162	-2.275
ECUADOR	Small	Medium II	0.746	-0.713	-0.536
EL SALVADOR	Small	Medium II	0.504	-0.899	-0.141
PARAGUAY	Small	Medium II	0.415	-0.099	0.506
ETHIOPIA	Small	Medium II	0.620	0.237	2.056
SUDAN	Small	Medium II	0.912	-0.356	1.481
CAMEROON	Small	Small	0.674	-0.054	-0.090
ICELAND	Small	Medium I	-0.001	0.525	0.040
SENEGAL	Small	Small	0.709	0.293	-0.090
TOGO	Small	Small	0.668	1.140	-0.233
CHAD	Small	Small	0.936	2.873	-0.770
SIERRA LEONE	Small	Small	1.035	0.134	0.614
JAMAICA	Small	Small	0.677	0.019	-1.569
NIGER	Small	Small	0.785	1.833	0.236
CENTRAL AFRICAN REPUBLIC	Small	Small	0.785	1.833	0.236
GABON	Small	Small	0.853	0.865	-0.675
KENYA	Small	Small	0.839	-0.317	-0.390
MALAGASSY	Small	Small	0.700	0.379	-0.061
MALAWI	Small	Small	0.761	1.928	0.793
TANZANIA	Small	Small	0.640	1.432	0.879

T A B L E 21

SUMMARY RESULTS DISCRIMINATE ANALYSIS CLASSIFICATION

INITIAL GROUP	NUMBER OF COUNTRIES	PREDICTED GROUP MEMBERSHIP			
		GROUP 1	GROUP 2	GROUP 3	GROUP 4
LARGE	14	13 (92.9%)	1 (7.1%)	0 (0.0%)	0 (0.0%)
MEDIUM I	11	1 (9.1%)	9 (81.8%)	1 (9.1%)	0 (0.0%)
MEDIUM II	10	0 (0.0%)	1 (10.0%)	9 (90.0%)	0 (0.0%)
SMALL	20	0 (0.0%)	2 (10.0%)	5 (25.0%)	13 (65.0%)

PERCENT OF GROUPED CASES CORRECTLY CLASSIFIED : 80.00%

94

inflationary patterns were manifested. In particular the differentiation between the low inflation--large and small--countries and the high inflation medium countries was relatively successful.

From these results it appears that there are in fact certain identifiable principles that determine the likely course (economic consequences) that world inflation will take as its impact is felt on an individual country. or group of countries.

At this point, however, it is not possible to make an estimate as to the optimal rate of inflation a country should strive for in modifying the impact of (a given rate of) world inflation. The statistical analysis presented only allows us to differentiate between the various countries on the basis of the inflation rates they actually experienced. If the choice of policies in these countries was misguided in the first place, any policy recommendations based on our analysis would be misplaced as well.

In this regard it is interesting to note that in practically every country, economists and policymakers have been apt to blame domestic inflation on 'imported inflation.' Inflation thus appears as a unique phenomenon which everybody imports and nobody exports. Even U.S. officials draw visions of global inflation to deflect criticism of their own price level failures.[8]

Of course the doctrine of imported inflation furnishes a comfortable rationalization for do-little public policies. If anti-inflationary policy is poorly implemented, then the resulting spurt in domestic prices can always be blamed on OPEC, world bankers, the Americans, and so on.

If inflation rates were more or less the same throughout the world, there might be some validity in these arguments. However, as a recent survey article (by economists sympathetic to the doctrine of global inflation) observed: "Nevertheless major discrepancies between the inflation rates experienced by different countries persisted and these divergencies need explaining."[9]

Essentially the rest of the study is concerned with this problem. Its aim is three-fold: (1) to consider the determinants of the domestic price level in the four country groups; (2) to identify that group of countries which has the greatest scope for countering world inflationary forces; and (3) to assess the economic consequences of world inflation on several countries within that group.

Using the discriminant analysis framework developed above, it will be shown that the Medium I countries have the greatest discretion over their internal rates of inflation (given a world rate of inflation). Since their domestic price level is not totally dependent on external price movements, they are referred to as semi-dependent.

The economic consequences of world inflation on these countries is then shown, after an examination of two of their members--Mexico and South Africa--to be largely a function of how their policymakers respond to increases in world prices, not necessarily what economic events are taking place in other countries or financial centers.

Notes

1. The original attempt being W. A. Lewis, The Theory of Economic Growth (London: Allan & Unwin, 1955).

2. Hollis Chenery, "Targets for Development," in B. Ward, The Widening Gap (New York: Columbia University Press, 1971).

3. Cf. the papers included in Austin Robinson, The Economic Consequences of the Size of Nations (London: Macmillan, 1963).

4. Victor Argy, "Structural Inflation in Developing Countries," Oxford Economic Papers (March 1970), pp. 73-85.

5. John Conlisk, "Cross-Country Inflation Evidence on the Moneyness of Time Deposits," Economic Record (June 1970), pp. 222-229.

6. Milton Ame Iyoha, "Inflation and Openness in Less Developed Economies: A Cross Section Analysis," Economic Development and Cultural Change (October 1973), pp. 31-37.

7. Several detailed descriptions of the discriminant analysis approach are available. One of the best is Jum Nunnally, Psychometric Theory (New York: McGraw Hill, 1978), Ch. 14. Others include John Overall and C. James Klett, Applied Multivariat Analysis (New York: McGraw Hill, 1972), Ch. 9-11; and John Van de Geer, Introduction to Multivariate Analysis for Social Sciences (San Francisco: W. H. Freeman, 1971).

8. Sidney Weintraub, "The Price Level in the Open Economy," Kyklos (No. 1, 1977), pp. 22-37.

9. D. Laidler and J. M. Parkin, "Inflation: A Survey," Economic Journal (December 1975), p. 783.

CHAPTER 7

A MONETARY MODEL OF IMPORTED INFLATION

Introduction

The discriminant analysis of inflationary patterns performed in the previous chapter did not include monetary variables. By abstracting money from other factors that may cause inflationary patterns to differ, we are able to directly determine whether money-price relationships vary between the four country groups, a proposition usually rejected out of hand by most monetarists,[1] yet a situation considered quite likely on both theoretical and empirical grounds by many other economists.[2]

The issues at hand are therefore:

1. What precisely have been the world trends in money and price?

2. Why did the world money supply increase so rapidly beginning in the late 1960s?

3. What is the causation between money and prices?

4. If the causation is exclusively from money to prices, why do observed rates of price increases in various countries and the four major country groupings differ somewhat?

5. Is this difference in country and group inflation rates inconsistent with the monetary theories of inflation and the balance of payments?

6. If this is the case, what are the implications for national economic policymaking?

World Money and Prices

There is no question that the world money stock exploded in all geographical areas between 1970 and 1973 (Tables 22-27) and was followed by an upsurge in world prices from 1973 to 1975, particularly in export and import prices (Tables 28 & 29). The reason for the

99

TABLE 22

THE MONEY SUPPLY IN DEVELOPED COUNTRIES, 1952-1976

(Yearly Average Rate)

Country	1952-1955	1955-1960	1960-1965	1965-1968	1968-1970	1970-1973	1973-1976	1973	1974	1975	1976
Australia	5.63	1.74	1.93	6.74	7.05	13.62	10.04	15.78	-0.99	23.34	9.12
Austria	11.58	7.46	8.58	5.98	7.07	15.19	10.58	8.67	4.96	17.17	9.94
Belgium	3.32	2.73	7.65	5.73	5.42	11.23	9.58	7.46	6.21	15.71	7.08
Canada	-	12.21	19.93	13.79	18.72	10.13	6.20	8.98	-2.90	20.89	2.03
Denmark	2.67	7.15	11.06	12.36	6.85	11.01	13.19	11.68	4.71	30.29	6.30
France	12.54	9.71	13.11	6.83	4.83	12.17	11.89	9.78	15.20	12.72	7.88
Germany	11.31	10.25	8.87	6.83	7.79	8.97	9.94	0.76	12.19	13.95	3.94
Italy	9.39	10.41	14.19	13.62	21.55	20.15	13.84	24.33	9.39	13.45	18.88
Japan	-	12.21	19.93	13.79	18.72	23.58	11.70	16.76	11.51	11.12	17.66
Netherlands	7.24	3.38	8.50	8.13	9.91	10.63	12.77	0.06	12.21	19.68	6.80
New Zealand	7.90	4.05	1.03	-0.30	5.04	21.85	7.12	26.56	3.12	9.69	8.68
Norway	3.64	3.07	6.43	10.00	10.37	27.69	1.80	59.94	-19.38	16.56	12.27
Sweden	1.51	6.42	8.07	33.13	3.79	9.06	13.25	10.13	25.08	8.78	6.76
Switzerland	3.45	7.25	8.76	7.81	11.31	7.39	3.60	-0.18	-1.09	4.36	7.72
United Kingdom	1.94	1.97	3.44	3.83	4.73	11.35	13.53	5.10	10.79	18.60	11.36
United States	6.09	8.26	14.93	7.32	8.74	7.25	4.69	5.82	3.13	5.37	5.59
(Average)	(6.30)	(6.77)	(9.78)	(9.72)	(9.49)	(13.83)	(9.61)	(13.23)	(5.88)	(15.11)	(8.88)

Source: Computed from International Monetary Fund, International Financial Statistics, May 1977, January 1978.

100

TABLE 23

THE MONEY SUPPLY IN DEVELOPING WESTERN HEMISPHERE, 1952-1976

(Yearly Average Rate)

Country	1952-1955	1955-1960	1960-1965	1965-1968	1968-1970	1970-1973	1973-1976	1973	1974	1975	1976
Caribbean and Central America											
Costa Rica	8.66	4.95	6.67	14.17	11.33	22.35	24.47	24.38	19.21	24.09	30.35
El Salvador	4.61	0.59	5.34	4.01	6.08	16.16	26.33	20.68	20.43	19.04	40.64
Jamaica	5.83	9.21	4.00	14.29	15.52	18.35	16.26	20.77	27.11	20.23	2.83
Latin America											
Colombia	13.18	15.61	19.55	18.06	18.84	22.97	23.99	30.74	17.82	20.07	34.74
Ecuador	4.31	7.74	9.07	16.02	19.75	23.58	29.88	34.89	50.76	10.83	31.12
Mexico	14.05	10.01	11.73	11.84	12.83	15.79	23.67	22.39	20.65	21.43	29.10
Paraguay	34.81	13.40	12.94	5.60	12.39	19.57	20.00	32.62	21.02	17.92	21.09
Venezuela	8.14	8.16	5.77	7.92	8.14	18.58	34.59	19.18	37.75	50.45	17.64
(Average)	(11.70)	(8.71)	(9.38)	(11.49)	(13.11)	(19.67)	(24.90)	(25.71)	(26.84)	(23.01)	(25.94)

Source: Computed from International Monetary Fund, International Financial Statistics, May 1977, January 1978.

101

TABLE 24

THE MONEY SUPPLY IN MEDIUM DEVELOPED COUNTRIES, 1972-1976

(Yearly Average Rate) Country	1952-1955	1955-1960	1960-1965	1965-1968	1968-1970	1970-1973	1973-1976	1973	1974	1975	1976
Finland	7.13	6.78	6.88	8.57	13.63	21.08	16.23	23.29	18.84	34.47	-1.75
Greece	30.79	14.26	15.70	12.84	8.41	19.70	19.44	23.42	19.79	16.44	22.17
Iceland	19.00	8.97	20.00	2.53	26.84	27.28	29.40	38.89	30.07	33.15	24.65
Israel	17.60	16.05	16.64	15.11	8.09	29.73	22.19	32.33	17.96	21.71	27.06
Portugal	6.52	6.99	6.44	9.05	6.96	21.39	3.29	35.42	10.21	24.53	
South Africa	2.62	-0.02	8.04	11.98	4.95	14.42	9.47	20.40	18.60	6.86	3.52
Spain	11.20	11.12	15.75	12.65	10.16	23.92	19.12	23.58	17.23	18.69	21.46
(Average)	(13.55)	(9.16)	(12.78)	(10.39)	(11.29)	(22.50)	(17.02)	(28.19)	(18.96)	(22.26)	(16.19)

Source: Computed from International Monetary Fund, International Financial Statistics, May 1977, January 1978.

102

TABLE 25

THE MONEY SUPPLY - AFRICA, 1960-1976

(Yearly Average Rate) Country	1960-1965	1965-1968	1968-1970	1970-1973	1973-1976	1973	1974	1975	1976
Cameroon	8.13	14.01	10.54	13.93	17.63	23.55	29.40	3.20	21.90
Central Africa	14.29	9.64	1.11	7.63	22.69	4.46	31.73	0.17	39.97
Chad	4.41	3.19	8.03	2.84	28.68	-1.29	53.75	10.54	25.35
Ethiopia	9.95	3.11	5.60	10.85	11.57	28.31	19.13	27.16	-8.31
Gabon	9.73	2.50	14.74	21.18	66.35	24.26	68.27	55.45	75.98
Ivory Coast	12.60	11.85	18.90	12.18	30.17	14.33	38.04	10.47	44.62
Kenya	-	10.48	22.11	17.02	13.68	27.50	3.99	13.05	24.98
Malagassy	5.86	8.51	8.29	7.46	11.70	7.46	18.53	2.09	15.18
Malawi	-	9.69	14.12	19.02	9.72	35.74	33.24	0.26	-1.11
Morocco	7.59	7.09	8.79	15.72	20.89	17.03	26.64	18.09	18.14
Niger	10.73	2.53	10.41	15.54	22.07	19.72	29.48	14.15	23.07
Senigal	-6.36	-0.70	10.30	8.56	29.06	12.86	53.44	10.98	26.23
Sierra Leone	2.89	9.19	2.57	18.64	14.30	24.08	13.63	9.88	19.61
Somallia	15.15	3.48	18.37	10.47	25.19	15.12	23.96	31.37	20.48
Sudan	10.72	8.34	18.09	15.42	22.10	22.33	30.42	14.50	21.89
Tanzania	-	13.27	10.32	16.50	25.51	17.34	28.83	23.19	24.57
Togo	13.01	13.12	15.96	4.42	41.77	-2.23	116.99	-14.05	52.78
(Average)	(8.48)	(7.61)	(11.66)	(12.79)	(24.30)	(17.09)	(36.44)	(13.56)	(26.20)

Source: Computed from International Monetary Fund, International Financial Statistics, May 1977, January 1978.

103

TABLE 26

THE MONEY SUPPLY IN THE MIDDLE EAST, 1955-1976

(Yearly Average Rate) Country	1955-1960	1960-1965	1965-1968	1968-1970	1970-1973	1973-1976	1973	1974	1975	1976
Cyprus	-	10.43	10.15	14.15	12.63	11.05	5.92	10.14	-3.91	29.41
Turkey	16.70	12.22	16.81	15.79	26.16	28.93	32.67	27.15	31.63	28.05
Egypt	3.55	10.09	3.31	2.75	15.46	22.94	21.78	24.73	23.08	21.04
Iran	17.43	10.42	12.35	10.48	29.40	33.93	29.75	37.17	20.13	45.78
Iraq	9.88	6.81	7.12	7.23	14.03	32.76	24.17	43.34	35.29	20.67
Jordan	8.33	12.62	23.01	9.48	9.21	23.70	21.07	22.24	28.36	20.63
Syria	14.24	8.49	14.64	11.95	17.49	31.32	20.50	45.90	25.72	23.46
Saudi Arabia	-	10.17	13.78	4.49	30.14	63.72	39.95	41.40	89.57	-
(Average)	(11.69)	(10.16)	(12.65)	(9.54)	(19.38)	(31.04)	(24.48)	(31.50)	(31.23)	(27.01)

Source: Computed from International Monetary Fund, International Financial Statistics, May 1977, January 1978.

104

TABLE 27

THE MONEY SUPPLY IN ASIA

(Yearly Average Rate)

Country	1952-1955	1955-1960	1960-1965	1965-1968	1968-1970	1970-1973	1973-1976	1973	1974	1975	1976
India	6.57	5.82	9.44	7.81	12.28	14.45	12.36	16.85	10.23	9.47	17.55
Indonesia	-	-	-	-	46.74	38.94	33.62	41.56	40.45	35.22	25.63
Korea	89.32	19.14	23.54	39.40	20.07	33.40	28.35	23.49	29.49	24.97	30.66
Malaysia	5.37	-1.60	5.33	4.19	9.88	21.71	12.06	37.61	8.54	7.25	20.88
Pakistan	7.12	7.91	7.00	12.66	9.23	16.56	16.02	11.31	1.46	13.78	35.30
Philippines	3.04	6.73	9.37	8.09	14.67	19.96	18.44	12.32	23.96	14.51	17.06
Sri Lanka	6.27	2.44	7.31	3.63	1.41	12.24	14.47	12.03	6.02	4.86	34.92
Thailand	12.48	6.89	4.91	4.11	6.23	15.77	10.65	21.00	9.45	6.34	16.40
(Average)	(18.60)	(6.76)	(9.56)	(11.41)	(15.06)	(21.63)	(18.25)	(22.02)	(16.20)	(14.55)	(24.80)

Source: Computed from International Monetary Fund, International Financial Statistics, May 1977, January 1978.

105

TABLE 28
INFLATION IN EXPORT PRICES

(Yearly Average Rate)

Area	1960-1965	1965-1968	1968-1970	1970-1973	1973-1976	1968	1969	1970	1971	1972	1973	1974	1975	1976
World	0.91	0.37	4.83	12.13	16.24	-1.09	3.30	6.38	5.00	8.57	23.68	42.55	8.46	2.29
Industrialized Countries	0.92	0.74	4.83	10.79	12.10	-1.09	3.30	6.38	5.00	8.57	19.30	25.74	11.70	1.05
Other Europe	2.99	-1.79	5.41	13.44	13.10	-5.26	3.33	-0.99	6.00	9.43	25.86	33.56	10.27	0.00
Australia, New Zealand, South Africa	1.43	-1.32	1.02	19.11	4.89	-1.01	3.06	4.17	1.00	14.85	45.69	18.34	-3.50	1.04
Other Western Hemisphere	2.74	-0.38	7.83	12.66	14.91	1.18	3.49	12.36	-4.00	8.33	37.50	30.77	1.08	15.43
Other Less Developed Areas	1.15	0.37	4.83	11.60	12.33	2.25	5.49	4.17	-3.00	5.15	36.27	37.41	-3.14	6.49
Oil Exporting Countries	-1.01	0.00	2.06	23.20	53.69	1.05	0.00	4.17	25.00	8.00	38.52	212.30	6.79	6.20
Other Asia	-0.77	-2.02	2.60	11.87	8.94	2.15	5.26	0.00	-2.00	3.06	38.61	40.00	-8.72	1.69
Other Africa	-	-	5.41	8.58	13.27	-	7.78	3.09	-8.00	5.43	31.96	46.88	1.06	-2.11

Source: Computed from International Monetary Fund, International Financial Statistics, May 1977, January 1978.

Note: Figures are growth rates computed from indexes of prices expressed in U.S. dollars.

106

TABLE 29

INFLATION IN IMPORT PRICES

(Yearly Average Rate)

Area	1960-1965	1965-1968	1968-1970	1970-1973	1973-1976	1968	1969	1970	1971	1972	1973	1974	1975	1976
World	0.44	0.00	3.70	11.60	15.83	-1.06	2.15	5.26	5.00	6.67	24.11	43.17	8.04	0.47
Industrialized Countries	0.45	0.36	4.26	11.60	15.83	-1.08	2.17	6.38	5.00	7.62	23.01	41.73	8.12	1.41
Other Europe	1.54	-1.06	4.26	11.87	16.54	-3.16	3.26	5.26	6.00	7.55	22.81	46.04	8.87	-0.45
Australia, New Zealand, South Africa	0.86	-0.35	3.14	11.33	16.11	-3.09	2.13	4.17	6.00	8.49	20.00	32.61	14.21	3.35
Other Less Developed Areas	1.04	-1.02	2.06	11.33	16.64	0.00	1.04	3.09	3.00	6.80	25.45	50.00	7.25	-1.35
Other Asia	0.80	-1.32	1.53	11.06	18.16	0.00	1.01	2.04	3.00	4.85	26.85	56.20	7.94	-2.16

Source: Computed from International Monetary Fund, International Financial Statistics, May 1977, January 1978.

Note: Figures are growth rates computed from indexes of prices expressed in U.S. dollars.

107

1970-1973 explosion was clearly not due to the collective eccentricity of the world's central banks but rather a series of developments beginning in the United States in the late 1960s.

The fiscal deficits of the United States incurred to pay for Vietnam expenditures induced an acceleration in the growth rate of the U.S. money supply and price level. Inflation then spread from the United States to other countries. A number of factors aided in the transmission of inflation throughout the world:[3]

1. The 'direct price influence' which worked commodity arbitrage and raised the price of traded goods everywhere.

2. The trade surpluses of other nations which were induced by the fact that U.S. income growth was higher than their own, as well as by deteriorating U.S. price competiveness, boosted foreign levels of production, income, and eventually prices when full employment was reached.

3. The 'Bretton Woods monetization channel' allowed U.S. balance of payments deficits to be paid for by the creation of U.S. dollar liabilities. Dollar inflows expanded the monetary base of many nations, further contributing to their own domestic inflation rates.

4. An acceleration of U.S. inflation undoubtedly raised domestic expectations of inflation directly. The result was even higher wage and price increases.

These factors were interrelated in that for each country higher prices for tradable goods, higher real output, and higher expected prices for nontradable goods, all raised that country's transaction demand for money. With the expansion of dollars and a monetary system facilitating their mobility, it was easy for these countries to attract the international reserves needed to bring the domestic money supply into equality with higher money demand. Domestic monetary supplies increased thus driving prices up even further.

The Money-Price Relationship

The direct money-price relationship postulated by monetarists, of course, is not new. The monetary hypothesis of inflation is in fact the oldest theory of price increase. Basically the theory relates international differences in inflation to the growth rates of money supply per unit of output. This proposition was tested by Anna Schwartz for the period 1952-1969 using a sample of 40 countries. The correlation coefficient was as high as 0.97, from which she concluded "the key to understanding secular price change, now as in the past, is the behavior of money stock per unit of output."[4] This interpretation is, of course, open to challenge because of the assumed direction of causality. Many economists have taken the position that the quantity of money is not something exogenously determined; rather it is an endogenously determined quantity that adjusts to expenditure decisions.

If this were the case, the monetarist position would be untenable. Recent research, however, using Granger causality tests[5] has examined the nature of the money-price relationship. Granger causality tests provide a way of testing for the direction of causation between two variables. It involves regressing one variable on its own past values and the past values of the other variable.

The lagged values of the 'dependent' variable are included in order to detrend the series and so reduce the probability of finding a relation between two variables which are not truly causally related, but which merely move up or down together over time.

For all countries tested by Bazdarich[6] for example, the money-supply growth apparently had a systematic effect on inflation with no reverse effect; i.e., the causation was from changes in money to changes in price and not the other way around.

The Monetarist World Money-Price Mechanism

If the causation from money to prices on a national level is accepted, then it is fairly easy to show the manner in which money and prices interact on a worldwide basis. If all countries had fixed exchange rates, the world economy would be identical to that of a federation of individual states such as the U.S. As with the U.S., mobility of dollars between states assures similarity of prices in all geographical areas. The same would apply to the world as a whole. The relevant money supply as far as the world is concerned would be the sum of the domestic money supplies of each national economy (converted to a common unit at the fixed exchange rates); its time path determined by the combined monetary policies of the individual countries.

Given this environment the relationship between money and the inflation rate in any particular country is viewed by monetarists as largely a result of the process whereby inflationary impulses are transmitted to it from other countries. As far as long-run equilibrium is concerned, the predictions of the monetary approach are quite clear cut. If the world economy were always in long-run equilibrium, any one country would be facing a level and structure of interest rates determined for it on world capital markets, and facing a price level and inflation rate (fully anticipated) also determined for it on world markets. It could operate at full employment only by conforming to these parameters.[7]

In this situation, domestic monetary policy would influence that economy's rate of inflation in the long run only to the extent that domestic monetary expansion or contraction influenced the change of the world money supply (and hence the rate of change of world prices). Domestic monetary policy in any individual country would, given the above assumptions, have its main long run effects not on that country's inflation, but on its balance of payments.

To summarize, the monetarist approach to the rate of inflation in the world economy is determined by the rate of the world monetary expansion relative to the world rate of real economic growth. Excessive money creation of one or more countries spreads through the world community and capital markets and establishes one world price level and one world level of interest rates. National price levels and national level of interest rates must conform to the international levels. There is no possibility for small open economies to escape the international rate of inflation. The international rate of inflation becomes the rate of inflation in each

110

country.

Monetary Theory Versus Reality

It is clear that these results are only valid in long run equilibrium; i.e., only in the long run does every country have the same rate of inflation. However, in the short run, inflation rates can and do differ from country to country. In fact, the four groups of countries identified in the previous chapter all have had somewhat different inflationary patterns. Why?

Changes in tariffs or in non-tariff barriers to trade could explain these divergences. It is unlikely that changes in either, however, could have been large enough and on such a widespread scale to account for the post-1973 acceleration in world inflation. An alternative explanation draws on the awkward but apparently fruitful distinction between the determination of the prices of tradable goods on the one hand and of non-tradables on the other, a distinction which corresponds to that made (as indicated in Chapter 3) in the Nordic literature between the output of the exposed and sheltered sectors of an economy. Non-tradables are simply those items which, because they must be consumed at the point of production, have only a domestic market. The argument is that it is not the overall price level, but only the price level of tradable goods that is determined on world markets.

Monetarists are aware of the fact that the segmentation of the economy into these two different sectors implies the application of two different theories of price formation, one for the tradable sector and one for the non-tradable sector. They argue that the two markets may be interrelated, not by the labor market but by the demand of tourists for non-tradable goods. This approach while ingenious is not altogether convincing, and there is no real reason to expect that the inflation rates in the two sectors will be the same even in the long run. If technical change in the two sectors is different in character, then the possibility of the marginal productivity schedules of labor shifting at different rates arises. For given output combinations and for a given rate of wage inflation, rates of price inflation will differ in such circumstances. They will also differ if, in a growing economy, the

111

division of aggregate demand between the output of the two sectors changes over time. But if inflation rates differ between these two sectors and if the overall domestic inflation rate is an average of the two, then we have ample scope for any one country's inflation rate to differ from that ruling in the rest of the world, and to differ persistently. A result obviously not consistent with basic monetarist theory.

Even on a more basic level, the monetary theory is suspect as a precise predictor of prices for individual countries. The process of transmitting changes in the inflation rate for non-tradables is likely to be subject to time lags; the domestic inflation rate thus can differ from that ruling in the rest of the world while such adjustments are taking place. There is no reason to suppose that the lags in question will be sufficiently short as to be negligible. The time that must elapse for an economy fully to adjust to a new inflation rate could conceivably be more appropriately measured in decades rather than in years.[8]

At issue is not the theoretical validity of the monetarist approach which (despite the arguments made above) we do not dispute. What we question is the general applicability of the theory.

As noted in Chapter 2, there is ample evidence that, at least until 1974, the variation in inflation between developing countries was much stronger than among industrial countries. It appears that at least for developing countries international economic integration is far from perfect. These observations point to the need for additional analysis and specifically a further elaboration of the world monetarist approach so as to account for this wide dispersion of national inflation rates.

A Monetarist Model of Imported Inflation

To test some of the major monetarist predictions, a macroeconomic model[9] was constructed as follows:

1. $M = kYP$

2. $P = a_1 P_d + a_2 P_{IMP}$

3. $a_1 = DS/Y$; $a_2 = IMP/Y$

4. $M = RES + CRD$

5. $RES = R_o + P_d X - a_2 P_{IMP}$

6. $E = f(P_d/P_{IMP})$

7. $IM = f(P_d/P_{IMP})$

8. $NO = DE + E - IMP$

9. $Y = DS + IMP/T$

10. $T = P_d/P_{IMP}$

Equation 1 states that in equilibrium the money supply is equal to the nominal amount of money demand, the latter being proportional to the nominal amount of gross domestic expenditures. This formulation is of course identical to the basic monetarist or quantity equation of the form $MV = PT$, where V is the income velocity of money, and T the real gross domestic expenditure. Equation 1 is the Cambridge version of the quantity theory where $k = 1/V$, but differs in that it is formulated in terms of expenditure rather than product.

Equation 1 emphasizes the critical element in the monetary theory--the motive for holding domestic money as for anticipated or potential expenditures at home, including those on both domestic and imported products, but excluding foreigner purchases of the country's exports. The shift in emphasis to expenditures from product shows itself mainly in the type of price indices used in the actual empirical testing.

Equation 2 defines, as in the Nordic theories, a price index of domestic expenditures as an average of the domestic product and foreign product prices. The weights (a_1 and a_2) are the proportions of domestic expenditure spent on the respective products (equation 3).

Equation 4 is an identity indicating that the money supply in any country is the sum of the foreign reserves (RES) and domestic credits (CRD) in that country's central bank portfolio.

113

Equation 5 is another tautology. It defines the
foreign reserves at the end of the period equal to the
amount at the beginning of the period (R_o) plus the
trade balance $(P_dX - a_2P_{IMP})$ during the period (assuming of course no net international capital flows).

Equations 6 and 7 indicate that the country's exports and imports are a function of that country's
domestic and the world price level. It should be noted
that the price of imports (P_{IMP}) is assumed to be the
foreign price converted to the domestic price by the
country's exchange rate.

Equation 8 states that the national output (NO) is
equal to domestic expenditures plus exports (E) minus
imports (IM). Equation 9 defines domestic expenditure
as the sum of domestic spending for both domestic product and foreign product.

Equation 10 defines the terms of trade as the ratio
of the price of the domestic product to that of the
foreign product, both stated in terms of the national
currency.

Beginning from a position of equilibrium and differentiating it is possible to derive (with the change
in domestic credit = 0) the following relationships:

11. $\Delta P = (MONTI + EXPI)(\Delta P_d - \Delta P_{IMP})$

indicating that the terms of trade effect of imported
inflation on the domestic price level has two components: (1) a monetary impact (MONTI) and a domestic
expenditure impact (EXPI). MONTI represents the change
in central bank foreign reserves as a ratio of the
initial domestic money supply resulting from a change
in the terms of trade, and is equal to:

12. $-[\Delta E/\Delta(P_d/P_{IMP}) - a_2/\Delta(P_d/P_{IMP}) + a_2] / IM$

MONTI should be positive if the export and import
elasticities are fairly large. In this case the trade
balance would improve with a decline in the terms of
trade.

MONTI can be negative, however, when the initial
volume of imports is sufficiently great so that the
increased import expenditures resulting from higher

114

import prices exceeds the sum of the indexed increase in exports and the reduction in imports. An illustration of the case is the large trade deficits sustained by many countries as a result of the 1973 increases in oil import prices.

EXPI measures the net proportionate change in the nation's real domestic expenditure resulting from changes in exports and imports induced by a change in the terms of trade. Thus a trade surplus resulting from a rise in import prices should be inflationary because of the induced domestic monetary expansion coupled with a resultant drain of resources away from the economy.

Also obtained from differentiating 1 through 10 and solving are:

13. $\Delta P_d = (1 - 1/Z) \Delta P_{IMP}$

and

14. $\Delta P = [1 - (1/Z) \Delta (1/T)] \Delta P_{IMP}$

where $Z = MONTI + EXPI + \Delta (1/T)$

Equations 13 through 15 indicate that the impact of imported inflation on the domestic prices depends systematically on the extent MONTI and EXPI on the one hand, and the size of the import ratio (i.e., imports divided by gross domestic expenditure) on the other. The former effects are directly related to the elasticities of substitution between foreign and domestic products. When these products are highly homogeneous-- i.e., when the elasticities of substitution between the two products in the import demand and export demand functions are both very large-- ΔP and ΔP_d will both approach ΔP_{IMP}. The same result is obtained in the world monetarist approach under the assumption of perfectly homogeneous products worldwide.

The import ratio a_2/T also enters into the picture in that other things being equal, the larger the import ratio, the larger will be the impact of imported inflation on domestic prices.

A major implication derived in the equations above is that in the absence of domestic credit expansion or

115

contraction, the impact of imported inflation on domestic prices should depend systematically on the degree of openness of the economy which in turn is determined by the substitutability between domestic products and foreign products on the one hand, and the ratio of imports to domestic expenditures on the other.

Operationally, product substitutability is reflected in the size of the induced change in the country's trade balance relative to both its domestic money supply and domestic expenditures. The larger the sum of these two ratios, and the larger the ratio of imports to domestic expenditures, the larger will be the impact of import price increases on domestic prices. Only in the extreme case where both the induced change in the trade balance and the import ratio are very large will the import price increases be fully reflected in the domestic price increases.

An Empirical Test of Monetarist Predictions

In order to test the monetary approach to world inflation, regressions were run on the four basic country groupings established in the regression analysis (large, Medium I, Medium II, and small). The time period in most cases covered the 1960-1976 period except for several countries whose time series started a bit after 1960 and those who had by mid-1978 not compiled their 1976 data. The analysis attempts to prove:

1. Whether inflation in the different groupings is a monetary phenomenon consistent with the quantity equation MV = PT, and

2. Whether imported inflation significantly affected inflation rates in these countries; i.e. in terms of the quantity equation, have changes in P_{IMP} significantly affected P.

The starting point of the empirical work is the basic monetarist model derived from the equation of exchange. More specifically let us assume a simple money demand function of the following form:

16. $M/PT = Y^a C^b$

where M is the exogenously determined nominal stock of

116

money, P is the price level, T is real income, and C is the expected cost of holding real balances.

Equation 16 can be solved for P and expressed in terms of growth rates (lower case letters) yields:

17. $p = m-(1-a)y - bc$

The nature of the relationships is clear and straightforward. The growth of money relative to output and cost of holding real balances will generate an increase in the rate of inflation. The growth of real income will cause decreases in the rate of inflation via the demand for real balances. Similarly, the rate of inflation is inversely related to the expected cost of holding real balances.

Equation 17 assumes instantaneous adjustment of money changes and no money illusion. Therefore, the tested form of the monetarist equation is:

18. $P = a + a_1m + a_2m(L1) + a_3M(L2) - a_4T$

Note that the lagged money variables not only are assumed to capture the lagged adjustment of changes in money and prices but also are a proxy for C. (L1) and (L2) indicate the rate of growth of the money supply in the previous year and the prior year to that, respectively.

With this format, any change in velocity will be captured by the constant term. In addition, this specification permits the money supply to affect prices with lags, whereas our formal model posits instantaneous adjustment. Both real GNP and real domestic expenditure were tried as explanatory variables.

The basic monetarist contention, as noted earlier, is that the causal relation is from money to prices and output. It follows that any persistent increase in money relative to output is a sufficient condition for inflation, and that the magnitude and the length of inflation is dependent on the magnitude and persistence of monetary growth. It is the increasing growth rate of money which yields uniformly inflationary pressures.

On the whole, the very simple quantity theory

specification works quite well for most countries
(Tables 30-33). On the whole Medium I countries showed
the best results using the quantity theory with Medium
II the poorest. For Medium I only Korea and Sri Lanka
(ranked as Medium II in the discriminant analysis)
showed poor results, the rest having an r^2 above 0.54.
For Medium I countries at least one money supply variable is statistically significant in every case but
Korea. Not surprising, the regression results do not
differ significantly whether real expenditures or real
output are used. Since a time series in real expenditures was not available for many of the countries, we
report only the results using real output as the explanatory variable.

On the whole regressions of import prices (the
current and lagged one and two years) tended to perform
(in terms of r^2) better than the crude quantity theory.
This was particularly true for the large and Medium II
groups, but not for Medium I where the average r^2 for
the quantity regressions was 0.63 and for the import
regression only slightly better at 0.66.

When both import prices and the money variables are
regressed together on domestic prices (Tables 34-37),
the result is to reduce coefficients of the money supply
variables as well as the values of the t statistic
associated with them. This is not surprising, since we
would expect rising import prices normally to increase
a country's foreign exchange reserves and thereby lead
to an expansion in its money supply--provided no official action were undertaken by the monetary authorities.
Thus, changes in import prices and in the money supply
are not truly independent of each other.

The following inferences may be drawn from the
regression results:

1. A very simple monetarist model is particularly
   adept in explaining inflation in developing
   (Medium I) countries.

2. Imported inflation appears to have contributed
   significantly to domestic inflation in all four
   groups of countries.

3. Imported inflation appears to have affected
   domestic prices more strongly in the developed

118

TABLE 30
SOURCES OF INFLATION - LARGE COUNTRIES

Country	Import Prices						Quantity Theory						
	A	P(L2)	P(L1)	P	r^2	F	A	M	M(L1)	M(L2)	Y	r^2	F
Australia	2.55	0.14 (4.72)	0.12 (5.18)	0.30 (5.79)	0.87	27.53	1.63	0.30 (1.85)	0.15 (1.87)	0.62 (5.08)	-0.57 (1.43)	0.76	8.70
Austria	4.00	0.18 (4.38)	0.14 (3.32)	0.21 (3.67)	0.77	14.54	0.84	0.17 (2.58)	0.18 (2.09)	0.30 (3.88)	-0.41 (2.43)	0.72	7.99
Belgium	4.31	1.00 (4.77)	0.07 (1.16)	0.17 (1.70)	0.69	9.00	-3.54	0.84 (5.38)	0.34 (1.56)	0.17 (0.81)	0.22 (0.57)	0.74	8.10
Canada	1.84	0.21 (3.09)	0.04 (4.38)	0.37 (3.79)	0.77	14.38	7.22	-0.02 (0.28)	0.06 (0.20)	0.04 (0.51)	-0.73 (1.62)	0.26	0.75
Denmark	5.32	0.06 (1.95)	0.06 (2.06)	0.25 (5.10)	0.74	11.34	10.49	-0.09 (0.10)	0.13 (1.09)	-0.05 (0.85)	-0.83 (3.50)	0.56	3.55
France	3.41	0.07 (2.26)	0.13 (3.74)	0.20 (5.10)	0.77	15.01	4.09	0.15 (0.75)	-0.01 (0.04)	-0.01 (0.01)	-	0.04	0.19
Germany	3.04	0.05 (1.56)	0.10 (2.16)	0.14 (2.62)	0.51	4.66	11.24	-0.21 (1.74)	-0.08 (1.89)	-0.15 (1.10)	-0.22 (1.33)	0.44	2.40
Italy	3.53	-0.01 (6.20)	0.16 (5.12)	0.16 (5.31)	0.89	30.99	8.77	-0.36 (1.49)	0.11 (0.51)	0.29 (1.91)	-0.83 (1.88)	0.47	2.41
Japan	5.89	0.05 (1.41)	0.04 (4.24)	0.22 (10.77)	0.91	45.36	16.78	-0.04 (2.09)	0.03 (1.00)	-0.04 (1.53)	-0.90 (3.99)	0.66	5.90
Netherlands	4.38	0.11 (3.18)	0.12 (3.08)	0.13 (2.69)	0.67	8.95	-1.84	0.29 (2.50)	0.27 (2.49)	0.26 (2.01)	-	0.56	5.50
New Zealand	3.03	0.19 (3.76)	0.17 (4.50)	0.20 (2.85)	0.78	14.17	6.35	0.18 (1.72)	0.01 (1.15)	0.19 (3.35)	-0.81 (1.97)	0.64	4.84
Norway	4.15	0.12 (3.57)	0.25 (3.75)	0.14 (1.88)	0.70	10.13	1.34	-0.03 (7.35)	-0.05 (1.44)	0.74 (5.91)	-0.30 (0.72)	0.88	2.29
Sweden	3.72	0.17 (4.98)	0.10 (2.80)	0.13 (2.69)	0.75	13.29	7.16	0.22 (2.50)	-0.11 (0.75)	0.17 (2.45)	-1.08 (3.74)	0.69	6.70
Switzerland	2.77	0.12 (0.26)	0.26 (3.76)	0.30 (4.08)	0.70	10.27	5.13	-0.22 (3.01)	0.04 (0.89)	0.21 (1.33)	-0.30 (1.50)	0.54	3.47
United Kingdom	3.31	0.16 (12.28)	0.29 (10.25)	0.10 (3.05)	0.95	88.37	6.09	0.34 (5.52)	0.44 (3.13)	0.13 (1.71)	-1.86 (4.83)	0.84	16.63

Source: Computed by Author.

119

TABLE 31

SOURCES OF INFLATION - MEDIUM INCOME COUNTRIES I

Country	Import Prices						Quantity Theory						
	A	P(L2)	P(L1)	P	r²	F	A	M	M(L1)	M(L2)	Y	r²	F
Greece	1.91	0.14 (8.19)	0.01 (6.97)	0.51 (10.60)	0.94	75.99	-4.96	0.47 (2.64)	0.08 (1.79)	0.52 (1.79)	-0.08 (2.08)	0.60	4.44
Spain	5.84	0.13 (3.41)	0.12 (4.24)	0.10 (2.49)	0.73	11.62	2.11	0.33 (3.45)	0.30 (3.32)	0.13 (2.68)	-0.77 (2.02)	0.76	9.56
Malaysia	-0.10	0.09 (2.22)	-0.08 (5.36)	0.60 (4.81)	0.84	18.93	-2.32	0.08 (2.62)	0.35 (7.26)	0.14 (2.57)	-	0.86	22.06
Mexico	10.83	0.54 (3.33)	-0.05 (1.20)	-0.18 (0.76)	0.50	4.37	20.11	0.31 (1.67)	-0.27 (0.96)	0.04 (1.66)	-1.47 (2.79)	0.54	3.57
Venezuela	0.75	0.19 (6.47)	0.15 (3.42)	0.11 (1.22)	0.81	18.35	-2.33	0.09 (7.66)	0.01 (1.43)	0.23 (2.88)	0.33 (1.63)	0.86	17.92
Egypt	2.71	0.19 (2.35)	0.16 (1.01)	0.05 (0.23)	0.33	2.20	0.72	-0.03 (2.48)	0.20 (3.30)	0.24 (2.46)	-	0.64	7.70
Sri Lanka	1.62	0.02 (0.10)	0.03 (2.88)	0.15 (4.26)	0.67	8.83	-0.35	-0.01 (0.17)	0.32 (1.92)	0.31 (1.33)	-	0.29	1.84
Korea	12.35	-0.33 (1.47)	0.96 (1.59)	-0.38 (1.08)	0.31	1.95	17.03	-0.12 (1.42)	-0.17 (1.21)	0.12 (1.23)	0.20 (0.41)	0.30	1.29
Israel	2.18	0.17 (3.50)	0.23 (3.50)	0.35 (3.44)	0.74	12.12	3.73	0.26 (2.02)	0.41 (2.28)	0.48 (3.08)	-1.66 (3.61)	0.73	7.94
Finland	3.30	0.15 (2.80)	0.20 (3.46)	0.21 (2.72)	0.68	9.08	5.40	0.09 (2.49)	0.28 (4.15)	0.08 (2.14)	-0.72 (2.86)	0.75	9.04

Source: Computed by Author.

TABLE 32

SOURCES OF INFLATION - MEDIUM INCOME COUNTRIES II

Country	A	Import Prices						Quantity Theory					
		P(L2)	P(L1)	P	r²	F	A	M	M(L1)	M(L2)	Y	r²	F
Nigeria	4.24	0.44 (3.35)	0.73 (0.97)	-0.26 (0.56)	0.49	4.17	1.27	0.25 (3.85)	0.09 (1.10)	0.05 (0.29)	-	0.55	5.37
Burma	2.69	0.83 (3.70)	0.21 (1.25)	0.52 (1.10)	0.57	5.50	2.85	0.35 (1.86)	0.06 (0.66)	0.31 (1.62)	-	0.35	2.57
India	4.77	-0.28 (3.59)	0.10 (4.52)	0.34 (3.93)	0.79	16.23	-0.85	0.32 (0.41)	0.28 (0.84)	0.17 (0.91)	-	0.12	0.57
Pakistan	2.03	-0.10 (4.16)	0.52 (6.93)	0.66 (3.30)	0.85	25.42	2.42	-0.01 (0.46)	0.01 (2.27)	0.50 (2.01)	-	0.42	3.13
Thailand	2.06	0.08 (1.76)	-0.05 (2.30)	0.34 (8.83)	0.87	27.79	8.13	-0.03 (1.15)	0.60 (3.06)	-0.01 (0.94)	-1.16 (1.83)	0.55	3.78
Colombia	9.18	1.73 (2.47)	-1.13 (0.03)	0.81 (1.85)	0.44	3.17	-20.60	0.80 (0.77)	0.24 (1.80)	1.16 (3.66)	-1.42 (0.84)	0.62	4.49

Source: Computed by Author.

121

TABLE 33

SOURCES OF INFLATION – SMALL COUNTRIES

Country	Import Prices						Quantity Theory						
	A	P(L2)	P(L1)	P	r²	F	A	M	M(L1)	M(L2)	Y	r²	F
Costa Rica	0.29	-0.16 (4.59)	0.54 (9.12)	0.66 (4.25)	0.91	40.78	1.01	0.11 (1.22)	0.31 (1.07)	0.20 (1.07)	-0.55 (0.73)	0.34	1.39
Ecuador	2.90	0.23 (8.66)	0.53 (0.11)	0.11 (0.81)	0.93	62.05	-2.76	0.24 (1.22)	0.27 (1.54)	0.06 (1.07)	—	0.89	35.91
El Salvador	0.79	0.16 (10.51)	0.31 (3.51)	0.61 (4.22)	0.83	19.56	4.81	0.11 (6.44)	0.19 (1.09)	0.35 (1.34)	—	0.23	1.20
Paraguay	2.84	-0.05 (5.34)	-0.01 (3.51)	0.68 (4.22)	0.50	4.33	-4.60	0.27 (1.08)	0.19 (1.66)	0.21 (1.12)	—	0.33	1.50
Ethiopia	-3.67	3.23 (5.11)	-1.13 (1.25)	0.72 (2.20)	0.83	9.61	1.95	0.19 (1.66)	0.76 (4.69)	-0.12 (1.43)	—	0.80	7.91
Sudan	1.46	-0.27 (2.18)	0.68 (1.08)	0.59 (1.79)	0.68	9.36	-8.19	-0.30 (1.19)	0.42 (1.95)	-0.12 (0.59)	—	0.55	5.24
Somalia	2.66	0.02 (2.33)	0.16 (1.74)	-0.11 (0.29)	0.46	2.86	0.24	0.63 (3.44)	0.07 (1.57)	0.10 (0.27)	—	0.24	1.08
Cameroon	1.60	0.08 (6.98)	0.16 (6.25)	0.43 (2.95)	0.91	32.19	-4.55	0.07 (0.42)	0.27 (1.57)	0.16 (0.76)	0.26 (0.25)	0.65	5.64
Iceland	11.27	0.04 (0.19)	0.04 (0.42)	0.10 (1.06)	0.09	0.45	4.97	0.23 (1.60)	0.42 (3.52)	-0.04 (1.41)	-0.67 (1.32)	0.41	2.12
Senegal	1.70	-0.21 (5.66)	0.91 (2.45)	-0.06 (0.46)	0.92	29.27	2.63	0.13 (1.70)	0.30 (1.94)	-0.03 (0.30)	—	0.84	14.38
Togo	1.00	0.24 (4.85)	0.42 (2.88)	0.06 (0.30)	0.80	10.62	-1.39	0.11 (1.27)	0.30 (1.94)	0.08 (0.50)	—	0.68	5.67
Chad	4.76	-0.41 (1.83)	0.77 (5.25)	-0.17 (1.43)	0.77	10.99	4.29	0.17 (1.77)	0.17 (3.40)	-0.09 (1.95)	—	0.65	6.20
Sierra Leone	2.73	0.27 (4.57)	0.46 (2.08)	-0.30 (0.13)	0.68	8.42	2.21	0.11 (3.52)	0.17 (1.74)	0.35 (1.89)	—	0.34	2.03
Jamaica	1.90	0.16 (6.48)	0.13 (8.83)	0.78 (6.19)	0.92	52.79	-2.04	0.07 (1.47)	0.31 (1.47)	0.15 (1.89)	—	0.52	4.72
Nigeria	3.09	1.32 (4.30)	-1.09 (2.46)	0.52 (2.27)	0.79	9.89	0.80	0.26 (1.86)	0.14 (2.40)	0.35 (2.50)	—	0.37	1.54
Central African Republic	4.89	-0.14 (2.99)	0.68 (2.48)	-0.26 (1.92)	0.66	5.79	3.07	0.18 (0.86)	0.17 (0.77)	-0.02 (0.77)	—	0.24	0.94
Gabon	2.22	0.61 (7.98)	0.58 (0.99)	-0.23 (1.35)	0.88	22.18	-0.29	0.34 (7.65)	0.34 (5.99)	0.06 (0.47)	—	0.91	31.54
Morocco	1.54	0.14 (3.20)	0.08 (2.97)	0.26 (7.45)	0.86	24.84	-2.91	0.30 (4.75)	0.10 (1.26)	0.25 (1.95)	—	0.70	9.34

Source: Computed by Author.

122

TABLE 34

SOURCES OF INFLATION - LARGE COUNTRIES

Country	A	P(L2)	Independent Variable P(L1)	P	M	M(L1)	M(L2)	Y	Period	r^2	F
Australia	0.94	0.14 (11.69)	0.18 (12.83)	0.17 (14.33)	0.04 (3.19)	0.26 (6.70)	0.19 (3.09)	-0.13 (1.05)	1960-1976	0.99	81.75
Austria	1.61	0.17 (7.57)	0.06 (5.73)	0.11 (6.34)	0.10 (1.92)	0.07 (2.09)	0.24 (4.22)	-0.22 (2.01)	1960-1976	0.95	22.89
Belgium	-4.26	0.26 (4.65)	0.20 (1.14)	0.04 (1.66)	0.59 (1.40)	0.22 (1.02)	0.13 (0.30)	0.42 (0.57)	1960-1975	0.78	4.16
Canada	0.59	0.27 (3.21)	-	0.40 (6.01)	0.04 (0.85)	0.03 (0.77)	0.05 (1.67)	-0.02 (0.07)	1960-1976	0.84	8.44
Denmark	7.80	-	0.01 (3.13)	0.23 (6.87)	0.05 (1.19)	0.08 (1.64)	-0.15 (1.03)	-0.47 (3.14)	1961-1976	0.90	12.01
France	3.22	0.07 (2.02)	0.12 (3.35)	0.21 (4.56)	0.01 (0.19)	0.07 (0.33)	-0.06 (0.52)	-	1960-1976	0.79	6.09
Germany	8.38	-	0.06 (2.54)	0.21 (2.97)	0.10 (0.02)	-0.34 (2.61)	-0.11 (0.86)	0.06 (0.31)	1960-1976	0.70	3.82
Italy	5.68	0.01 (5.32)	0.16 (4.40)	0.17 (4.56)	-0.05 (0.45)	0.05 (0.29)	-0.12 (0.73)	-0.07 (0.17)	1960-1975	0.90	9.91
Japan	0.32	0.07 (1.54)	0.06 (4.62)	0.23 (11.72)	0.09 (0.78)	0.06 (0.66)	0.11 (2.29)	0.08 (0.31)	1960-1976	0.95	23.92
Netherlands	0.24	-	0.06 (5.20)	0.20 (3.81)	0.11 (0.52)	0.37 (4.99)	-0.02 (0.17)	-	1960-1976	0.86	13.35
New Zealand	4.67	0.13 (4.11)	0.19 (4.92)	0.11 (3.11)	0.08 (1.17)	0.08 (0.99)	0.02 (0.63)	-0.56 (1.89)	1960-1975	0.88	8.15
Norway	5.56	0.14 (8.05)	0.08 (8.46)	0.02 (5.23)	-0.18 (3.34)	0.14 (2.20)	0.67 (5.18)	-0.69 (2.15)	1960-1976	0.96	30.17
Sweden	5.98	0.16 (7.32)	0.16 (4.12)	0.01 (3.97)	0.20 (1.95)	-0.22 (3.13)	0.01 (0.56)	-0.49 (2.28)	1960-1976	0.92	15.08
Switzerland	1.91	0.13 (0.29)	0.19 (4.22)	0.30 (4.58)	-0.02 (0.80)	0.08 (1.83)	0.19 (1.63)	-0.29 (0.85)	1960-1976	0.84	6.60
United Kingdom	3.85	0.10 (13.26)	0.21 (10.97)	0.09 (3.40)	0.11 (1.13)	0.16 (1.34)	0.01 (0.04)	-0.56 (1.81	1960-1976	0.97	44.89

Source: Computed by Author.

123

TABLE 35

SOURCES OF INFLATION - MEDIUM INCOME COUNTRIES I

Country	A	Independent Variable							Period	r^2	F
		P(L2)	P(L1)	P	M	M(L1)	M(L2)	Y			
Greece	-1.12	0.10 (7.82)	-	0.50 (12.10)	0.13 (0.71)	-0.06 (0.10)	0.14 (0.11)	0.02 (0.11)	1960-1976	0.95	34.92
South Africa	1.54	0.02 (9.29)	0.15 (4.77)	0.23 (3.65)	0.06 (1.29)	0.10 (1.27)	0.06 (0.91)	-0.14 (0.41)	1960-1976	0.93	18.11
Spain	1.70	0.10 (4.91)	0.09 (3.78)	0.04 (2.88)	0.11 (1.87)	0.29 (2.20)	-0.01 (0.07)	-0.11 (0.28)	1960-1976	0.86	7.88
Malaysia	0.58	0.11 (2.26)	-	0.57 (7.33)	-0.09 (1.20)	0.05 (1.04)	-0.06 (0.34)	-	1962-1976	0.87	12.29
Mexico	23.09	0.84 (3.72)	-	-	-0.30 (1.60)	-0.37 (1.97)	-0.26 (1.06)	-0.30 (0.39)	1960-1976	0.66	4.32
Venezuela	-2.10	0.15 (7.36)	0.11 (2.75)	-	0.01 (0.56)	-0.02 (1.32)	0.24 (2.59)	0.36 (1.53)	1960-1975	0.89	12.14
Egypt	0.77	-	-	0.04 (2.05)	-0.05 (1.37)	0.20 (3.12)	0.24 (2.57)	-	1960-1975	0.64	5.38
Sri Lanka	2.21	0.03 (0.12)	0.04 (2.57)	0.15 (3.81)	-0.02 (0.02)	0.04 (0.22)	0.06 (0.58)	-	1960-1976	0.68	3.59
Korea	17.89	0.48 (2.46)	-	-	-0.14 (1.29)	-0.20 (1.95)	0.06 (0.75)	0.16 (0.32)	1960-1976	0.56	2.76
Israel	9.77	0.07 (3.69)	0.16 (3.64)	0.28 (3.70)	-0.05 (0.34)	0.16 (0.10)	0.10 (0.07)	-1.11 (2.32)	1960-1976	0.84	6.58
Finland	5.88	-	0.13 (4.74)	0.17 (3.39)	-0.05 (2.23)	0.21 (1.93)	0.01 (1.17)	-0.61 (2.46)	1960-1976	0.83	8.35

Source: Computed by Author.

124

TABLE 36

SOURCES OF INFLATION - MEDIUM INCOME COUNTRIES II

Country	A	Independent Variable							Period	r^2	F
		P(L2)	P(L1)	P	M	M(L1)	M(L2)	Y			
Nigeria	2.40	0.49 (3.54)	–	–	0.19 (1.95)	0.04 (0.24)	-0.05 (0.26)	–	1960-1976	0.58	4.12
Burma	0.96	1.01 (3.68)	–	0.50 (1.40)	0.09 (0.22)	-0.06 (0.22)	0.21 (1.29)	–	1960-1975	0.63	3.46
India	3.02	–	–	0.39 (4.07)	0.03 (0.20)	-0.01 (0.12)	-0.02 (0.16)	–	1960-1976	0.58	4.15
Pakistan	1.14	0.13 (4.56)	0.44 (7.60)	0.48 (3.62)	-0.18 (1.09)	0.23 (1.93)	0.11 (0.85)	–	1960-1976	0.91	16.21
Philippines	2.58	–	–	0.15 (3.21)	0.06 (1.10)	0.13 (0.37)	0.54 (2.59)	-0.98 (0.76)	1961-1976	0.65	3.79
Thailand	-1.63	0.06 (1.76)	–	0.31 (9.04)	0.02 (0.46)	0.10 (1.85)	0.06 (0.25)	0.28 (0.68)	1960-1976	0.90	14.83
Colombia	-15.63	0.13 (2.61)	–	0.08 (1.42)	0.74 (0.16)	0.15 (0.25)	1.06 (2.33)	-1.59 (0.80)	1960-1975	0.62	2.49

Source: Computed by Author.

125

TABLE 5?

SOURCES OF INFLATION - SMALL COUNTRIES

Country	A	Independent Variable							Period	r^2	F
		P(L2)	P(L1)	P	M	M(L1)	M(L2)	T			
Costa Rica	3.50	0.17 (3.77)	-	0.99 (8.04)	-0.02 (0.68)	-0.04 (0.17)	-0.10 (0.88)	-0.44 (1.24)	1961-1976	0.90	13.61
Ecuador	1.30	0.23 (8.36)	0.39 (10.05)	0.05 (0.28)	0.08 (0.69)	0.09 (1.25)	-0.02 (0.29)	-	1960-1976	0.95	29.29
El Salvador	-1.58	-	0.28 (7.85)	0.41 (6.55)	0.14 (1.08)	0.06 (0.68)	-0.07 (1.85)	0.41 (3.04)	1960-1975	0.93	19.79
Paraguay	0.01	-	-	0.56 (3.44)	0.14 (0.56)	0.06 (0.02)	0.09 (0.75)	-0.20 (0.21)	1960-1976	0.54	2.55
Ethiopia	-1.68	-	-	1.90 (10.30)	-0.27 (3.15)	0.46 (4.34)	-0.12 (1.32)	-	1966-1976	0.96	34.13
Sudan	-2.88	-	0.26 (1.15)	0.55 (4.84)	0.30 (1.23)	0.12 (0.46)	-0.02 (0.09)	-	1960-1976	0.71	5.30
Somalia	1.86	0.05 (2.23)	0.66 (1.66)	-	-0.13 (0.79)	0.06 (0.17)	0.09 (0.75)	-	1963-1976	0.53	1.79
Cameroon	2.17	0.10 (8.26)	0.59 (7.98)	0.10 (1.98)	-0.01 (0.73)	-0.16 (2.19)	-	-	1964-1976	0.95	28.38
Iceland	0.42	-	-	0.07 (1.14)	0.27 (1.70)	0.36 (1.82)	0.02 (0.07)	-0.30 (0.69)	1960-1976	0.42	1.61
Senegal	1.44	-	0.55 (9.66)	0.11 (0.56)	-0.03 (1.85)	0.09 (1.24)	-0.02 (0.45)	-	1965-1976	0.94	19.75
Togo	-1.65	0.26 (4.95)	0.11 (1.85)	0.27 (2.49)	0.05 (0.32)	0.11 (2.12)	0.05 (0.49)	-	1965-1976	0.86	7.10
Chad	4.33	-	0.24 (4.01)	-	0.03 (0.56)	0.08 (1.13)	-0.08 (1.60)	-	1963-1976	0.69	5.06
Sierra Leone	3.59	0.43 (4.35)	0.38 (1.97)	0.03 (0.12)	-0.18 (1.23)	0.08 (0.48)	-0.06 (0.33)	-	1961-1976	0.73	4.12
Jamaica	1.81	0.11 (0.11)	0.17 (0.73)	0.73 (5.83)	-0.06 (0.80)	0.02 (0.09)	0.07 (0.94)	-	1960-1976	0.93	23.68
Nigeria	2.60	0.74 (3.25)	-	-	0.11 (0.57)	0.01 (0.14)	-0.08 (0.42)	-	1965-1976	0.61	2.78
Central African Republic	3.67	-	0.37 (3.38)	-	0.07 (0.07)	0.04 (0.53)	-0.04 (0.41)	-	1964-1976	0.60	3.02
Gabon	0.24	-	0.22 (8.78)	-	-0.02 (0.94)	0.30 (3.52)	0.04 (0.24)	-	1963-1976	0.91	22.64
Morocco	-0.80	0.07 (3.43)	0.04 (3.18)	0.20 (7.98)	0.10 (1.60)	0.10 (1.18)	0.10 (0.90)	-	1960-1975	0.91	15.06

Source: Computed by Author.

126

countries and in the small rather than in the
Medium I and Medium II groups. Clearly this
finding illustrates the danger of relying on
the import ratio as the sole measure of the
economic impact of world inflation on individual countries.

Conclusions

The major finding of the empirical work is that
the monetarist theory of imported inflation goes a long
way in explaining the observed patterns of inflation.
The money-price mechanism specified by that theory does
not work uniformly, but instead is modified somewhat by
national economic characteristics. Any forecast of the
inflationary impact world economic changes might have
on an individual country would likely be off the mark
unless it was known which of the basic country groupings
that country belonged.

The monetary approach by itself, therefore, lacks
a convincing explanation of existing international price
differences. It seems that besides different methods
to measure price levels in the different countries,
differences in the rates of inflation between countries
could be due to at least four different causes:
(1) different national monetary policies; (2) different
fiscal policies; (3) different importance of tradable
and non-tradable goods; and (4) product differentiation
between domestic and foreign goods.

For instance the relatively greater importance of
import prices over monetary variables in explaining the
inflation rates in the developed countries helps explain
the wider dispersion of inflation rates among the developing countries than among the developed countries, to the
extent that the developing countries are less well integrated into the world economy. This final observation
has several important implications, the most important
of which is that an independent monetary policy may be
less feasible for the developed (and small) countries
than for the Medium I countries. This conclusion was
counter to the usual monetarist contention that central
banks are totally helpless in coping with imported inflation.

Instead the environment in Medium I countries may

be conducive to enabling monetary policy to become an effective instrument in stabilizing domestic prices in the face of price increases abroad. Clearly the economic consequences of world inflation are somewhat different for countries belonging to this group, as opposed to one of the other three groups.

Notes

1. Cf. David Meiselman, "Worldwide Inflation: A Monetarist View," in Patrick Boarman and David Tuerck eds., World Monetary Disorder: National Policies vs. International Imperatives (New York: Praeger Publishers), pp. 21-65.

2. For example, Manfred Willms, "Comment on Laidler and Nobay," in E. Claassen and P. Salin, ed., Recent Issues in International Monetary Economics (Amsterdam: North Holland Publishing Company, 1976), pp. 309-310.

3. A more detailed account is given by Hans Genberg and Alexander K. Swoboda, "Causes and Origins of the Current Worldwide Inflation," in Erik Jundberg, ed., Inflation Theory and Anti-Inflation Policy (Boulder: Westview Press, 1977), pp. 72-91.

4. Anna J. Schwartz, "Secular Price Change in Historical Perspective," Journal of Money Credit and Banking (February 1973), p. 264.

5. For a full exposition of this technique, see Christopher Sims, "Money, Income, and Causality," American Economic Review (September 1972).

6. Michael Bazdarich, "Inflation and Monetary Accommodation in the Pacific Basin," Federal Reserve Bank of San Francisco, Economic Review (Summer 1978), pp. 23-36.

7. D. Laidler and J. M. Parkin, "Inflation--A Survey," Economic Journal (December 1975), pp. 783-784.

8. As admitted by Milton Friedman in "The Role of Monetary Policy," American Economic Review (March 1968), pp. 1-17.

9. The model is similar and draws on one developed by Hang-Sheng Cheng and Nicholas P. Sargen in their "Central Bank Policy Towards Inflation," Federal Reserve Bank of San Francisco, Business Review (Spring 1975), pp. 31-41.

CHAPTER 8

INFLATION AND MONETARY AUTONOMY

Introduction

Inflation rates have varied somewhat between countries, particularly between the medium sized countries and the other groups identified above. Yet, inflationary patterns among the large group countries and those in the small group have been fairly similar.

The empirical work in the previous chapter also indicated that import prices had played a more important role in the inflationary experience of the large and small sized countries, but the money supply was much more important in accounting for the price changes in the Medium I group.

The Role of Monetary Policy

One possible explanation of these patterns is that the Medium I group of countries tends to pursue different monetary policies than the large and small sized countries.

While plausible, this explanation runs counter to one of the major mechanisms stressed by the monetary theorists; i.e., that increased economic interdependence between countries has restricted the scope of national economic policymaking. Nowhere, they argue, has this interdependence been more confining than in the sphere of monetary policy. Monetary linkages between financial markets have reduced the ability of individual monetary authorities to conduct an independent monetary policy.

Effectiveness of Monetary Policy

Clearly, financial markets under fixed exchange rates are at the present time linked by a high degree of capital mobility which limits the control of any individual monetary authority over its money supply and interest rates. With capital movements responsive to relative interest rate incentives, a change in

131

monetary policy in any one market induced offsetting
capital flows which in turn would modify the domestic
impact of that policy. Moreover, offsetting capital
flows transmit the impact of the change in monetary
policy from one country to another.

Capital mobility thus poses a significant threat
to monetary independence. Indeed if, as the monetarists
often implicitly assume, capital mobility were perfect--
if the assets and liabilities of different countries
were perfect substitutes--then monetary policy would in
any particular country lose all of its effectiveness
unless the national monetary authorities could influence
the level of interest rates in the rest of the world--
obviously an option not open to many, if any, countries.

Attempts to change bank reserves, for example,
would result in capital flows that completely offset
the change in reserves. With monetary policy ineffective and with capital flows offsetting the impact of
any domestic disturbances, interest rates in all financial markets would be equalized. In this limiting case,
there would be one world money supply and one world
interest rate and one inflationary pattern in all countries.

Movement Toward Integration

The increasing popularity of the monetarist theory
coincides with an apparent trend in institutional
developments beginning in the 1950s toward moving more
in the direction necessary for major assumptions to be
valid.

The postwar years have seen a gradual liberalization of tariffs between industrialized countries.
These reductions have been largely the result of successive rounds of negotiations of the General Agreement
on Tariffs and Trade. The result has been the market
for many manufactured goods has become a single world
market.

The second important feature of the international
economy since the end of the Second World War (at
least until its breakdown in the early years of this
decade) has been the common practice of most countries
in maintaining fixed or relatively fixed exchange rates.
As part of the Bretton Woods Agreement the United States

132

agreed to fix the price of the dollar in terms of
gold, and all other countries which were signatores
to the International Monetary Fund agreed to peg their
currencies to the dollar. The exchange rate changes
were permitted only in conditions of a fundamental disequilibrium, and that occurred infrequently (until the
late 1960s).

The existence of fixed exchange rates in a world
in which the markets for the products of industrialized
countries have become increasingly integrated has, according to the monetarists, one extremely important implication. It means that the world economy has become
very similar to a country with the nations of the world
comparable to regions within that country. Much as
within a country, there is one ruling market price; i.e.,
one effective price in the world as a whole to which
individual country's prices must adjust.

The third and final important feature the monetarists point out is the introduction of currency convertibility by many developed countries in 1958 and the OECD
Code of Liberalization of Capital Movements. At present
the Eurocurrency markets dominated in the 1960s by the
Euro-dollar market are a highly competitive international network of short term capital markets and the Euro-
bond markets a highly competitive network of longer term
capital markets so that it probably does make sense to
think of interest rates being determined in a global
rather than insular setting.

Non-Monetarist Cases

With limited capital mobility and imperfect substitution, monetary independence would still be limited in
scope. The contrast of the monetarist world described
above with monetary policy in a closed economy, however,
is one of degree rather than kind; the monetary authorities in this instance must cope with capital flows which
weaken their control over monetary conditions, but they
retain the power to alter the national money supply and
interest rates.[1]

Along these lines the concept of autonomous monetary policy is important because it refers to a situation under which the monetary authority of a country
can implement policies designed to alleviate internal
economic problems without being hindered by economic

and financial relationships with other countries. The concept is therefore closely related to that of monetary dependence or the inability of the authorities to control their domestic money supply.

In evaluating the degree of monetary autonomy, the following conditions are of importance:

1. The degree to which the economy is resilient to changes in the rest of the world. This would depend inter alia on: (1) the level and rate at which domestic real per capita incomes are increasing over a relevant period, and (b) the extent of unemployment of existing resources.

2. The degree to which the economy depends on the rest of the world to maintain and increase internal levels of employment, output, demand, and prices (generating factors).

3. The degree to which monetary and financial institutions (as well as individuals and government) have a high propensity to invest in foreign assets.

4. The degree to which the autonomous elements in the monetary system attach importance to financing the 'generating' factors not only by lending to them more of their funds than to other sectors (independent sectors) but also lending to these generating sectors at an increasing rate of comparison with other sectors.

These considerations underly the empirical work that follows.

Scope of Monetary Policy

In examining the autonomy of monetary policy attention should be focused on analyses of the money supply process. Although the basic framework of analysis is similar in all economies--developed, less developed or underdeveloped--the money supply process itself is likely to be highly differentiated, depending on a variety of factors, such as the openness of the economy, the level of development of the financial markets, their degree of integration, and so on. If the economy is insulated, monetary policy should have a far more active impact on the money supply variations than it would in an open economy where short term capital movements are unhampered.

In this context, the central bank should be viewed as a strategic institution--in terms of both its internationality and its statutory powers. In the advanced countries monetary policies are designed mainly to manage money and credit so as to maintain internal and external equilibrium. Obviously, their integration into the world economic system greatly limits their ability to do this. In the developing countries, monetary policy has to be concerned with the building of an economic system that will reduce economic dependence and render the economy more amenable to control from inside. For these countries limited contact with world financial markets undoubtedly permits them a greater degree of autonomy in this regard.

If these observations are in fact the case, the relative degree of monetary autonomy may be an important factor in explaining the similar patterns of inflation experienced by the large countries and the somewhat dissimilar patterns of inflation observed for the Medium I countries.

Overview

For most small developing countries, the empirical tests that follow suggest that most of the large group countries can be classified as dependent monetary economies. However, some elements of monetary dependence are present even in the small group countries, especially since modern communications have broken national barriers and have brought nearly all economies into a network of interrelationships.

The Medium I countries, however, may be able because they are less integrated into the international system, to pursue an independent monetary policy, and thus maintain for some period of time a fixed exchange rate and an inflation pattern different from that of their major trading partners.

135

Notes

1. Richard Herring and Richard Marston, National Monetary Policies and International Financial Markets (Amsterdam: North Holland Publishing Company, 1977), p. 2.

CHAPTER 9

EMPIRICAL TESTS FOR MONETARY AUTONOMY

Introduction

National authorities have tried to insulate their economies from the impact of foreign inflation and its economic consequences. They have devised neutralizing measures which can be grouped under the four basic headings alluded to in connection with the policy options available to correct balance of payments disequilibria: (1) to alter the exchange rate; (2) to impose import controls; (3) to finance external surpluses and deficits out of the official reserves; and (4) to deflate the economy.

Stabilization programs often include one or more of these policies in conjunction with a wide variety of related measures. The limited effectiveness of these stabilization efforts, however, is evidenced by the generality of inflationary trends in all of them. This lack of success can probably be attributed to two major causes: (1) the inadequacy of national stabilization programs to contain the domestically generated inflation, and (2) the nature of international inflation being such as to negate the attempts of the authorities at stabilization.

In this regard it is important to recall that the main thrust of the monetarist theory is that so long as countries maintain fixed exchange rates, they cannot in the long run avoid a common rate of inflation. Worldwide inflation can only be avoided according to this theory by repeated currency appreciation. There is a further less obvious corollary: if a country maintains its fixed exchange rate but tries to stop inflation with monetary and fiscal policy, it is highly likely to wind up with the worst possible of results, unabated inflation combined with unemployment of men and productive capacity.

The fundamental point is that the central bank has no control over the domestic supply of money. This is an extremely important point, given the fact that so much monetary theory and empirical analysis has been conducted in terms of the supply of money as a key economic variable and policy instrument.[1]

137

A Model of Monetary Autonomy

Whether or not the central bank in an open economy can effectively control the domestic money supply and thereby maintain domestic price stability in the face of imported inflation depends on several factors. Using the monetarist model[2] developed in Chapter 7 and setting $\Delta P_{IMP} = 0$, equations (1) through (10) in that chapter can be solved to obtain:

1. $\Delta M = 1(1 - MONTI/Z) \Delta CRED$

2. $RES = -(MONTI/Z) \Delta CRED$

Equations (1) and (2) indicate that expansions (or contractions) in central bank domestic credit will be partially effective in expanding (or contracting) domestic money supply--but not fully effective, because of the resultant reserve loss (or gain).

Equation 1 suggests that domestic credit expansion will have a positive effect on domestic money supply, regardless of the degree of openness of the economy. Of course this result is at variance with that stressed by the monetarists; i.e., that the monetary authorities cannot control the domestic money supply in an open economy (since domestic credit expansion will be offset by foreign reserve losses).

The modifications of the basic monetarist position made by equations (1) and (2) should make that model a more realistic depiction of the real world. The monetarist models were originally designed only for the conditions existing in the advanced countries, and the highly theoretical small open countries. Despite increased integration of world markets, the inclusion of countries such as the medium groups always introduces an element of non-homogeneity into product markets. The basic differences between the standard version of the monetarist model and the one developed here are that: (1) this model incorporates product differentiation into the analysis whereas the monetarist models assume homogeneous products, and (2) this model assumes the demand for real balances is a function of real domestic expenditure whereas the monetarist models assume them to be a function of real national income.

As a result of these modifications to the monetarist model, any expansion in domestic credit now causes an increase in the nominal demand for money (through an import surplus) and a rise in the prices of domestic expenditures (both of which will induce the public to hold a larger amount of domestic money).

In sum monetarists: (1) by assuming homogeneous products rule out any induced change in the domestic price level; (2) by relating demand for real balances to real income, rather than real expenditure, also preclude any effect changes in trade balances might have on the demand for real balances.

Because of the modifications introduced above, the central bank now has at least partial control over the domestic money supply. Domestic credit can, therefore, be adjusted to check imported inflation; i.e., by setting $\Delta P = 0$, we obtain from equations 1 - 10 in Chapter 7:

3. $\Delta CRED/M = -[(MONTI + EXPI)/\Delta Y] \Delta P_{IMP}$

which states that if a trade surplus results from inflation abroad, the required credit contraction to maintain domestic price stability will be larger: (1) the closer domestic and foreign products are substitutes for each other; and (2) the larger the ratio of imports is to domestic expenditures.

Policy Implications

To summarize the modified monetarist model as represented in equations 1 - 3 above implies that:

1. In the absence of domestic credit expansion or contraction, the impact of imported inflation on domestic prices will depend systematically on the degree of openness of the economy which in turn will be determined by the substitutability between domestic products and foreign products and the ratio of imports to domestic expenditures.

    Operationally, product substitutability is reflected in the model by the size of the induced change in the country's trade balance relative to both its domestic money supply and its domestic expenditures. The larger the sum of these two ratios, and the larger the ratio of imports to domestic expenditures, the larger will be the impact of price increases on domestic prices. Only in the extreme case where both the induced change in the trade balance and the import ratio are very large will import price increases be fully reflected in domestic price increases.

2. The central bank in an open economy can have at least partial control over the domestic money supply, depending upon its degree of openness (as defined above). The monetary mechanism operates through the effect of domestic credit expansion or contraction on the domestic money supply (as a result of induced changes in domestic demand for money which are brought about by changes in real expenditures and domestic prices).

3. It follows from these considerations that the central bank through its credit policies has the potential to effectively combat imported inflation.

4. Finally, the usual method of combating imported inflation, the sterilization of capital inflows (adjustments by the central bank of its credits to offset fluctuations in its foreign assets), would not be sufficient to achieve domestic price stability (due to the reduction in the supply of goods to the domestic economy-- the resource effect).

Practical Considerations Governing the Use of Monetary Policy

The model as outlined is clearly incomplete in that it deals only with the efficacy of central bank price stabilization policy in an open economy. The feasibility and desirability of pursuing anti-inflationary measures are separate matters.

First, the duration of inflation abroad may be critical in determining a central bank's ability to continue altering domestic credit as a means of combating imported inflation. Clearly, any policy that relies on credit contraction cannot be used indefinitely. Central bank credit policies are then only viable as a means of dealing with relatively short term fluctuations in international prices. Secular trends require other measures.

Second, central banks in many of the Medium I and II, as well as the small country, group economies are frequently new and inexperienced with the problems of monetary management. In addition "commerce" banks, while more established, have little experience in this area; i.e., often they were originally foreign controlled and were created principally to provide credit for trade (mainly the financing of imports and exports) and plantation agriculture.

In general the governments of these countries have left the commercial banks to their traditional roles and have created development corporations to provide both short and long term capital to the agricultural and industrial sectors. As a result most of these countries have not developed very sophisticated capital markets. The market for government securities is also very limited. Underdevelopment in the entire financial sector is a serious restraint on the central bank's use of traditional instruments such as open market operations, variable reserve requirements, and discount policy, to control the level of money and credit.

Thirdly, even if a central bank is in a position to effectively use open market operations or variable reserve requirements, a policy of systematic sterilization of foreign assets through domestic credit contraction is tantamount to a deliberate switch in the banks portfolio from domestic assets to foreign assets. This implies (assuming a fixed amount of domestic savings) a substitution toward investments in liquid foreign assets away from domestic capital formation. The desirability of such a policy may be questioned, especially in the Medium I and II as well as the small countries, where national savings are usually very limited and capital formation is a constraint on economic growth.

The effectiveness of central bank policy for price stabilization thus depends upon circumstances. Central banks generally should be able to use domestic credit policy to maintain domestic price stability: (a) when world inflation abroad is of relative short duration; (b) when the economy is relatively closed (as in the case of the medium group countries); (c) when domestic capital markets are developed to the extent allowing

the central bank a certain amount of flexibility in
pursuing domestic credit policy. The feasibility and
the desirability of central bank action may be doubtful
when none of these conditions are fulfilled. In this
situation domestic price stability may not be feasible
without other measures such as adjustments in the exchange rate.

Empirical Test of Monetary Autonomy

All of these considerations are rather moot unless
the money supply as an actual not just a theoretical
matter can be controlled. If changes in domestic credit are fully offset by changes in international reserves, monetary policy will be ineffective in combating imported inflation. To determine the degree of
monetary autonomy possessed by our sample countries the
following regression was performed for each:

$$R = a + a_1 R_w + a_2 C + a_3 E$$

where R = percent change in central bank foreign assets,
C = percent change in central bank domestic assets, and
E = percent change in the exchange rate (domestic cur-
rency units/U.S. dollar lagged one year).

The domestic credit variable (Tables 38-41) had
large negative coefficients which were statistically
significant for all the large developed countries, but
not for most of the Medium I and II countries. In large
part the small countries, as was the case for the empirical tests performed in earlier chapters, followed a
pattern similar to that of the large countries. In
general the world reserve variable was also highly significant for the developed countries and a number of small
countries but not for the medium countries. Thus, the
results suggest that independent monetary policy under
a relatively fixed exchange rate regime may be relatively more difficult if not impossible for the developed
countries and many smaller economies. At the same time,
the scope for credit control may be rather extensive
in the medium sized countries.

The results are suggestive not conclusive. An
equally plausible explanation might be that the large
(and perhaps a few small) countries pursued deliberate
sterilization policies whereas for some reason the
medium countries did not. This possibility must be

142

$$\underline{T} \underline{A} \underline{B} \underline{L} \underline{E} \quad 38$$

TEST FOR MONETARY AUTONOMY -- LARGE COUNTRIES

DISCRIMINANT ANALYSIS GROUPING

COUNTRY	A	C	RW	E(L)	r^2	F
AUSTRALIA	-1.14	-0.33 (4.89)	2.04 (3.91)	-1.01 (1.24)	0.76	13.58
AUSTRIA	9.57	-0.62 (2.72)	0.34 (1.26)	0.25 (0.33)	0.41	3.03
CANADA	5.72	-0.17 (4.65)	0.57 (2.37)	-0.34 (0.34)	0.68	9.13
FINLAND	7.56	-0.32 (2.61)	0.82 (0.90)	-0.73 (0.65)	0.38	2.66
FRANCE	28.13	-1.09 (5.28)	0.34 (0.51)	2.53 (2.13)	0.72	10.89
GERMANY	9.43	0.59 (4.55)	0.65 (1.25)	-1.06 (1.55)	0.66	8.23
JAPAN	13.34	-0.75 (5.92)	2.29 (2.80)	-0.31 (.17)	0.77	14.33
SWEDEN	6.11	-0.48 (4.95)	1.58 (3.19)	-0.45 (0.24)	0.72	11.57
U.K.	-3.39	-0.53 (2.36)	2.84 (2.57)	1.28 (0.47)	0.49	4.13

143

TEST FOR MONETARY AUTONOMY -- MEDIUM I COUNTRIES
(DISCRIMINANT ANALYSIS GROUPING)

COUNTRY	A	C	RW	E(L)	r^2	F
ITALY	15.26	-0.35 (0.30)	1.48 (0.70)	1.93 (0.33)	0.05	0.23
GREECE	4.76	-0.26 (0.06)	1.52 (2.16)	3.43 (0.59)	0.28	1.68
SOUTH AFRICA	34.68	-0.40 (2.63)	-1.01 (1.03)	0.86 (0.25)	0.38	2.67
SPAIN	2.91	-0.15 (2.56)	1.89 (0.35)	-3.39 (2.73)	0.52	4.71
MALAYSIA	13.30	-0.09 (1.70)	0.26 (0.62)	0.12 (0.42)	0.20	1.10
MEXICO	1.91	0.02 (0.59)	0.71 (3.09)	-1.47 (3.36)	0.62	7.08
VENEZUELA	2.04	0.20 (0.06)	2.21 (1.86)	0.40 (0.32)	0.21	1.19
EGYPT	2.07	0.64 (1.19)	-0.54 (0.53)	0.84 (0.67)	0.13	0.66
KOREA	84.44	0.09 (0.20)	-3.02 (0.92)	0.91 (1.20)	0.15	0.78
ISRAEL	32.73	-0.44 (1.47)	1.38 (1.06)	-0.06 (0.10)	0.20	1.10
ALGERIA	23.89	-1.02 (2.51)	0.70 (1.36)	4.70 (2.83)	0.67	5.39
COSTA RICA	8.69	-0.95 (1.71)	2.65 (2.55)	-1.66 (1.12)	0.45	3.57
ICELAND	26.11	0.01 (0.38)	-0.07 (0.23)	-0.52 (1.12)	0.10	0.49

T A B L E 40
TEST FOR MONETARY AUTONOMY -- MEDIUM II COUNTRIES
(DISCRIMINANT ANALYSIS GROUPING)

COUNTRY	A	C	RW	E(L)	r^2	F
SRI LANKA	14.04	-0.62 (0.71)	0.57 (0.46)	-0.04 (0.02)	0.07	0.34
NIGERIA	64.24	-0.96 (1.40)	5.23 (0.87)	2.93 (0.13)	0.19	0.92
INDIA	39.73	-2.88 (1.97)	0.60 (0.86)	0.26 (0.68)	0.28	1.70
PAKISTAN	39.11	-2.86 (2.03)	0.62 (0.88)	0.42 (0.50)	0.28	1.71
PHILIPPINES	30.28	-1.03 (1.67)	2.77 (2.15)	0.50 (1.21)	0.41	2.97
THAILAND	14.46	-0.20 (2.71)	-0.13 (0.39)	2.64 (0.47)	0.37	2.58
COLOMBIA	12.71	0.83 (0.79)	0.21 (0.06)	-0.63 (0.45)	0.06	0.28
MOROCCO	25.94	-0.92 (2.73)	0.20 (0.63)	1.45 (1.14)	0.41	3.04
ECUADOR	10.25	0.15 (0.17)	0.86 (1.07)	-1.08 (0.49)	0.10	0.47
EL SALVADOR	3.01	-0.01 (0.24)	1.17 (1.33)	-	0.12	0.91
PARAGUAY	55.42	-0.61 (0.83)	-0.22 (0.27)	4.56 (1.60)	0.20	1.11
ETHIOPIA	4.28	0.46 (4.37)	-0.38 (0.57)	4.03 (1.41)	0.64	7.14
SUDAN	-89.87	4.68 (2.16)	0.28 (1.03)	18.04 (2.78)	0.51	4.48

145

TEST FOR MONETARY AUTONOMY -- SMALL COUNTRIES
(DISCRIMINANT ANALYSIS GROUPING)

COUNTRY	A	C	RW	E(L)	r^2	F
CAMEROON	24.87	-1.15 (1.70)	0.11 (0.06)	3.09 (2.45)	0.43	2.97
SENEGAL	-16.82	-0.50 (2.24)	2.93 (1.20)	-4.47 (5.31)	0.78	11.55
TOGO	15.26	-0.06 (2.21)	0.26 (0.94)	2.08 (1.25)	0.51	2.44
CHAD	254.90	-3.51 (2.34)	-6.51 (0.21)	38.35 (2.93)	0.54	4.70
JAMAICA	6.92	-0.39 (2.89(	1.13 (1.48)	-1.65 (1.15)	0.48	3.96
GABON	29.91	-0.73 (1.85)	1.72 (0.90)	-2.99 (1.39)	0.34	2.06
MALAGASSY	-4.61	-0.37 (2.08)	1.12 (2.20)	-0.94 (0.64)	0.49	3.18
MALAWI	44.54	-0.16 (1.22)	-1.43 (0.66)	2.48 (0.85)	0.27	0.88
TANZANIA	13.27	-0.29 (3.06)	1.02 (1.08)	-10.82 (1.26)	0.67	4.04
SOMALIA	30.71	0.59 (3.93)	-1.45 (1.19)	-4.37 (0.80)	0.59	5.83

examined before any conclusions as to monetary autonomy can be drawn.

The Possibility of Sterilization Activity

As a first step, consider the assets of a foreign central bank as composed of domestic assets (e.g. government securities, loans to commercial banks) and foreign assets. These are counterbalanced by central bank liabilities, the equivalent in the U.S. of member bank reserves.[3] This gives:

4. $D + R = B$

where D = domestic assets of the central bank, R = foreign assets of the central bank (usually denominated in dollars), and B = monetary base of the central bank (central bank money).

The monetary base for the country (B) is linked to the domestic money supply (M) by the relationship:

5. $M = mB$

where m is the money multiplier (which if need be can be decomposed into its components reflecting the financial preferences of the public and the banking system).

In the United States the principal foreign component of the monetary base is the gold stock. For most countries, however, the central bank's holdings of foreign assets are the principal foreign component of the monetary base. Since a nation's money supply is ultimately dependent on the size of the central bank's monetary base, control of that variable is essential if a country is to alter its rate of inflation.

For incremental changes, (4) can be written as:

6. $\Delta D + \Delta R = \Delta B$

or

7. $\Delta R = \Delta B - \Delta D$

Here, ΔR represents the change in a country's holdings of foreign exchange reserves and corresponds to one definition of the balance of payments.

147

Thus, for a given time interval, say a year, ΔR would be the change in the balance of payments, ΔB the change in the monetary base, and ΔD the change in domestic assets held by the central bank. If through open market operations or their lending to commercial banks the monetary authorities have complete control over D, they are in a position to offset movements in its foreign exchange reserve component. Such action would result in a negative correlation between ΔD and ΔR.

It is possible for the reverse to occur; i.e., capital flows offsetting the central bank's decision regarding the desired change in D. This could occur, for example, if the monetary authorities decided not to satisfy increases in the demand for money. In this instance the increase in the domestic component of the monetary base would not be sufficient to satisfy this demand. Given the supply of money, the outcome would be a rise in domestic interest rates.

Widening domestic-foreign interest differentials, however, would cause the excess demand for money to be satisfied from abroad (through an increased capital inflow and a balance of payments surplus). The resulting balance of payments would reflect the fact that domestic money demand exceeded domestic money supply. When finally the excess demand for money was satisfied, the balance of payments would revert back to zero. A negative relationship between ΔR and ΔD is, therefore, consistent with either mechanism.

During the period 1960-1976, the change in the domestic component of the monetary base of the large group countries was in general very significantly and negatively related to the movement in their foreign component (Table 42). The overall goodness of fit in these simple regressions is generally acceptable.

In most cases changes in foreign assets explained over 60 percent of the variation in the change in the domestic component of the monetary base.

The results were not nearly as satisfactory for the medium country groups, with Spain and Thailand being the only countries experiencing a statistical pattern similar to the large countries. The small countries on the other hand tended as usual to have a pattern similar to the large countries, although (as

148

Table 42

Relationship between change in Foreign Assets and the change in Domestic Assets

(Groupings based on Discriminant Analysis)

Country	Intercept	Coefficient	r^2
Large Group			
Australia	269.0805	-0.5357	0.2921
Austria	0.2941	-0.0712	0.4122
Canada	0.5619	-1.1620	0.5952
Finland	405.8063	-1.0111	0.3639
France	6.5960	-0.7129	0.6640
Germany	3.5254	-0.4024	0.3679
Japan	956.1011	-1.1428	0.6486
Sweden	1.5206	-1.2307	0.7385
U K	601.9108	-1.6287	0.7151
Medium I			
Italy	2105.4767	-2.6778	0.2256
Greece	8.9052	0.3148	0.0167
South Africa	123.3657	-0.4519	0.2151
Spain	50.8095	-1.1302	0.5613
Malaysia	37.9066	-0.0525	0.1419
Mexico	4.0861	5.1899	0.1856
Venezuela	42.1153	0.0236	0.2474
Egypt	276.6080	-0.1335	0.00003
Korea	90.3426	.0301	0.0009
Israel	479.4003	0.7141	0.3114
Algeria	629.2175	-0.2562	0.1248
Costa Rica	94.6730	0.3686	0.0388
Iceland	2585.3428	-0.9557	0.0685
Medium II			
Sri Lanka	201.2130	0.5032	0.1015
Nigeria	56.4678	-0.0423	0.0981
India	4.5373	-0.2695	0.0552

Table (Contd)

Country	Intercept	Coefficient	r^2
Pakistan	1022.8129	-0.0127	0.0001
Philippines	552.5207	0.0085	0.0001
Thailand	1.5983	-0.4818	0.4437
Colombia	1223.8739	1.2163	0.3113
Morocco	245.6505	-0.1344	0.0181
Ecuador	810.7802	0.0155	0.0004
El Salvador	63.3018	0.7773	0.2181
Paraguay	638.9545	-0.0581	0.0125
Ethiopia	38.6528	-0.2075	0.0267
Sudan	27.4630	-1.0722	0.0586
Small			
Cameroon	2.7551	-0.4365	0.3274
Senegal	2.1726	-0.5944	0.2155
Togo	480.8922	-0.1061	0.3914
Chad	0.8426	-0.8719	0.4784
Jamaica	27.1325	-1.6919	0.4965
Niger	659.2818	0.2350	0.2203
Central African Republic	0.6725	-0.5661	0.1779
Gabon	0.3167	0.1752	0.3827
Malagassy	1.7726	-1.1383	0.4422
Malawi	5.6498	-0.3843	0.2617
Tanzania	442.3489	-1.1209	0.1762
Somalia	42.8391	-0.2493	0.0141

measured by the r^2) the relationship was not as satisfactory.

While the regressions confirm the negative rela-
tionship between ΔD and ΔR for several of our country
groups, causation has not yet been established. Additional information is needed to establish whether or
not some central banks were able to sterilize foreign
exchange inflows, and thus maintain some degree of
monetary autonomy. An examination of the movements in
the United States monetary base should resolve the
issue.

The U.S. Monetary Base and National Money Supplies

If in fact central banks were capable of sterili-
zing foreign exchange influences on their monetary
bases, then we should not expect to find that changes
in the monetary base of the United States[4] (the country
to which most of the other countries pegged their exchange rate for much of the sample period) strongly
influenced their domestic money supplies. This was not
the case. Changes in the money supplies of all our
four groups of countries were fairly closely related to
changes in the U.S. monetary base. The change in the
U.S. monetary base is statistically significant in the
majority of cases (Table 43) with the correlation coefficient averaging 0.3675, 0.4450, 0.4029, and 0.4612
for the large, Medium I, Medium II, and small countries,
respectively.

It is not surprising to find that changes in the
U.S. monetary base were significant in explaining
changes in foreign money supplies. Given the commitment
by most nations to a system of relatively fixed exchange
rates, and given the continual rise in the rate of
growth of the U.S. monetary base (from 2.0 percent in
1959-1962 to 8.1 percent in 1973), it was not simply
chance that most industrial nations experienced rapid
increases in the rates of growth of their money supplies.[5] The evidence seems to indicate that while many
nations could in the short run sterilize some of the
undesired increase in their monetary bases caused by
the inflow of U.S. dollars, they would not achieve long
sterilization and thus controls over their money supplies.

T A B L E 43

RELATIONSHIP BETWEEN CHANGES IN THE U.S. MONETARY BASE AND NATIONAL MONEY SUPPLIES
(Groupings based on Discrimination Analysis)

COUNTRY	INTERCEPT	COEFFICIENT	r^2
LARGE GROUP			
AUSTRALIA	24.0781	84.9448	0.3444
AUSTRIA	3.0539	0.7766	0.2770
FINLAND	18.4057	115.1646	0.4082
FRANCE*	11.7833	2.7067	0.3886
GERMANY	4.1786	0.9827	0.3494
JAPAN	1250.9300	406.6074	0.4646
SWEDEN*	0.4808	0.2333	0.3071
U.K.*	121.3185	160.5217	0.4008
MEDIUM I			
ITALY	1737.5717	490.1921	0.3238
GREECE	3.6448	1.0495	0.2842
SOUTH AFRICA	93.7990	23.1941	0.2130
SPAIN	23.0719	18.7122	0.4394
MALAYSIA	-2.3052	53.3697	0.4026
MEXICO	1.5399	1.2235	0.4306
VENEZUELA	-332.9058	384.0485	0.4172
EGYPT	-1.1310	23.8320	0.4813
KOREA	-10.5400	21.7102	0.5507
ISRAEL	-30.4250	171.6610	0.6024
ALGERIA	441.9237	351.2180	0.2854
COSTA RICA	-58.5770	56.9363	0.7095
ICELAND	-222.1636	263.1215	0.6450
MEDIUM II			
SRI LANKA	0.0264	37.9535	0.3075
NIGERIA	-106.1738	68.1423	0.4241
INDIA	2.3849	0.8891	0.5707
PAKISTAN	-29.0645	374.9885	0.3957
PHILIPPINES	175.9015	95.4040	0.3403
THAILAND	0.4502	0.3042	0.4330
COLOMBIA*	-2864.0468	2224.8470	0.4641
MOROCCO*	118.2586	146.4717	0.4420

T A B L E 4 3 (Con't.)

COUNTRY	INTERCEPT	COEFFICIENT	r^2
ECUADOR*	-311.9153	419.5164	0.5530
EL SALVADOR	-13.2982	13.5659	0.4944
PARAGUAY	340.1224	190.1862	0.2895
ETHIOPIA	6.4738	8.9584	0.2927
SUDAN*	5.0066	2.8315	0.2313
SMALL			
CAMEROON	1.5966	0.7373	0.2231
SENEGAL*	-7.3488	2.4381	0.7109
TOGO*	-2902.5526	1018.2776	0.4359
CHAD*	-0.5222	0.3030	0.4894
JAMAICA	0.9667	3.0595	0.4223
NIGER	-372.9592	330.4341	0.5302
CENTRAL AFRICAN REPUBLIC*	-0.1817	0.2011	0.4768
GABON*	-0.7004	1.0869	0.2949
MALAGASSY*	-0.4947	0.7799	0.9063
SOMALIA	4.6712	11.4064	0.1221

NOTE: * indicates best relationship found with U.S. monetary base lagged one year.

Conclusions--Observations on Semi-Dependence

The empirical tests presented above indicate that independent monetary policy appears to be much less feasible for the large and small group countries than for the medium sized countries. This finding helps explain the wider dispersion of inflation rates among the developing (medium sized) countries than among the developed countries. Presumably the developing countries are less well integrated into the world economy, and this is reflected by the fact that capital movements in and out of these countries is not as responsive to changes in their interest rates vis a vis the world rate as is the case for the large group countries. The small (developing) countries are so open to trade and capital flows that they have little chance in even attempting to pursue an independent monetary policy.

In this regard it is accurate to classify the small and large countries (excluding the U.S.) as dependent monetary economies. The medium group countries appear to be capable of controlling to various degrees their money supplies and thus domestic rates of inflation. They are in this sense semi-dependent economies.

Notes

1. See for example the essays by Milton Friedman in his The Optimum Quantity of Money (Chicago: Aldine Publishing Company, 1969).

2. A similar approach was taken by Hang-Sheng Cheng and Nicholas Sargen in "Central Bank Policy Towards Inflation," Federal Reserve Bank of San Francisco, Business Review (Spring 1975), pp. 31-41.

3. M. W. Holtrop, Money in an Open Economy (Leiden: H. E. Stenfert Kroese, 1972), for an elaboration on these points.

4. Joseph Bisignano, "The Interdependence of National Monetary Policies," Federal Reserve Bank of San Francisco, Business Review (Spring 1975), pp. 41-48.

5. Edward Shaw, "International Money and International Inflation: 1958-1973," Federal Reserve Bank of San Francisco, Business Review (Spring 1975), pp. 5-17.

CHAPTER 10

MONETARY ARRANGEMENTS IN A SEMI-DEPENDENT COUNTRY:

THE CASE OF MEXICO

Introduction

The term semi-dependent was used at the end of
Chapter 9 to refer to a group of countries (the two
medium sized groups) that had, based on several econo-
metric tests, appeared to have some degree of control
over their domestic money supplies, and therefore internal rates of inflation. By definition it follows
that dependent countries would have little or no control over these variables.

The term dependence (but not semi-dependence) has
been used extensively and loosely in the literature.[1]
From our point of view it is obviously important to be
precise about the underlying causes of dependence, and
the related concepts of semi-dependence and independence. Clearly the classification within which a country finds itself will ultimately determine the likely
economic consequences world inflation will have for it
in the future.

A first step in this direction is the examination
of the manner in which the term 'dependence' has been
used in the literature; a second step is to then specify the formal conditions that are required before an
economy can be classified as monetary dependent, semi-
dependent and independent.

Economic Dependence as Used in the Literature

As is only to be expected when a word in common use
is given a special connotation and ascribed uncommon
characteristics, a fairly large amount of confusion has
arisen over what 'dependence' means. In conventional
economic parlance, a country may be described as being
'dependent' on foreign trade or foreign technology; or
a process of great complexity may be said to involve
greater 'interdependence' between different workers; or
the world may be said to become more 'interdependent'
because of increasing international trade and invest-

155

ment.

In such usage, there is no hint of anything undesirable (on the contrary, most conventional economists would regard more interdependence as a good
thing), nor is there any implication of a process of
causation: dependence is defined with reference to
some particular objective economic fact and says nothing in a descriptive or causal sense about the condition of the economy as a whole.[2]

In the literature on monetary problems, the terms
'dependent economies,' 'dependent monetary economies,'
'dependent systems,' and 'dependent export economies,'
have been used interchangeably and not always in such
a way that precise meanings could be attached to these
terms. In some instances nothing more than a political
system that was formally 'colonial' has been enough to
earn one of these particular labels, while in others it
may simply be the absence of a central bank.

The problem of clarity with regard to terminology
comes up in this area because the idea surrounding the
concept of economic dependence has not received systematic treatment as a quantitative concept. As a result
the term has been applied somewhat uncritically to a
number of situations in which it conveys the idea that
economic relationships between a country and other countries tend to be unequal and one-sided rather than equal
and mutual. It thus deals with relative power in the
field of international economic relations.

Economic dependence then is essentially the mani-
festation of unequal power relations between countries.
It follows that by this definition, economic circumstances in another (superordinate) country are the most
important factor conditioning the economic welfare of
the subordinate country. Economically independent countries can prosper on their own momentum; economically
dependent countries can do so only if circumstances in
the dominant country are favorable. A situation of unequal power clearly exists, and it is the subordinate
country's dependence on circumstances in the dominant
country for its prosperity that provides the qualitative nature of dependence.[3]

In the usage of the Dependencia School, for example, 'dependence' is meant to describe certain characteristics (economic as well as social and political) of

the economy as a whole, and is intended to trace certain processes which are causally linked to its underdevelopment and which are expected to adversely affect its development in the future.[4]

Implicit in current writings of the dependencia economists is the idea that economic dependence is an undesirable state of affairs, whatever the size of average incomes, and that it should be cured. This proposition is usually discussed along two lines. First, it is assumed as a positive proposition that economic dependence is an inherently unstable state which among other things renders ineffective attempts to predict economic performance and therefore to plan for economic growth. The premise here is that dependence on external economic factors implies an inability to countervail any adverse movement in these factors. Second, as a normative proposition, it is accepted that economic dependence is a state of inherent inequality which as such is condemned. Not only do disparities in international power operate to widen the degree of international inequality, but the localization of activity within the dependent country serves to reinforce and extend internal inequality.[5]

Many qualitative elements in this dominance/dependence system have been identified--the concentration of decisionmaking in the developed countries, the international forces making for the polarization of industry in the rich countries, the operations of multinational corporations, the alleged control of world prices by rich countries, the technological monopoly of the developed countries, and the terms on which technology is transferred to poor countries, and even cultural dependence.[6]

Five ways in which economic dependence is manifested in developing countries are usually cited as:

1. dependence through foreign ownernhip and control of key sectors of the economy;

2. dependence through foreign aid;

3. dependence through trade;

4. dependence through reliance of foreign human resources and foreign know-how;

157

5. dependence through imported consumption and production patterns.

But these are general problems facing to one extent or another all developing countries. When we describe countries as dependent by virtue of their ability to conduct monetary policy, we have a more global meaning in mind.

Critique of the Dependency Concept

One sometimes gets the impression on reading the literature that 'dependence' is defined in a circular manner: in one context less developed countries are poor because they are dependent, and any characteristics that they display signify dependence. In such tautologous definitions, 'dependence' tends to be identified with the features of these countries which the economist in question happens to particularly dislike as a verifiable explanation of the processes at work in the less developed world.

A concept of dependence which is to serve a useful analytical purpose, however, must satisfy two criteria:[7]

1. It must lay down certain characteristics of dependent economies which are not found in nondependent ones.

2. These characteristics must be shown to affect adversely the course and pattern of development of the dependent countries.

If the first criterion is not satisfied and crucial features of dependence are to be found in both dependent and non-dependent economies, obviously the whole conceptual scheme is defective. If the second is not satisfied, and peculiar features of dependence are not demonstrated to be causally related to the continuance of underdevelopment, the analytical purpose of the whole exercise is not served, and we end up with a catalogue of socio-economic indicators which are singularly unhelpful for understanding economic problems.

The concept of dependence need not be confined to developing countries, yet perhaps because it always has been applied in that manner accounts for its inability to provide very useful insights into national economic

158

problems.

If, however, we approach the problem of dependency without the initial two-fold classification of industrial and developed, it is possible to gain a number of valuable insights relevant for economic policymaking.

Operational Definitions

Using the initial approach of Thomas,[8] there are two necessary conditions which must be simultaneously evaluated in an economy before it can be categorized as a 'dependent' economy. These are:

1. The degree to which the economy is resilient to changes taking place in the rest of the world. This depends on: (a) the level and rate at which domestic real per capita incomes are increasing over a relevant period of time; and (b) the extent of unemployment of existing resources.

2. The degree to which the economy depends on the rest of the world to maintain the increased internal levels of employment, output, demand, and prices.

The first group of conditions refer to the existence of resilience factors (since they state in economic terms the ability of the community to sustain sudden and erratic changes in the second set of conditions). The second group of conditions are generating factors (since they indicate the degree to which internal income, price, output, and employment changes depend upon events in the rest of the world).

Two further conditions are necessary before the economy is classified as a 'dependent' monetary economy. These are:

1. Monetary and financial institutions (as well as individuals and government) must have a high propensity to invest in foreign assets to the extent that their peculiar types of speculation do not make this impossible.

2. The autonomous elements in the monetary system must attach greater importance to financing

159

the generating factors, not by lending to them more of their funds than to the other sectors (independent sectors) but must also be lending these generating factors at an increasing rate in the comparison with other sectors.

While the presence of all these conditions in an economy is largely a matter of degree, the monetary dependence concept developed meets the two criteria outlined above. For example, while the advanced open economies have many of the characteristics of dependence, e.g. a high export/national income ratio, these in the context of their wealth would not be enough to make them dependent economies in the same sense as the smaller developing countries.

The Small Country Group

The ability of many small countries to conduct monetary policy has been severely limited for a number of reasons. Many of the countries belonging to the small country group have recently been the colonies of a European power (or have been at some stage of their history). Their economies are usually integrated into those of the mother country in such a way that they are hardly more than a locus of production of a number of fragments tenuously held together largely by government controls.

Because their small size limits the scope of the domestic market, monopolistic conditions of production and exchange usually prevail in these economies. Manufacturing in most cases is limited to the low level of domestic purchasing power and is confined mainly to import substitution assembly plant operations. High levels of unemployment and underemployment of labor may exist while income distribution is frequently highly skewed. There may be significant economic and social dualism while industrial linkages are normally very marginal. The propensity to import is very high, and there is a wide divergence between the structure and pattern of domestic consumption and domestic production.

The economies of the small developing countries are, therefore, highly open both structurally and functionally. Structural openness relates to the fact that foreign trade and payments dominate domestic

160

economic transaction. Exports, therefore, play a crucial role and contribute more to the determination of income levels and employment than investment changes as in the Keynesian type models. Functional openness of these economies leads to the integration of domestic money and capital market institutions with other branches of the multinational corporations and with the metropolitan countries. Thus, both the real sector and the financial sector are controlled from outside.

In general there is a high degree of capital mobility between the small developing countries and the world's major financial centers; i.e., since these countries' financial markets are unable to compete in either breadth and depth or resiliency, a substantial portion of domestic savings is channelled overseas and the remainder is utilized mainly to finance imports. Given their usual high ratio of foreign to domestic investments, long term capital inflows become crucial to the operation of these economic systems; the inflows finance expansion in domestic production.

Small developing countries certainly meet the two criteria outlined above for classification as monetary dependent as well as dependent economies. The conditions existing in the large countries (except of course the United States) place them in the monetary dependent group (because they cannot control their money supplies). However as confirmed by their structural characteristics and the discriminant analysis performed above, large countries, with regard to the environment from which they encounter world inflationary forces, belong in a group distinct from the smaller nations.

While most small developing countries can be classified as 'dependent' monetary economies, some elements of monetary dependence are present even in the larger developing countries, especially since modern communications have broken national barriers and have brought nearly all economies into a network of financial interrelationships.

The Medium II group countries, however, usually have an environment in which central bank policy instruments are still quite rudimentary. Open market operations are often infeasible since central banks hold few marketable domestic assets, especially in countries where the development of domestic money markets has been, as in the case of India, stifled by an official low interest rate policy. Central bank discount policy is often ineffective at a time when the banking sector is already awash with liquidity arising from balance of payments surpluses. Adjustments in reserve requirements are sometimes subject to statutory ceilings. For lack of alternatives, many central banks have relied largely on moral suasion to control the growth of domestic credit. Altogether the room for maneuver is most often extremely limited.

Many of these deficiencies are present but to a lesser extent in the Medium I countries. For that reason they are classified here as semi-dependent economies. An examination of the monetary arrangements in one of these countries--Mexico--illustrates these points and provides a more detailed insight into the type of environment from which semi-dependent countries must conduct anti-inflationary policy.

Instruments of Central Bank Monetary Policy

There are a number of instruments available to the monetary authorities in semi-dependent countries, each effective[9] to one degree or another in controlling the domestic money supply and thus the domestic level of inflation. The main instruments of monetary policy include:[10] (1) the discount, (2) open market operations, (3) reserve ratios, (4) rediscounting, (5) public sector credit, (6) selective credit controls, (7) import deposits, (8) exchange controls, and (9) exchange rate adjustments.

Most of the illustrations that follow are for Mexico,[11] a country that has been one of the more successful countries in perfecting the use of many of these tools.

The Central Bank of Mexico

Article 28 of the Mexican Political Constitution states that issuance of bank notes remains the right of a single agency of the Mexican government: the Banco de Mexico. In 1917 the Constitutional Congress expressly provided for the establishment of the Banco de Mexico, but not until 1925 did the central bank begin to emerge from the myraid of existing private financial institutions. In the Banco de Mexico Organic Law

162

of 1936, the central bank finally obtained full control of monetary reserves and had authority over the issuance and placement of bank notes. In 1941, it became even more powerful with the enactment of the Legal Reserve Requirement Law, which conceded to it legal command over reserves. Other banking laws of the 1940s and early 1950s along with those of 1970 established the bank's role of adviser and executor of monetary policy, but reserved final responsibility of such policy to the federal government.

The growth of the Mexican central bank is similar to that of the U.S. Federal Reserve System, with some significant exceptions. Whereas the Federal Reserve Act of 1913 was designed to establish the Federal Reserve System as an agency semi-independent from the government, the Bank of Mexico was established as an integral part of the federal government. Thus government and bank policies are considered synonymous, and consequently the central bank may be viewed as an essential arm of the federal government's overall policy objectives.

In some instances, however, the central bank resembles the Federal Reserve System in that both are responsible for initiating and advising the executive authority on monetary policy issues. The Bank of Mexico like the Federal Reserve System, can set required reserve ratios for commercial banks and other financial intermediaries. The central bank issues paper currency that is a liability of the bank, just as Federal Reserve notes are liabilities of the U.S. Federal Reserve System. The day to day functions of the two banks are similar, in that both are clearing houses for the daily activities of the banking community and both may act as the banker of the federal government. Though the Federal Reserve System and the central bank of Mexico both carry government and community bank deposits only the central bank deals directly with the public by making loans or holding personal demand deposits.

One of the most important administrative functions of the Bank of Mexico is the selective allocation of credit via its various policy tools. While both the U.S. and Mexican monetary authorities act as clearing houses for government bonds, only the Mexican central bank uses required reserves as an effective tool to promote bond purchases. The discount window of the Federal Reserve is used to provide liquidity for banks,

and in some instances, to attempt to influence the interest rates, whereas the central bank of Mexico ac-
tively uses the discount window selectively to increase
liquidity among banks, sectors, and regions. In short,
the central bank of Mexico acts as a director and executor of government financial and monetary policy in
the context of a developing country, while the Federal
Reserve System is the autonomous initiator, director,
and executor of monetary policy in an economy that is
developed and that plays a unique role in the world
monetary system.

The Bank Rate

The bank rate is the classical monetary policy
designed either to expand or to contract domestic credit so as to maintain equilibrium in the economy. In
practice, however, unless an economy is virtually
closed with regard to both current and capital financial
transactions, the chances of pursuing an independent
interest rate policy are constrained by developments in
the international economy. The effectiveness of changes
in the bank rate in a country like Mexico is further
limited by the shortage of loanable funds and the relationship of the multinational corporations who in large
part have their head offices in the United States.

If interest rates are low in Mexico in relation to
those in the U.S., there is a tendency for domestic
funds to be transferred to that country. This is faci-
litated by the partial integration of the two countries' money and capital markets and the stable exchange
rate between the peso and the dollar. Foreign business
will tend to borrow locally instead of in the U.S.,
since it is cheaper to do so. This action will result
in a decline in capital inflows and reduce the volume
of credit available to Mexican businesses and individuals.
On the other hand, if domestic interest rates are too
high in relation to those in the U.S., there will be a
tendency for 'hot money' to flow into Mexico, possibly
resulting in an inflationary situation.

With regard to Mexico, several observers have
argued that the interest rate differential is a major
factor contributing to Mexican success in attracting
foreign capital and generating capital account surpluses, and that these differentials in interest rates
between Mexico and other countries have been an impor-

164

tant policy tool for the central bank of Mexico. On the other hand, one could easily contend that these differentials are set in the marketplace and reflect the difference in risk between Mexican and world (U.S.) securities.

While it is clear that nominal levels of interest rates in Mexico can and do differ from the nominal rates for similar types of securities in the United States, Europe or Japan, the reason for this disparity is a matter of debate.

It is clear, however, that the financial assets of the two countries differ in at least two basic attributes--the currency in which they are denominated and the legal jurisdiction in which they are issued. Because assets are denominated in different currencies, the future price relationship may differ from the current price relationship if the exchange rate is changed. Investor concern with possible changes in exchange rates involves exchange risk; their concern with possible changes in exchange controls involves political risk.

If investors were certain about the future exchange rates and were concerned that exchange controls might be raised or lowered by the Mexican authorities (or the U.S. authorities for that matter), then interest rates on similar assets denominated in dollars or pesos would differ only by the anticipated rate of change in the exchange rate. And if investors were certain about the future of exchange controls and knew that exchange rates would remain unchanged, then interest rates on assets issued in the two countries should differ by no more than the effective cost of these controls.

Because investors are uncertain about exchange rates in the future, they may be reluctant to sell securities denominated in dollars, for example, and buy Mexican securities with higher interest rates denominated in pesos, even if the interest rate differentials exceed the expected change in the exchange rate.

Reluctance of this sort simply reflects investor's concern with possible losses if the actual change in the exchange rate exceeds the mean expected change. Uncertainty of this sort acts as a barrier to the shift of funds among the two currencies and their respective financial centers--Mexico City and New York. Consequently, at any moment the observed interest rate differentials on similar assets but denominated in different currencies--or dollars and pesos--reflect investors' expectations of future exchange rates and the payment if any demanded by investors for bearing uncertainty about possible changes in the peso-dollar exchange rate.

Determining that investors do not regard the assets produced in the two countries as perfect substitutes for each other is a necessary condition for some degree of Mexican monetary independence; it is not a sufficient condition. Investors might regard these assets as close substitutes. Examination of correlation suggests that the changes in the Mexican and U.S. rates are related. Investor foresight, however, is imperfect, and because of exchange risk and political risk, U.S. investors may be reluctant to shift funds to Mexico to take advantage of small differences in expected yields. The sufficient condition for Mexican monetary independence is that, given the currency preferences of investors and their willingness to bear risk, the authorities can readily sterilize the volume of capital flows. There is no evidence that the Mexican monetary authorities are in a position to accomplish this feat.

It is also difficult to argue that the Mexican capital market is isolated from other financial centers, when as early as 1963 foreign financing paid for almost 25 percent of public investment. In 1971 Mexico borrowed $1.378 billion from abroad, of which $1.047 billion was borrowed by the government. These figures are remarkable considering that foreign borrowings were equivalent to 4 percent of GNP. These figures leave little doubt that Mexico is susceptible to the influence of foreign capital markets.

Open Market Operations

Open market operations involve the central bank's intervention into the market on its own initiative to buy or sell government securities in order to effect changes in the domestic money supply. The efficacy of open market operations, therefore, presupposes the existence of a broad and active securities market. This exists to only a limited degree in Mexico as well as in most of the semi-dependent countries.

Thus, while announced government policies have
been directed at maintaining a rate of interest on
Mexican bonds sufficiently high to attract foreign
savings, this high rate of interest may in large part
be due to a liquidity and risk premium paid on Mexican bonds. There is no developed secondary bond market in Mexico, and as a result the actual price of
bonds is not determined in a well functioning market
as is the case in the United States.

The central bank of Mexico in fact has no open
market committee to control the monetary base through
purchases and sales of government securities. The
compulsory deposit, required reserve mechanism laws
of 1941, 1949, and 1958, allow it an alternative to
the open market mechanism. A target rate of deposit
growth may be established by the central bank for individual commercial banks. Those that cannot attract
reserves sufficient to meet the prescribed annual rate
of increase in deposits may borrow reserves from the
central bank, thus allowing commercial banks that are
below the target rate to borrow funds. At the same
time the central bank allows loans to those commercial
banks whose deposit growth exceeds the target.

Reserve Ratios

Variable reserve ratios of commercial banks have
been used effectively as a tool of monetary policy in
a number of developing countries.

Although it may be objected to as interfering
with the market mechanism, this system is in general
a direct means of stabilizing money and credit conditions and the balance of payments. Whenever there is
excessive liquidity in the banking system, there is
a temptation on the part of banks to expand credit,
thus transferring international inflation to the domestic economy. The central bank can prevent this by
raising the ratio of required reserves on deposits,
thereby reducing the bank's ability to expand credit.
Funds thus sterilized could presumably be channelled
to productive sectors through rediscounting facilities
or maintained by the bank as part of its stabilization
policy.

167

Mexico's reserve requirements are very complicated. While all the nation's financial institutions must maintain required reserves with the central bank, only deposit banks have the ability to create money. There are two types of reserves. One is the traditional non-interest bearing deposits of the banks at the Banco de Mexico, while the second can be held in the form of low interest bearing government securities. The second form of reserve requirement is a tool that is used by the government to transfer savings from the private to the public sector. It will not, however, affect the money supply.

The transfer is regulated by a committee of the central bank utilizing the required reserve ratios. In essence these procedures are the Mexican version of the Open Market Committee of the U.S. Federal Reserve System.

There are several important points related to the Mexican monetary procedure. First, since deficit spending depends upon transfers of funds from the private to the public sector through the banking system, the government becomes dependent upon the private and semi-governmental banking system for funds.

Second, if any policy of the government disturbs the amount of savings captured by the domestic banking system, the ability of the system to finance government expenditures are lessened.

Third, if the rate of growth of the government deficit financed by this transfer is greater than the savings rate, the availability of liquidity to the private sector is lowered.

Fourth, and perhaps the most important point, is that the Mexican reserve mechanism does not carry the traditional money multiplier effect that the required reserve ratios in other countries usually do. In the U.S., for example, an increase in the reserve requirement will lower the multiplier, and therefore, lower the money supply. In Mexico this may not happen as in the early 1970s when the authorities increased the marginal reserve requirements in an effort to slow the growth in the supply of money. It appears that this policy had only marginal success.

Subsequent studies by the members of the central bank of Mexico have indicated that the use of these reserve requirements to control the money supply has had little effect; i.e., the main impact of changes of the reserve requirements are in the money multiplier not the supply of money.

Rediscounting Facilities and Loans to Commercial Banks

As lender of last resort, the central bank in most semi-dependent countries is usually in a position to influence credit expansion or contraction through its rediscounting and loan facilities to commercial banks. These facilities can also help to make the bank rate effective and influence the allocation of credit. But the potential of these facilities for effecting an independent monetary policy is limited by a number of factors.

1. In several of the semi-dependent countries the central bank is a relatively new institution. It will take some time before the commercial banks become adjusted to its presence and to the use of its facilities.

2. Often many of the commercial banks are branches of overseas banks. They tend to use their head office facilities when they are short of funds and to reduce their indebtedness when they are in surplus.

3. Commercial banks in these countries often find it more economical to finance import requirements--often an important element in their portfolios--through their head offices.

4. Commercial banks operating in some of the semi-dependent countries are branches of large multinational banks with assets many times that of the central bank. If as is often the case the resources of the central bank are limited, the amount of funds available for rediscounting facilities and loans to commercial banks may be inadequate to influence domestic monetary conditions.

5. In the more open semi-dependent countries, the

169

central bank has to be very cautious in making loans to commercial banks since this could contribute to the country's balance of payments problems (because of the high propensity to import).

The experience in a number of the semi-dependent countries has been that as the economy develops and becomes more diversified, the influence of the central bank obtains more influence over the policies of the commercial banks. Moreover, as in the case of Mexico where there are no foreign banks and the commercial banks have become localized and grounded in the domestic economy, the scope for monetary policy has improved.

In Mexico where the discount mechanism has been used to regulate the rate of growth in deposits of individual banks, the central bank of Mexico may use the discount window at its discretion to stimulate deposits in given commercial banks and, during most of the period after 1954, has maintained a specific target rate of growth in deposits for the various types of commercial banks. Whether or not an individual bank was expanding its deposits at this rate was in fact an important element in the central bank's decision to make funds available. Naturally, the discount mechanism had other uses that infringed upon its use solely for controlling the expansion of deposits; but where possible, it was frequently utilized to maintain a steady growth in deposits for the financial sector as a whole and among individual banks.

The central bank of Mexico has also exercised limited control over the placement of public debt instruments in commercial banks through its discount window. Although published discount rates are established, the actual rate for any specific commercial paper loan has been left to the discretion of the central bank. Thus through its variable discount rate, it can influence the placement of credit to particular industries. The window also provides support for commercial banks experiencing short term losses of deposits. The discount window permits the central bank not only to be the lender of last resort, but also to serve as vehicle to control the money base in the short run. In addition, it allows the bank to maintain some control over domestically financed government borrowing.

Public Sector Credit

The central bank usually acts as the government's banker. Because government income and expenditure are significant in the semi-dependent countries, the operations of government accounts have a significant affect on the money supply. Payments by the government serve to increase the stock of money held by the rest of the community, while the government's receipts tend to reduce it. It goes without saying that if deficits are financed by borrowing from the central bank, the money supply is quite likely to increase and inflation result.

Since in Mexico it is relatively easy for the government to borrow from the central bank, there has from time to time been a tendency for the authorities to misuse this facility. Historically this has led to balance of payments problems and widespread inflation.

Public sector credit is an important constraint on monetary policy in Mexico. The tax structure has not been able to raise revenues in line with government expenditures. The bank from time to time has been obliged then to finance the government's deficit, when in fact it would, based on its own goals for the economy, have preferred to restrain monetary expansion.

Selective Credit Controls

Although selective credit controls are a useful policy instrument, their application in semi-dependent countries has often been limited by conflicts between various policy goals. In the highly open countries, credit creation has not necessarily led to internally generated inflation. Because in these countries, domestic output is easily supplemented by imports, a balance of payments problem usually arises instead.

Import Deposits

The use of pre-deposits on imports, while not prevalent in Mexico, is becoming popular in a number of the semi-dependent countries. The purpose of this instrument is to increase the cost of credit and thereby restrict its availability for import expenditure (while at the same time mopping up excessive liquidity). Several structural factors in these countries, however,

171

tend to militate against its effectiveness.

First, the financial institutions often make credit available to finance the pre-deposit requirement. Such loans are riskless and the deposit in itself guarantees the loans. Also, the financing of imports is often undertaken by commercial banks simply in order to maintain their level of profits. Because the banks are likely to loose customers unless they provide for import needs, the pre-deposit requirements are often made by shifting funds that would have been lent to other uses.

The effectiveness of import deposits is therefore dependent on the simultaneous imposition of direct controls and adequate arrangements to absorb liquidity at the time when deposits are refunded.

Exchange Controls

Exchange controls like import deposits are not used in Mexico. In other semi-developed economies, however, exchange controls are considered important in preventing domestic savings from leaving the country. Furthermore, since the openness of these economies limits the effectiveness of monetary policy and its potential for independent action, exchange controls may enable the authorities to achieve some degree of monetary independence. The case for exchange controls is therefore based on the need to insulate the domestic economy against adverse financial conditions overseas and give the domestic monetary authorities greater power to regulate capital outflows (and of course capital inflows during inflationary periods).

The chief arguments against exchange controls are largely psychological, and no doubt these play a role in Mexico's reluctance to introduce these measures. As soon as exchange controls are imposed, investors in foreign countries may feel that this is the prelude to devaluation and hence divert their savings away from Mexican assets. The result in the case of Mexico might be sizable enough to offset any possible benefits derived from their imposition.

Exchange Rate Policy

Changes in the exchange rate are primarily intended to bring the balance of payments into equilibrium. In the case of the semi-dependent countries, however, changes in the exchange rate may be either passive or active. Passive changes reflect a decision to follow the international currency to which the currency of the country is linked. Active changes in exchange rates by the monetary authorities of the semi-dependent countries are deliberate policy actions in the sense that action is taken to change the exchange rate or to establish multiple exchange rates for purely internal economic reasons notwithstanding the position of the currency to which the domestic currency is pegged.

Mexico has had only two recent devaluations, 1954 and 1976. Hence, the country has adopted in large part a passive exchange rate policy. There are two schools of thought, however, in Mexico on the pursuance of an active exchange rate policy. First, there are those who regard devaluation as a strategic policy decision to foster the country's economic development. Second, there are those who contend that given the underlying structural rigidities in the Mexican economy, devaluation as a policy prescription would be disadvantageous to the domestic economy.

From time to time, the former (particularly prior to the 1976 devaluation) have contended that the peso was heavily over-valued, and that this was the basic reason for the country's high and steadily mounting unemployment.

The latter group usually argues that the supply of many products was inelastic. Hence, devaluation as such could not help the export sector and would tend to move the terms of trade against the country. On the other hand, the devaluation itself would be inflationary since the economy imports many essential intermediate and capital goods. If the demand for money is stable, a large inflow of funds would take place to satisfy the increased transactions demand for money. Further increases in price that result from this inflow might throw the country into a devaluation-wage-price spiral.

Conclusions

The main purposes of monetary policy in semi-dependent countries should be to develop institutions capable of increasing savings and transferring these funds into the most productive investments; and secondly, in association with other kinds of policy, to facilitate the process of structural transformation and domestic economic integration. Both processes have been shown to take place best in an environment of price stability. The monetary authorities have numerous tools to aid them in this regard.

Mexico's experience indicates that in spite of dependence on the developed countries, particularly the U.S., the country has the potential for pursuing autonomous monetary policies. There is little doubt that the economy has developed to such a stage where at least potentially skillful management of the money supply in combination with an incomes policy could reduce unemployment without serious inflationary and balance of payments problems.

Following the increase in worldwide inflation after 1970, developments in Mexico--double digit inflation, devaluation, a large balance of payments deficit, and an unemployment rate of almost 40 percent after a decade and a half of stability and high growth--seem to contradict, however, the notion that the Mexican authorities can pursue monetary policy with any degree of autonomy, or at least have more than marginal control over their domestic money supply.

The two chapters that follow examine Mexico's recent series of economic setbacks to see if in fact the economy's basic characteristics placing it in the semi-dependent country classification have in turn prevented the country from dealing with developments in the world economy--developments which if unchecked would have grave economic consequences for the economy.

Notes

1. Cf. T. dos Santos, "The Structure of Dependence," American Economic Review (May 1970), pp. 231-236; O. Sunkel, "National Development Policy and External Dependence in Latin America," Journal of Development Studies (October 1969), pp. 23-48; and Norman

Girvan, "The Development of Dependency Economics in the Caribbean and Latin America: Review and Comparison," Social and Economic Studies (March 1973), pp. 1-33, for a flavor of this approach.

2. Sanjaya Lall, "Is Dependence a Useful Concept in Analyzing Underdevelopment?" World Development (Nos. 11 & 12, 1975), p. 799.

3. The approach taken by William Demas. See his "Economic Independence: Conceptual and Policy Issues in the Commonwealth Caribbean," in Percy Selwin, ed., Development Policy in Small Countries (New York: Holmes & Meier Publishers, 1975), pp. 191-207.

4. O. Sunkel, "Big Business and Dependencia," Foreign Affairs (April 1972), pp. 517-534.

5. Havelock Brewster, "Economic Dependence: A Quantitative Interpretation," Social and Economic Studies (March 1973), pp. 90-95.

6. O. Sunkel, "Translational Capitalism and National Disintegration in Latin America," Social and Economic Studies (March 1973), pp. 132-176.

7. Lall, op. cit., p. 800.

8. Clive Thomas, Monetary and Financial Arrangements in a Dependent Monetary Economy: A Study of British Guiana 1945-1962 (Kingston Jamaica: Institute of Social and Economic Research, 1965), pp. 3-4. Also see his The Structure Performance and Prospects of Central Banking in the Caribbean (Kingston Jamaica: The Institute of Social and Economic Research, 1972).

9. An interesting approach is Eprime Eshag, "The Relative Efficacy of Monetary Policy in Selected Industrial and Less-Developed Countries," Economic Journal (June 1971), pp. 294-305. See, however, Tom Mayer, "The Relative Efficacy of Monetary Policy in Selected Industrial and Less-Developed Countries: A Comment," Economic Journal (December 1972), pp. 1368-1371.

10. Asgar Ally, "The Potential for Autonomous Monetary Policy in Small Developing Countries," in Percy Selwin, op. cit., pp. 144-163. W. T. Newlyn takes a somewhat different approach. See his "Monetary Analysis and Policy in Financially Dependent Economies,"

in I. G. Stewart, ed., Economic Development and Structural Change (Edinburgh: Edinburgh University Press, 1969), pp. 71-82.

    11. The following examination of the Mexican financial system was gleaned from a number of sources. The interested reader should consult the following for a more detailed examination of the country's monetary institutions: Dwight Brothers and Leopoldo Solis, Mexican Financial Development (Austin: University of Texas Press, 1966); Raymond Goldsmith, The Financial Experience of Mexico (Paris OECD, 1966); B. Griffiths, Mexican Monetary Policy and Economic Development (New York: Praeger Publishers, 1972); and D. Sykes Wilford, Monetary Policy and the Open Economy: Mexico's Experience (New York: Praeger Publishers, 1977).

CHAPTER 11

INFLATION IN MEXICO

Introduction

Given space limitations, it is not possible to
consider on an individual basis the impact of the recent worldwide inflation on each of the semi-dependent
countries identified above. While the discriminant
and cross-section analysis performed in previous chapters shed light in this area, a more detailed examination of inflationary patterns experienced by individual
countries is necessary before any firm conclusions can
be drawn.

The Experiences of Mexico and South Africa

Mexico and South Africa were selected for detailed
analysis largely because each country has published
relatively complete and accurate statistics covering
the period under question. In addition, each country
illustrates quite clearly one aspect of the inflationary process in semi-dependent countries.

The Mexican experience illustrates:

1. That the nature of the money supply mechanism
   in these countries is critical in determining
   the economic consequences of world inflation
   on their domestic economies.

2. That because the authorities in semi-developed
   countries can to some extent control their
   domestic money supplies, improper application
   of monetary policy may result in the domestic
   rate of inflation remaining above the world
   rate for some time (even while maintaining a
   fixed exchange rate).

3. That the ability of monetary authorities to
   use monetary policy effectively in combating
   world inflation depends critically on the
   development of the country's fiscal system.

The South African experience illustrates that inflation in the semi-dependent countries has been a mixture of demand and cost pressures, and that many of these pressures have stemmed from the government's incorrect policy response to an initial inflationary impulse from abroad. As with Mexico, the result of government actions has been that domestic rates of inflation have lasted longer and have been higher than that for the world economy.

Despite their many similarities, both South Africa and Mexico both illustrate the diversity of patterns that inflation may take, a fact that makes generalized policy prescriptions very hazardous for the semi-dependent country.

Rationale for Selecting Mexico

There are five major reasons for using the Mexican experience to illustrate the economic consequences of world inflation on semi-dependent countries. First, of course, the country was, through the cross-section regressions and discriminant analysis, identified as a semi-dependent country. Second, as indicated in the previous chapter, Mexico has a relatively well developed financial system--one capable of exerting control over the domestic money supply. Third, there was a distinct break in the country's pattern of inflation with the advent of worldwide inflationary pressures in the early 1970s. Fourth, between 1954 and 1976 the country maintained a fixed exchange rate with the United States. Stability of the exchange rate enabled the country's inflationary patterns to be examined within the framework of the monetary approach to the balance of payments, an approach particularly adept at identifying the precise relationships between external inflation, the money supply, and the patterns of domestic inflation. And fifth, Mexico is in close geographic proximity to the United States; a majority of Mexico's foreign investors are American, and much of its trade is with the United States. Such a relationship is especially useful in examining the country's inflationary patterns since the United States may serve as a proxy for the 'rest of the world' in the analysis of Mexican inflation.

Mexican economic policy and the institutions that implement it have evolved over the years to the point where they are beginning to take on some of the characteristics usually associated with the industrialized countries. In general during the 1955-1970 period, the authorities were able to successfully pursue the country's traditional goals of price stability with growth. After 1970, however, these same policies appeared incapable of dealing with the problems posed by world inflationary pressures.

The economic consequences of world inflation on the Mexican economy cannot be evaluated without a proper understanding of the nature of these policies, the mechanisms through which they operated, and their capacity for accommodating the increased demands placed on them after 1970.

Background--The 1940-1970 Period

The development of the Mexican economy over the three decades 1940-1970 and especially over the period 1955-1970 has been hailed by many economists as the outstanding success story of Latin America and indeed of the whole underdeveloped world, something akin to that of Japan. It was this performance that led Tom E. Davis to conclude that "three decades of continuous rapid growth differentiates the performance of the Mexican economy from that of other Latin American nations," and that "the sustained economic expansion of Mexico surpasses even that of the presently developed countries during the period of their most rapid economic growth."[1]

Between 1940 and 1970 the growth rate of Mexican gross national product (GNP) in real terms averaged approximately 6 percent which, when account is taken of the increase in population of approximately 3.5 percent per annum, implied a growth rate in GNP per capita of around 2.5 percent. No country in Latin America experienced such a high average growth rate and for so long a period. In addition, Mexico during most of this period had a rather modest rate of inflation. During the period 1940-1970, the annual rate of increase in the cost of living index was only 4 percent whereas Peru averaged 9.2 percent, Colombia 10.6 percent, Chile 37.1 percent, Argentina 64.8 percent, and Brazil 193.2 percent.

Overall inflation figures for Mexico are, however, slightly misleading. The period 1940-1970 can be

179

divided into two fairly distinct subperiods--the first
extending from 1940 to the devaluation of 1954 (when
increases in the cost of living averaged 13.0 percent
per annum and the peso was twice devalued), and the
second from 1955-1970 (when the rate of inflation
averaged only 4.8 percent and there were no devaluations).[2]

Economic Strategy

Favorable conditions in the world economy, particularly the expansion of the United States economy,
undoubtedly assisted in Mexico's achievements. It is
clear, however, that Mexico's growth with price stability was largely the result of a number of economic
policies implemented during this time, especially after
1955.

These policies form the Mexican development strategy, the main elements of which were: (1) the maintenance of economic policies which were strongly conducive to the growth of private savings and investment; (2) the maintenance of a fixed exchange rate,
achieved by the avoidance of a faster rate of inflation
than that experienced by the country's major trading
partners; and (3) the sectoral allocation of public
resources in a way that was favorable to the growth of
the private sector.[3]

While government spending continued to rise in
absolute terms throughout the period, its deficits were
financed increasingly in a non-inflationary manner;
i.e., the rapid development of private savings and the
ability of the government through its monetary policies
to draw on these resources meant that the public sector's
deficits were financed less and less by credits obtained from the central bank.

While the government did make some gradual improvements in the tax system's capacity for raising revenues,
further fiscal reforms were constrained by official
feeling that to stimulate the growth of the private
sector: (1) the tax ratio should be kept low, and
(2) that prices of goods and services produced by the
public sector enterprises and used by the private
sector should also be kept low (even if this meant
that many public firms suffered losses). While the
country's revenue system remained underdeveloped, the

country's relatively low level of government expenditure meant that the public deficit did not rise above 2.5 percent of GDP (a low level by Latin American standards). Most of the deficit was financed by domestic savings mobilized by the banking system. Over time however borrowing in international markets resulted in the build-up of a fairly substantial debt burden. By 1970 the average debt service ratio was 25 percent, a relatively high but not an excessive figure for a developing country.

The growth of private savings was the major factor enabling the public sector to borrow heavily without excessively pre-empting credit flows to the private sector or creating inflationary pressures. To stimulate growth of these funds, the authorities offered a nominal interest rate of 9 percent or more on fully liquid deposits (or bonds). Pesos were freely convertible into dollars under conditions of minimal exchange risk at a fixed exchange rate maintained by the central bank. Since the price level was increasing by only 2 to 3 percent per annum, the real rate of interest to savers was 6 to 7 percent, a rate well above that of comparable foreign assets. To further increase the attractiveness of Mexican assets, only 10 percent of the interest received was taxed, regardless of the saver's income bracket.

As a result of these measures, private savings continued to increase all through the 1955-1970 period. By the mid-1960s the country was in a position to finance its public sector deficit while keeping the growth of the money supply more or less equal to the growth of real income. Fiscal expenditures also grew at a rate not significantly different from the rate of growth of real income.

To summarize, fiscal conservatism and private sector funding of the government deficit through transfers of financial savings were the key elements in the government's development strategy throughout the 1960s, a development strategy whose success was measured in terms of high rates of real growth and based largely on the maintenance of price stability.

Consistency of Economic Policy and Price Stability

Although some of the price increases in specific

years can be attributed to cost-push factors and to specific institutional developments, the long term trend of the absolute price level was very similar to the trend of money supply expansion, and there was a very close correlation between the money supply (coins and currency in circulation plus demand deposits), and the price level (see Chapter 12 below).

The money supply in Mexico is determined by central bank monetary expansion, bank reserve policies (deposit/ reserve ratio), and the public's preference between holding currency and deposits (deposit/currency ratio).[4] Public sector borrowing was the main factor responsible for increasing the money supply between 1955 and 1970. Borrowing by public sector enterprises was mainly responsible up to 1963 with federal government borrowing predominating between 1964 and 1970.

The result of these patterns was a growth in domestic credit times foreign reserves over high powered money of 7 to 8 percent annually, and the rate of domestic inflation very close to that of the United States. Given the country's underlying structure and economic institutions, it appeared that by 1970 the economy could grow at 7 percent per annum and that the fiscal deficits and associated expansion of the money supply were such that the monetary authorities could easily contain inflation to the rate likely to exist in the United States. Past trends in the Mexican economy implied that if the desired rate of inflation was 4 percent per annum, monetary expansion had to be confined to 13 percent; at 5 percent it could not exceed 15 percent. These levels were completely compatible with past trends in government expenditures and revenues.

By 1970, the public sector was pre-empting about 40 percent of the net annual increment in bank credits and given the conditions existing at that time, it would be possible for the government to increase its rate of borrowing as a ratio of GDP by about 0.6 to 0.7 percentage points without necessarily raising the historical (1960s) level of inflation. The transfer of this amount of resources by the banking system from the private to the public sector, however, would not only reduce credit availability to the private sector, but might begin to place strains on the financial system. To avoid potential problems that might develop in the private sector and financial sector, it appeared that net borrowing by the public sector from the banking

182

system should probably not greatly exceed 3 percent of GDP during the early 1970s. This figure was still higher than the historical average of 2.7 percent, but lower than what it would be if the public sector continued to pre-empt 40 percent of banking resources at the margin. In terms of past trends, this rate implied a maximum increase of 0.3 percent of GDP.

Limitations of Mexico's Development Strategy

While Mexico achieved high rates of growth combined with price stability all during the 1960s, a number of problems were also developing. Economic expansion did not generate sufficient new employment opportunities to absorb a working age population (which by 1970 was increasing at a rate of about 3 percent a year). By the end of the 1960s, about 40 percent of the labor force was either unemployed or (accounting for a much larger proportion) only marginally employed in relatively unproductive (and hence poorly paid) occupations.[5] There is also ample evidence that the income distribution was becoming more unequal all during this period.

Public investment in some sectors (notably steel and agriculture) appeared inadequate. Shortages of many basic products were, as a result of low rates of capacity expansion, beginning to develop. Low levels of investment resulted in many cases (particularly hydrocarbons) from simple lack of funds (associated with the maintenance of low product prices which failed to generate sufficient revenues).

In short, while the productive capacity that had been installed during the inflationary years of the 1940s and 1950s (to 1956) permitted growth to proceed into the 1960s with price stability, and while the private sector continued to respond to profit incentives, the country's pattern of growth was not matching the burgeoning social and economic needs of the country.

Finally, inflationary pressures began to be felt. After having edged upward at a rate of less than 3 percent annually in 1967 and 1968, the consumer price index rose by around 3.5 to 3.7 percent in 1969. In 1970 inflation reached 4.8 percent.

Trends in the balance of payments reflected many

183

of these problems. The deficit on current account (balance of goods and services) was $375.7 million in 1965. By 1970 it was $908.8 million. Between 1965 and 1970, the deficit was financed in large part by direct and indirect foreign borrowing. Long term capital inflows represented 68 percent of the current account deficit during this period with short term finance providing the remainder.

Mexico was caught in a typical dilemma of that experienced by many semi-dependent countries during this time. Its rapid growth required the importation of raw materials and intermediate goods. Exports in part due to the growing domestic needs and a slowdown in agricultural development were not growing at a rate adequate to satisfy the nation's import requirements. The fixed (and by now overvalued) exchange rate also hindered the growth of exports. During 1965-1970, merchandize exports grew by only 3 percent, while imports grew at 9 percent per year. The result was a 16 percent per annum growth in the (merchandize) trade deficit.

A number of observers[6] urged the government to take action through devaluation of the peso, taxes on import intensive items, measures designed to increase the competitiveness of domestic manufactures abroad, and other means necessary to alleviate the deficit. Instead most of the burden fell on foreign borrowing, with net long term capital inflows increasing at an astounding rate of 90 percent annually, totalling $2.2 billion by 1970. Of this amount, loans increased by 34 percent annually, and foreign direct investment by only 5.5 percent.

Most of the borrowing was undertaken by the public sector. By 1970 the accumulated government foreign debt was over $7 billion and interest payments since 1965 had quadrupled. From the viewpoint of the balance of payments, the appearance of stability was increasingly misleading.

A number of Mexico's economic problems were, therefore, increasing. To deal with them effectively would require a change in the country's development strategy. Major changes in both tax and expenditure policy were clearly needed. Unfortunately, the high real growth rates of the 1960s and the appearance of stability apparently lulled many officials into a false sense of

184

security. Other officials not so easily convinced of
the strategy's success still resisted any fundamental
alterations on the grounds that any change in policy
would create uncertainty causing domestic and foreign
capital to leave the country.

The Post-1970 Period--Overview

The administration of President Echeverria (1970-
1976) ushered in a new group of officials who felt that
a sharp break with the past strategy was necessary. It
was their belief that a number of problems, particularly
unemployment and inequality in income, could only be
solved through a massive expansion of public sector
programs and expenditures.

The authorities, while greatly expanding the scope
of the state in the workings of the economy, did not
make any major changes in the federal revenue system or
basic institutions that had developed over the previous
15 years. They were apparently unaware that the forms
of monetary and fiscal policy that were utilized successfully during this period of stability required not
only a rather limited role of the government in the
economy but also world economic stability. The 1970s
saw disequilibrium in the world economy, worldwide inflation, and world recession; these shocks were extremely disruptive to the Mexican economy. Over time, the
economy experienced more and more difficulty in maintaining an acceptable growth rate and an increase in
prices commensurate with those taking place in the U.S.

Developments in 1972

After a brief recession in 1971, 1972 looked like
the beginnings of a new era of expansion. GDP grew by
more than 7 percent, prices rose by 5 percent, the
public sector greatly increased its expenditures, and
the private sector also increased its level of investment. The only negative factor was a massive increase
in the money supply. Monetary expansion that year was
beginning to accelerate at unprecedented rates of over
20 percent (Table 44). While some of this increase was
a result of the government's inability to increase tax
revenues in the light of increased expenditures, part
of the increase was also associated with the new problem of increased international liquidity and world

TABLE 44

MEXICO: PRICES AND MONEY

(Rates of change over one year)

	Wholesale price index	Consumer price index	Total domestic credit	Quasi-money	Money Supply	Domestic credit Bank of Mexico
December 1970	5.4	4.8	18.3	21.6	10.5	12.0
December 1971	2.2	4.4	12.6	18.2	8.2	11.3
March 1972	2.2	4.4	9.4	16.2	12.5	6.7
June 1972	2.6	5.1	13.9	16.3	15.1	15.6
September 1972	3.0	5.1	14.9	17.2	18.0	17.3
December 1972	5.4	5.6	17.8	16.6	21.1	22.4
January 1973	7.3	6.7	18.4	17.2	20.0	22.6
February 1973	8.2	7.2	19.0	16.3	21.7	20.5
March 1973	8.7	8.6	21.3	16.7	24.0	26.4
April 1973	10.0	8.6	21.5	15.0	26.6	29.8
May 1973	13.3	9.5	20.8	16.3	25.4	25.3
June 1973	13.3	9.6	19.8	13.7	24.4	23.0
July 1973	15.9	12.0	22.1	13.0	26.1	30.5
August 1973	18.1	13.0	20.5	11.5	25.8	27.3
September 1973	21.4	15.3	19.0	10.7	26.4	28.0
October 1973	23.0	16.7	18.6	10.0	25.4	31.0
November 1973	23.4	17.4	16.9	8.3	25.4	31.1
December 1973	25.2	21.4	14.6	9.4	24.1	30.4

Source: Bank of Mexico

inflation.

The 1973-1975 Period

In the first months of 1973, prices began to rise much faster than at any time since the early 1950s. By December the annual rate of inflation, measured by the consumer price index, had risen to 21.4 percent (Table 44), while the mean-to-mean increase was 12.1 percent (as compared with a rate of growth of only 5 percent the year before). In terms of current output, economic performance in 1973 was superficially satisfactory in view of the rate of real GDP growth (7.6 percent) being one of the highest ever recorded.

There were also signs that the economy was beginning to encounter a number of new forces whose implications were not understood by the government and whose response to them would have a profoundly negative impact on the country's growth pattern.

The first new phenomena was the appearance of the negative interest rate differential between the Mexican and the international (Eurodollar) market interest rates. The second was the afore mentioned sudden and steep increase in domestic prices. The results of these two factors were immediate: (1) the rate of increase of financial savings declined to the lowest level in many years (8 percent through December compared with an annual rate of 17 percent in 1972); (2) the inflow of private short term capital (U.S. $544 million in 1972) was replaced by a new outflow (of U.S. $675 million); (3) private fixed capital investment not only stagnated and even declined in real terms (in 1975); and (4) there was a record overall public sector deficit, reaching 6.4 percent of GDP.[7]

A major share of the limited total volume of private financial savings was pre-empted by the government to finance part of this deficit; one billion dollars of foreign borrowings (2 percent of GDP) were used to finance the rest. The large public deficit, together with the need to import fuels and foodstuffs (at rising prices due to world inflation) caused a rapid deterioration in the current account deficit of the balance of payments (Table 45). The external deficit was financed almost entirely by public borrowing, some of which was required to offset short term capital movements.

187

TABLE 45

MEXICO: BALANCE OF PAYMENTS, 1970-1976

(Millions of dollars)

	1970	1971	1972	1973	1974	1975	1976
Balance of Goods and Services	-908.8	-703.1	-761.5	-1175.4	-2558.1	-3768.9	-3023.7
Exports Goods and Services	3147.7	3192.9	3800.6	4828.4	6342.5	6303.0	6971.4
Imports Goods and Services	4056.3	3895.4	4562.1	6003.8	8900.6	10071.9	9995.1
Errors, Omissions and Short Term Capital	505.5	194.3	233.3	-378.4	-135.8	-406.0	-2119.4
Variation in Revenues	102.1	200.0	264.7	122.3	36.9	165.1	-333.1

Source: Banco de Mexico, Informe Anual, various issues.

In retrospect 1973 marked the end of an historical pattern of Mexican economic growth. That year saw the beginnings of an interplay between three sets of forces which are still (1978) continuing to cause major changes in the economy.

The first was a firm intention on the part of the authorities to continue to increase public expenditures in response to what it feared as social and economic imperatives irrespective of its ability to finance these expenditures in a non-inflationary manner.

The second was an evident disinclination of the private sector to continue investing as much as it had in the 1960s. In part this behavior was caused by the inflation that was more or less out of control and the deterioration in the balance of payments.

The third (and most important in terms of this study) change was increasing world inflation, and beginning in the fall of 1973, the series of shocks to the world economy which were to continue for several years. Developments in the world economy had three important economic consequences for Mexico. First, in 1973 the country was still a net petroleum imported and the increase in international oil prices therefore had an adverse effect on the balance of payments. Second, because developments in the world economy had an especially severe impact on the United States, Mexico's exports--about two-thirds of which go to the United States--were adversely affected. And also the expansion in world liquidity and inflation made it extremely difficult for the authorities, given the country's existing financial structure, to adjust interest rates upwards fast enough in order to attract private savings while at the same time maintaining control over the domestic money supply.

As it turned out, the combined effect of continued expansion of the public sector, the absence of tax reform, and international inflation proved to be much stronger than whatever forces were pushing in the direction of financial stability.

The net result was that domestic prices increased far more rapidly during the 1973-1975 period than at any time since the early 1950s (average deflator for 1973-1975 having risen on the average by 17 percent per year as compared with 4.0 percent during 1966-1972

(Table 46). The balance of payments deficit on current
account rose from an average of 2.4 percent of GDP in
1966-1972 to an average of 4.1 percent of GDP in 1973-
1975. The deficit of the consolidated public sector
rose from an average of 2.7 percent of GDP in 1966-
1972 to an average of 7.3 percent of GDP in 1973-1975.

The current account deficit continued to worsen.
From the 1971 level of $726 million, it reached $3,769
million in 1975 with the trend continuing in 1976.

The current account deficit was financed essentially in the same manner as previously; foreign direct investment was relied upon but only to supplement the
main source of borrowing which was foreign loans. Foreign loans to government grew from $286 million in 1971
to $3,054 million in 1975 (the same trend continuing
through mid-1976).

Because the government through the central bank
was able to pre-empt nearly all of the flow of private
savings for its own uses, businesses were forced into
rapidly increasing rates of foreign indebtedness. As
a result registered borrowings by the private sector
rose from $61 million in 1970 to $424 million in 1975.
While interest payments accelerated as a result of this
borrowing, the rate of growth of foreign credits was so
large that the interest share of net capital inflows
actually declined.

Economic Consequences of World Inflation

In terms of domestic and foreign breakdown between
domestic and foreign influences on (1) domestic prices,
and (2) the evolution of the country's balance of payments in 1973-1975, it is obvious that not all of the
blame for the growing domestic inflation and balance
of payments deficits can be traced directly to the
government's mismanagement of the economy.

While the trend of domestic prices was closely
linked to monetary expansion, about 30 percent (Table
47) of the cost pressures which led (in 1973) to the
increase in the consumer price increase were caused by
changes in the prices of internationally traded goods.
The responsibility of world inflation for the inflation
in Mexico decreased after that, and by 1975 the balance
was strongly tilted toward domestic forces (mainly the

TABLE 46

MEXICO: PRICE INCREASES, 1960-1977

(Average annual increase)

Year	Consumer Price Index	Wholesale Price Index	GDP Deflator	Export Price Index	Import Price Index	Terms of Trade Index
1960	4.8	4.9	4.8	-	-	-
1961	1.8	0.8	3.3	4.0	4.1	-0.4
1962	0.9	1.9	3.0	-1.4	6.4	-7.3
1963	0.7	0.4	3.1	6.0	0.0	6.0
1964	2.4	4.3	5.8	4.2	9.0	-4.3
1965	3.5	2.0	2.2	-1.5	0.0	-1.5
1966	4.2	1.2	3.9	3.3	0.3	2.9
1967	3.0	2.9	2.9	2.5	1.1	1.5
1968	1.4	2.0	2.4	1.1	-0.7	1.8
1969	3.9	2.5	3.9	3.3	3.9	-0.7
1970	5.2	5.8	4.4	6.7	7.1	-3.0
1971	5.7	3.8	4.5	3.7	6.4	-2.6
1972	5.0	2.7	5.6	6.7	9.6	-2.6
1973	11.3	15.8	12.4	15.2	22.7	-6.1
1974	22.5	22.5	24.0	26.6	24.6	1.6
1975	16.8	10.5	18.2	15.6	7.1	8.0
1976	16.1	22.3	N/A	N/A	N/A	N/A
1977	26.4	41.1	N/A	N/A	N/A	N/A

Source: International Monetary Fund, International Financial Statistics (May 1978), Bank of Mexico.

191

TABLE 47

MEXICO: DOMESTIC COST PRESSURES INDUCED BY WORLD INFLATION

Year	Change in Import Prices (Average Annual Increase)	Share of Imports in Total Costs	Cost Pressures Induced by Changes in Import Prices (Average Annual Increase)	Change in Consumer Price Index (Average Annual Increase)	Cost Pressures Induced by Changes in Import Prices (Percentage of Total)
1970	7.1	0.15[1]	1.1	5.2	21.2
1971	6.4	0.15	1.0	5.7	17.5
1972	9.6	0.15	1.4	5.0	28.0
1973	22.7	0.15	3.4	11.3	30.1
1974	24.6	0.15	3.7	22.5	16.4
1975	7.1	0.15	1.1	16.8	6.1
1976	3.6[2]	0.15	0.5	16.1	3.1
1977	4.8[2]	0.15	0.7	26.4	2.7

Source: International Monetary Fund, International Financial Statistics (May 1978), Bank of Mexico.

Notes: (1) Assumed to be 15 percent.
        (2) The United States export price increase.

192

public sector deficit).

With regard to the balance of payments, there are two points worth noting. First, the drastic deterioration in real export performance in 1975, and to some extent also in 1974, can be largely attributed to the world recession (particularly as it affected the United States). The recession appears to explain a preponderant--but by no means the entire--part of the decline in real exports. The overvalued peso also began playing an important role at this time.

Second, the growth of the resources gap was not only a result of the growth of real imports and the decline in real exports. It was also to some degree the result of a deterioration in terms of trade from 1966-1972, when the index was 95.7 (compared with 1960= 100.0), to 1973-1975 when it fell to an average of 89.7.

Conclusions

In all, it would be misleading to suggest that the recent deterioration in Mexico's economic indicators could be explained mainly by internal forces. There is no doubt that the transmission of world inflation and other external forces greatly magnified the problems associated with what would in any case have been a difficult set of structural changes which had been more or less forced on the new 1970 administration. While it is impossible to evaluate what might have happened in the last three years if the world environment had been more stable, the condition of the international economy impeded the conduct of economic policy.

Indirect effects--the strains placed on the ability of the financial system to mobilize savings, the complicating of what might otherwise have been a rather straightforward application of monetary-fiscal policy, and the eventual forcing of the government into a series of economic blunders (postponement of devaluation, stepped up borrowing at high rates of interest simply to support the peso, and other policy miscalculations which probably would not have happened if the authorities had had no control over the money supply)-- were the major economic consequences of world inflation on the Mexican economy.

Notes

1. Tom E. Davis, ed., Mexico's Recent Economic Growth: The Mexican View (Austin: University of Texas Press, 1967), p. 3.

2. Several other divisions are possible. See Roger D. Hansen, Mexican Economic Development: The Roots of Rapid Growth (Washington: National Planning Association, 1971) for an alternative approach.

3. Clark Reynolds, "Why Mexico's Stabilizing Development was Actually Destabilizing," paper presented to the Joint Economic Committee, Subcommittee on Inter-American Relationships hearing on "Recent Developments in Mexico and their Economic Implications for the United States." (Washington, D.C., January 17, 1977), p. 8.

4. An excellent description of the Mexican money supply mechanism is given in D. Sykes Wilford, Monetary Policy and the Open Economy: Mexico's Experience (New York, Praeger Publishers, 1977), Ch. 5.

5. Cf. David Felix, "Income Inequality in Mexico," Current History (March 1977), pp. 111-114; and Calvin Blain, "Echeverria's Economic Policy," Current History (March 1977), pp. 124-127 for recent accounts of this period.

6. For example: Redvers Opie, "The Last Informe of President Echeverria: Inflation and Devaluation," American Chamber of Commerce of Mexico, Economic Report (September 10, 1976).

7. Account taken from Analisis--76: The Mexican Economy (Mexico City: Publicaciones Ejecutivas de Mexico, 1977).

CHAPTER 12

MONETARY AND INFLATIONARY MECHANISMS IN MEXICO

Introduction

One of the more interesting patterns exhibited by
the Mexican economy after 1970 was the relatively small
impact increases in the prices of internationally
traded goods had on the domestic price level, in part
due to the fact that Mexico's imports only account for
about 12 to 15 percent of GDP. While the direct effects
of world inflation on the economy appear to have been
only marginal (particularly after 1974), its indirect
effects may have been much more instrumental in determining the country's inflationary patterns.

During the mid-1970s, Mexico's rate of inflation
began to diverge from that experienced in the United
States (Table 48) indicating that the monetary authorities may have some control over the domestic money
supply and thus the country's rate of inflation. An
examination of the country's monetary mechanisms
should reveal the major forces underlying the country's
recent acceleration in inflation and the role external
factors played in shaping these price movements.

Money and Inflation in Mexico

As a first step in the analysis, the following
model was developed for Mexico. In attempting to determine the inflationary impact on the economy stemming
from increases in the supply of money, the model seeks
to: (1) discover the dynamic process by which monetary
expansion in Mexico affects the level of domestic
prices; (2) ascertain the role of past acceleration of
inflation upon the current rate of price rise; and
(3) clarify somewhat the role that wage changes play
in the country's inflationary process.

The following form for the model was derived from
the quantity theory of money.[1] The quantity theory
holds that the demand for cash balances in real terms
is given by:

(1) $\log (M/P) = a + b_1 r + b_2 \log Y$

TABLE 48

COMPARISON OF MEXICO-UNITED STATES INFLATION RATES

	Consumer Price Index		Rate of Change of Consumer Prices		Wholesale Price Index		Rate of Change of Wholesale Prices	
	U.S.	Mexico	U.S.	Mexico	U.S.	Mexico	U.S.	Mexico
1960	55.0	43.4	-	-	54.3	47.3	-	-
1961	55.6	44.2	1.1	1.8	54.1	47.7	-0.4	0.8
1962	56.2	44.6	1.1	0.9	54.2	48.6	0.2	1.9
1963	56.9	44.9	1.2	0.7	54.0	48.8	-0.4	0.4
1964	57.6	46.0	1.2	2.4	54.1	50.9	0.2	4.3
1965	58.6	47.6	1.7	3.5	55.2	51.9	2.0	2.0
1966	60.4	49.6	3.1	4.2	57.1	52.5	3.4	1.2
1967	62.0	51.1	2.6	3.0	57.2	54.0	0.2	2.9
1968	64.6	51.8	4.2	1.4	58.6	55.1	2.4	2.0
1969	68.1	53.8	5.4	3.9	60.9	56.5	3.9	2.5
1970	72.1	56.6	5.9	5.2	63.1	59.8	3.6	5.8
1971	75.2	59.6	4.3	5.3	65.2	62.1	3.3	3.8
1972	77.7	62.8	3.3	5.4	68.1	63.8	4.4	2.7
1973	82.6	69.9	6.3	11.3	77.0	73.9	13.1	15.8
1974	91.6	85.6	10.9	22.5	91.5	90.5	18.8	22.5
1975	100.0	100.0	9.2	16.8	100.0	100.0	9.3	10.5
1976	105.8	116.1	5.8	16.1	104.6	122.3	4.6	22.3
1977	112.7	146.7	6.5	26.4	111.0	172.6	6.1	41.1

Source: International Monetary Fund, International Financial Statistics, May 1978.

where M = the money supply defined as currency and coin and demand deposits; P = the GDP deflator; r = the interest rate (representing the opportunity cost of holding money), and Y = gross domestic product in constant prices.

Differentiating this equation with respect to time we get:

(2) $d(\log M)/dt - d(\log P)/dt = a + b_1 dr/dt + b_2 d(\log Y)/dt$

Rearranging terms, we then get the basic form of the monetarist model:

(3) $d(\log P)/dt = -a + d(\log M)/dt - b_1 dr/dt - b_2 d(\log Y)/dt$

Since (d) the real interest rate in Mexico due to government controls rarely changes, and because credit is rationed by most banks, a better indication of the opportunity cost of holding money is some measure of the expected rate of inflation such as dA/dt, where A is equal to the difference between the rate of inflation in the previous year and the rate of inflation two years prior.

This is a rather naive version of a distributed lag function developed by Cagen[2] in his study of hyper-inflations. Following Cagen, an expected rate of inflation, PE, was derived as follows:

(4) $PE - PE(L) = a[P(L) - PE(L)]$

$0 < a < 1$

Where a = the coefficient of price expectation. This formulation implies that PE can be constructed as an exponentially weighted average of price changes in previous periods.

This technique assumes the following geometrically declining distributed lag:[3]

(5) $PE = \sum_{i=0}^{\infty} a(1 - B)^i P(L)$

197

By trying out different values for "a", we can construct the associated PE series. The series that best reflects the level of expectations is assured to be the one which gives the highest r^2. In this study the "a" which maximized r^2 was approximately 0.40, its low value an indication of the historically stable price level in Mexico. The relative low value of "a" indicates that inflation in Mexico has not (until recent years at least) acted as a significant tax on money holdings.

(6) $\quad d(\log P)/dt = -a + d(\log M)/dt - b_1 d(PE)/dt -$

$$b_2 d(\log Y)/dt$$

In his study of Chilean inflation, Harberger derived a similar equation:

(7) $\quad d(\log P)/dt = -a - b_1 d(\log Y)/dt + b_2 d(\log M)/dt$

$$+ b_3 [d(\log M)/dt](L) + b_4 dA/dt +$$

$$b_5 d(\log W)/dt$$

The major difference between equations (6) and (7) is the use of A by Harberger rather than PE and his inclusion of the wage variable.

In order to analyze the direct impact of changes in the money supply on the rate of inflation in Mexico, we tested both formulations (equations 6 and 7) using annual data for the period 1955-1975. The statistical analysis used conventional least squares regression techniques. All the variables are stated as percentage changes with the variables used in the regressions defined as follows:

Y = percentage change in gross domestic product

M = percentage change in the money supply (currency and coin plus demand deposits)

PGDPD = percentage change in the gross domestic product price deflator

QM = percentage change in quasi-money, defined in the International Monetary Fund Financial Statistics

W = percentage change in wages: monthly earnings
as computed in International Monetary Fund,
International Financial Statistics

PE = expected rate of inflation with an adjustment
coefficient of 0.40

A = the rate of inflation in the previous year
minus that of two years prior

(L) = last years value

(L_2) = the value two years prior

The results are as follows. In equation (1)
(Table 49), a regression using M and M(L) yielded a
fairly good explanation of changes in the gross domestic
product price deflator [r^2 = (0.69)], and the coefficients adding up close to one, indicating the general
validity of the approach. When Harberger's (A) was
used (equation 2), the results improved somewhat. The
best relationship was when both the Y and W terms were
included (equation 3) in the regression and (A) replaced
by our measure of the potential rate of inflation (PE).
Quasi-money[4] as defined by the International Monetary
Fund was also a factor in explaining Mexican inflation
(equation 4), but its low statistical significance must
relegate its role in the inflationary process to a
minor one.

The final regression (5) confirms that one of the
necessary conditions for the quantity theory of money
to be applicable to the Mexican context; i.e., a stable
demand for real balances, existed during this period.
This nearly statistically perfect equation (5) bears
out the hypothesis that the demand for money in real
terms in Mexico is proportional to the level of national income (as noted earlier this was the basis for
monetary policy during the 1955-1970 period). The
value of the coefficient is 1.037; i.e., there is
nearly a one to one relationship between money and
income. This value is entirely consistent with that
predicated by the monetarist models of inflation and
the monetary approach to the balance of payments.[5]

Monetary Mechanisms in Mexico

There are several indirect tests that can be used

199

TABLE 49

MEXICO: TEST OF QUANTITY THEORY OF MONEY

(billion pesos)

1. $PGDP = -5.851 + 0.596M + 0.401M(L)$
   $(3.1) \quad (2.1)$
   $r^2 = 0.4413$
   $F = 7.1$

2. $PGDP = 08.110 + 0.332M + 0.320M(L) + 0.508M(L2) + 0.480A$
   $(4.0) \quad (2.7) \quad (3.1) \quad (2.0)$
   $r^2 = 0.6922$
   $F = 9.0$

3. $PGDP = 04.563 + 0.016M + 0.480Y + 0.121W + 0.721PE$
   $(11.2) \quad (15.3) \quad (4.5) \quad (2.6)$
   $r^2 = 0.9617$
   $F = 100.4$

4. $PGDP = -9.165 + 0.191M + 0.216M(L) + 0.377M(L2) + 0.130QM(L) + 0.439W$
   $(5.1) \quad (3.5) \quad (4.0) \quad (3.2) \quad (2.7)$
   $r^2 = 0.8263$
   $F = 14.3$

5. $\log (M/PGDPD) = -1.020 + 1.037 \log Y$
   (43.3)
   $r^2 = 0.990$
   $F = 1877.1$

Source: Computed by author.

to determine the extent to which the Mexican authorities possess monetary autonomy.

1. If the authorities could in fact control the money supply and chose to use their power to stabilize the level of aggregate demand, certain patterns in private and public expenditures would develop over time. These patterns would be evidence that the country possesses some degree of monetary autonomy.

2. If the authorities had complete control over the domestic money supply, movements in money and the reserves of the central bank would not be closely correlated--the foreign sector would not be a significant factor in constraining the ability of the authorities to conduct policy.

These two propositions are tested below.

Effectiveness of Mexican Monetary Policy in Stabilizing Demand

An indirect test of whether or not the Mexican authorities have some control (and have used it) over the domestic money supply is whether fluctuations in the nation's money supply have tended to offset fluctuations in economic activity.

Successful stabilizing movements of public and private expenditures require that when one is abnormally high, the other should be abnormally low. Since the absolute levels of these variables are growing through time, the normal level of expenditure may be assumed to be the predicted trend value. To determine whether the money supply has been under the control of the authorities, in the sense they have been able to use monetary policy to stabilize the level of economic activity, the following method was developed:[6]

1. Using logarithms, equations of the general form $Y_t = a \cdot (1 + g)^t$ were specified where (a) is the value of (Y) in the first year, (g) is the percentage annual rate of growth, and Y_t is private autonomous expenditure, public expenditure (or some component of these aggregates). The predicted values of Y were

201

calculated from these coefficients.

2. The annual deviations from the trend for public expenditures and private autonomous expenditures were calculated and then correlated.

Clearly if movements in the public and private expenditure series are offsetting (and thus stabilizing), a significantly large negative correlation in the deviations of these series should exist. This pattern did exist (Tables 50 & 51) during the 1960-1975 period.

The movement of the residuals of private expenditures and public expenditures not only moved in contrary directions, but their trend deviations were of comparable magnitude. This pattern cannot be the result of fiscal policy since the statistical information on which such a policy would have to be based was not available to the authorities during most of this period. Furthermore, it can be shown that public expenditures follow their own cycle associated with the six-year presidential term.[7]

Thus it must be private investment which was forced to adjust in some manner to the movements in public expenditure. The only policy tool which the authorities manipulated frequently enough and with sufficient power to control private investment effectively was the ratio of reserves which private banks are required to deposit with the central bank. If the market for loanable funds was marked by excess demand (a plausible assumption for this period), then this tool was powerful enough to force private investment to move in a counter-cyclical way. This is confirmed in part by the fact that in a technical sense the authorities would have had no difficulties in implementing a policy of this sort; i.e., because the Mexican government's deficit is closely linked to the supply of money and the supply of money is in turn closely linked to the balance of payments,[8] and the need for a change in policy would be quickly signaled (to the authorities) through these variables. It should be noted, however, that the negative correlations between the two series were less distinct in the 1970s than in the 1960s, indicating perhaps the authorities' gradual loss of control over the money supply.

The ability to use monetary policy in this manner stems from the way in which the public deficit, changes

202

TABLE 50

MEXICO: TREND REGRESSIONS, 1960-1975

(1960 prices)

1. $APE = 15.73(1.0578)^t$ $r^2 = 0.7441$
        $t = 6.38$

2. $PE = 16.44(1.0802)^t$ $r^2 = 0.9322$
        $t = 13.87$

3. $DG = 1.452(1.1606)^t$ $r^2 = 0.7933$
        $t = 7.33$

4. $GE = 19.69(1.0747)^t$ $r^2 = .9400$
        $t = 14.82$

5. $GC = 9.22(1.0844)^t$ $r^2 = .9870$
        $t = 32.54$

6. $GI = 10.44(1.0656)^t$ $r^2 = .8046$
        $t = 7.59$

Source: Compiled by author.

Where: APE = Autonomous private expenditure = PI + DG
        PE = Private investment
        DG = Domestic resource gap
        GE = Government expenditure = GC + GI
        GC = Government consumption
        GI = Government investment

TABLE 51

MEXICO: REGRESSIONS, RESIDUALS ON RESIDUALS, 1960-1975

(1960 prices)

---

1. APE(RESID) = 0.3964 - 0.5469GI(RESID)
(5.01) $r^2 = .6423$

2. APE(RESID) = 0.4806 - 0.7291GE(RESID)
(6.38) $r^2 = .2438$

3. APE(RESID) = 0.0716 - 0.1818GC(RESID)
(3.77) $r^2 = .5035$

4. PE(RESID) = 0.0211 - 1.0639GE(RESID)
(6.47) $r^2 = .7496$

5. PI(RESID) = 0.0385 - 0.8497GI(RESID)
(6.21) $r^2 = .7338$

6. PI(RESID) = -0.0298 - 0.2140GC(RESID)
(2.63) $r^2 = .3303$

7. DG(RESID) = -0.1323 - 0.80196GE(RESID)
(2.21) $r^2 = .2595$

8. DG(RESID) = -0.0195 - 0.5191GI(RESID)
(1.67) $r^2 = .1670$

9. DG(RESID) = -0.3599 - 0.3010GC(RESID)
(2.12) $r^2 = .2428$

Source: Compiled by author

in the money supply, and movements in the balance of payments are related. The nature of the Mexican economy and the behavior of Mexican wealth holders are such that rapid expansion or contraction of the money supply will ultimately appear in the capital account of the balance of payments.[9]

As shown above, the demand for cash balances by Mexicans appears to be a markedly constant fraction of money national income, implying little or no speculative demand for money. Short run movements in the interest rate have been fairly limited, and the domestic securities markets are quite thin, especially so since by far the greater part of government securities are held in the form of required reserves by various financial institutions.[10] It follows that even if there were a speculative demand for peso balances, such balances could not have shifted greatly, which for our purposes is equivalent to their non-existence.

In contrast, the impact of changes in the money supply on the balance of payments does appear to a certain extent to work through interest rate differentials and resulting shifts in portfolios. It follows that given a stable transactions demand for money and the absence of a speculative demand, we would expect that balances for transactions needs would be a simple function of time. If the money supply were too small to support the current level of expenditures, those who had access to foreign sources of credit would be willing to pay some interest premium and run some foreign exchange risk for the sake of increasing their liquidity. Thus short-term capital would flow into Mexico. In the opposite situation, with an excess of money above transactions needs, individuals will shift some of their balances into dollar assets, thereby diminishing their expected losses in the event of a devaluation of the peso. In the process capital will flow out of the country. Since foreign central banks do not hold peso balances in their reserves, these capital movements will be immediately reflected in changes in Mexico's foreign exchange reserves.

In the long run, expansion or contraction of foreign exchange reserves through expanding or contracting the monetary base should shift the money supply to a level consistent with the level of money GNP. Similarly, the level of money GNP would also tend to rise or fall to consistency with the money supply because the

205

credit available for private investment would expand or contract with the supply of money. But if movements in the public deficit are sharp, the GNP might not be able to catch up to the money supply for some time; inflation would result and the central bank might lose an entirely unacceptable quantity of foreign exchange or become concerned about the increase in the short-term foreign indebtedness of the economy. This sequence of events began in Mexico with the advent of world inflation.

Mexico's problems in the 1970s stemmed from the fact that the existing policy tools and institutions which had worked so well to maintain growth with stability in the 1960s were very limited in their power to meet all of the demands placed on them in the 1970s.[11]

More precisely, the success of the reserve ratio as a policy tool depends on three special conditions. The first is that the financial system must be developed to a stage where it is able to capture a significant portion of society's savings, but not, as currently the case in Mexico,[12] developed to the point where the broadness of the securities market and the variety of types of financial institutions make it possible for enterprises to raise substantial funds outside the institutions that can be controlled by reserve requirements.

By the 1970s many Mexican firms were circumventing the domestic financial system by obtaining commercial bank loans from abroad.[13]

The second requirement is that demand for investable funds must be so high at the going interest rate that only restraint rather than stimulation of the private sector is required. This may be a rather general phenomenon in countries which are growing rapidly. In this situation rates of profit should be high for two reasons, shortages of capital relative to labor and quasi-rents that will be large when output is growing rapidly. This situation existed in the 1960s. With the slowdown of growth in the 1970s and the government's anti-business statements (often couched in Marxian terminology), however, caused a number of businessmen to postpone their investment plans. The third condition for the usefulness of the reserve ratio is that other policy tools must be able to avoid situations in which the appropriate response with respect to

aggregate demand is different from that dictated by
the balance of payments; i.e., balance of payments
must not be increasing so rapidly as to constrain the
authorities from pursuing a contractionary monetary
policy.

To summarize, given the institutional arrangements
existing in Mexico, success in controlling the money
supply depends on maintaining a high rate of return to
investment. It also depends on avoiding any long-run
balance of payments deficit. Finally, the effectiveness of the reserve ratio to combat future crises can
be eroded by relying on it too heavily to capture
resources for the public sector. In the 1970s, the
ratio drifted upward as a consequence of increasing
government expenditures unmatched by tax increases.
At that time the authorities found themselves without
the ability to use this instrument of control to fight
excess demand. Combined with the fact that the social
and economic priorities of the government dictated
increases in federal government expenditures, the
authorities gradually lost control over the money
supply (in the sense of expanding the money supply at
a rate faster than what they considered optimal).[14]

The Influence of the Foreign Sector on the Mexican Money Supply

The analysis used to examine this issue is based
on a Prais-Polack[15] monetary model adapted for the
Mexican economy. This model was chosen because it has
as one of its central features a money supply function
which explicitly includes foreign trade.

The Prais model is essentially a classical one
where substantially full employment of resources is
assumed and the major cause of changes in money income
is changes in the stock of money. It is a short run
model in which the capital stock is assumed to be fixed
and is specified as follows:

(1) $\bar{L} = KY$

(2) $\dfrac{\Delta L}{\Delta t} = X - M$

(3) $E = Y + a(L - \bar{L})$

(4) M = mY

(5) X = X(t)

(6) Y = E + X - M

where: Γ = desired liquidity
L = actual liquidity
E = expenditure
M = imports
X = exports
Y = income
a = liquidity reaction parameter

As can be seen from equation (1), a constant velocity of money (K = 1/V) is assumed. The two unique aspects of the model are: (1) that changes in liquidity, roughly speaking the money supply, are determined by conditions in the balance of trade as indicated in equation (2); and (2) that domestic expenditures are equal to income but are suppressed by any excess of desired liquidity over actual liquidity--the larger is the liquidity reaction parameter--(a), the faster is the adjustment to disequilibria in the money market.

In this model, given the constant velocity of money assumption, the most crucial variable becomes the marginal propensity to import because the adjustment to any exogenous disturbance occurs in the foreign sector.

Before the Prais model can be tested to see the degree to which it is capable of predicting movements in major macroeconomic variables in Mexico, it must be reformulated for empirical testing. Regressions were run on a model of the form:

(1) $\Delta M_d = a_{11} + a_{12} \Delta Y$

(2) $\Delta M_s = a_{21} + a_{22}D + a_{23}B + a_{24}L$

(3) $\Delta M_d = \Delta M_s$

(4) $B = X - IM$

(5) $IM = a_{51} + a_{52}Y$

(6) $X = X(t)$

(7) $L = L(t)$

(8) $\Delta DC = d(t)$

where ΔM_d = change in money demand; ΔM_s = change in money supply; ΔY = change in income; X = exports; IM = imports; ΔDC = net claims of banking system on the government; L = long term capital movements; and B = trade balance.

The estimates for the parameters for the period 1956-1974 are as follows:

(1') $\Delta M_d = 689.5 + 0.1022\Delta Y \qquad r^2 = 0.8603$
$\qquad\qquad\quad (10.23) \qquad\qquad\qquad F = 104.7$

(2') $\Delta M_s = 1487.4 + 0.2147B + 0.5285L + 221.7170\,\Delta DC$
$\qquad\qquad\quad (21.1) \qquad (6.7) \qquad\quad (4.3)$

$\qquad\qquad\qquad\qquad\qquad\qquad r^2 = 0.9712$
$\qquad\qquad\qquad\qquad\qquad\qquad F = 168.7$

(3') $IM = -3.3 + 0.1252Y \qquad r^2 = .9521$
$\qquad\qquad\quad (18.4) \qquad\qquad\qquad F = 337.9$

By combining equations (1') and (2'), it is possible to obtain the money multipliers of external variables on money national income.

From the equilibrium condition (3) $\Delta M_d = \Delta M_s$ we have:

$689.5 + 0.1022\,\Delta Y = 1487.4 + 0.2147B + 0.5285L +$

$\qquad\qquad\qquad\qquad 221.7170\,\Delta DC$

or

$\Delta Y = 7807.2 + 2.1008B + 5.1712L + 2169.3\,\Delta DC$

Next the data were directly estimated in this (3') reduced form of the model yielding:

(4') $\Delta Y = 7359.4 + 2.8671B + 2.6225L + 1715.08\,\Delta DC$
$\qquad\qquad\quad (21.1) \qquad (6.6) \qquad\quad (4.3)$

$\qquad\qquad\qquad\qquad\qquad\qquad r^2 = .9712$
$\qquad\qquad\qquad\qquad\qquad\qquad F = 168.75$

The hypothesis of a significant difference between

209

the coefficient estimates of (3') and (4') could not be accepted in any case at the 95 percent confidence level.

Thus by use of a simple quantity theory model which explicitly includes the foreign sector in the money supply function, we are able to explain approximately 97 percent of the variation in Mexican money income. Although the data are limited and the model crude, our results suggest that a model based on the quantity theory of money which includes external disturbances on the money stock explains most of the fluctuation in money income in Mexico.

The results place some doubt on whether the authorities can pursue a completely independent monetary policy while maintaining a fixed exchange rate and protecting the nation's level of international monetary reserves. For example, the results indicate that an increase in the money stock, indicative of an expansionary monetary policy, will lead to either: (1) a subsequent decrease in international reserves and the money supply (when all adjustments in the foreign sector have been completed), or (2) if adjustments do not take place in the foreign sector, a continuous balance of payments problem (assuming a fixed exchange rate). In either case, the expansive monetary policy cannot be sustained indefinitely.

Suppose the monetary authorities do attempt an expansionary monetary policy. Actual liquidity will become greater than desired liquidity. As expenditures rise, equation (3) above indicates that subsequent increases in money income and imports will occur (from equations 4 and 6). The increase in imports will lead to a reduction in international reserves and liquidity (equation 2). If equilibrium in the balance of payments is to be restored (given a fixed exchange rate), then imports and income must fall. The fall in income is likely to offset any possible benefits derived from the expansionary policy.

The results of the external influence test is only suggestive and can not really be accepted as it stands. For one thing, interest differentials between Mexico and the U.S. were not explicitly introduced. Even if they were, the control of the Mexican rates by the authorities might not enable many real forces to be identified.

210

Given this fact and the limitations of any statistical analysis, a more thorough examination of the workings of Mexican monetary policy is necessary before any conclusion can be made as to the degree of autonomy possessed by the central bank. The first step in this analysis is to examine in more detail the conduct of monetary policy by the central bank, especially in the 1970-1974 period when it appeared that the bank was beginning to have increasing difficulties in controlling the domestic money supply.

Mexico's Recent Monetary Experiences

During most of the 1950s and 1960s when the rate of growth in the world money supply and price levels was relatively low, Mexico's monetary system worked well. The rate of growth in domestic credit (adjusted by the ratio of domestic credit to high powered money) in Mexico grew at a rate similar to that of real income. Given the growth rate in world money supply, the price level, and the Mexican financial sector, the relatively slow growth of domestic credit was consistent with the assumptions underlying the monetary approach to the balance of payments; i.e., the monetary authorities had no control over the money supply. External forces caused the money supply to increase at a rate required to maintain a positive balance of payments with a fixed exchange rate.

It is difficult, however, to conclude simply from these trends that the authorities had no control over the Mexican money supply. The trends themselves provide no evidence that the authorities may have wanted to alter (and were unsuccessful) the expansion of the money supply from that actually being experienced. Certainly the rather slow rate of expansion of money and credit during this period was in line with the government's development strategy of growth with price stability.

Beginning in 1970[16], there is strong evidence that the authorities wished to alter the pattern of monetary expansion and were only partially successful. In both 1970 and 1971 the authorities attempted to tighten credit in order to combat what they considered to be a too rapid rate of monetary expansion. The major tool used to accomplish this goal was an increase in the reserve requirement. Their intention was to reduce the

211

money multiplier and decrease the need for domestic credit creation, since more private capital could be diverted to the public sector. Though the effects of this policy were to keep domestic credit from growing at a rate less than the world rate of growth in the money supply and also lower the money multiplier, it did not significantly lower the rate of growth in the domestic money supply. During 1971 foreign reserves scaled by the ratio of foreign reserves over high powered money (that is the growth in high powered money due to reserves) increased by 7.76 percent.

One effect of the policy, however, was to lower the assets of the central bank held in the form of government fixed interest securities and to increase its holdings of international reserves. In 1971 for example growth of foreign reserves (multiplied by foreign reserves over high powered money) was almost twice the growth rate in domestic credit (multiplied by domestic credit over high powered money). These trends imply that the restrictive monetary policy carried out in 1970 and 1971 was responsible for the reserve inflow; i.e., the reserve inflows (at a time when the balance of trade was worsening) were the direct result of an increasing demand for money and were necessary to equilibrate the economy's demand and supply of money at the existing price level and exchange rate, a result that would seemingly rule out any ability of the authorities to control the money supply.

To conclusively prove, however, that the Mexican authorities had no control over the domestic supply of money, it must be shown: (1) that they were not able to maintain an interest rate differential between Mexican securities and those prevailing in the United States and Euromarkets; and (2) that even if a differential was established by the authorities, they were not able to manipulate it in order to achieve the central bank target goal for financial savings.

Mexican-U.S. Interest Rates

As noted in Chapter 11 interest differentials do exist between Mexico and other financial markets. Some economists have argued that these differentials are maintained by the central bank and that this policy has been a major factor contributing to Mexican success in attracting foreign capital and in generating capital

212

account surpluses. Clark Reynolds,[17] R. W. Goldsmith,[18] and Robert Bennet,[19] for example, have in fact suggested that differentials in interest rates between Mexico and other countries have been one of the central bank's most important policy tools used for controlling the domestic money supply. A number of other economists,[20] however, feel that these differentials are outside of the bank's control, and that they are set in the marketplace reflecting differences in risk between Mexican and world (U.S.) securities.

It has been shown that in fact Mexican and U.S. rates do differ (Figure 8) for securities of similar maturity. Levels of nominal interest rates in Mexico and the United States could differ in equilibrium for many reasons. If the two markets are linked with arbitrage easily undertaken, these differences however cannot be such that the nominal rate of return (adjusted for transportation costs, risk, and liquidity) on a Mexican instrument is considered consistently higher or lower than on foreign debt instruments. While one can appeal to international arbitrage of debt instruments to insure equilibrium rates of return on Mexican issues vis a vis the United States, there is no conclusive evidence that these forces are at work to the extent necessary to call their capital markets completely unified. Thus based on existing interest differentials between Mexico and the U.S., the authorities have the potential to pursue an independent (at least within limits) monetary policy.

Financial Savings

Financial savings began to decline in the early 1970s. Whereas these savings had increased by 17.6 percent in 1970 and 14.8 percent in 1971, their growth fell to 10.3 percent during 1972. The decline in financial savings meant that the central bank was faced with the alternative of reducing total domestic credit, or of expanding credit by expanding the money supply. Given the government's attempt to expand the economy at that time (1972), they chose the latter.

The growth of the money supply by a greater extent than would have been necessary merely in order to stimulate the economy is therefore explained in part by a slackening of monetary savings. Corresponding to a six to nine months lag between changes in the excess

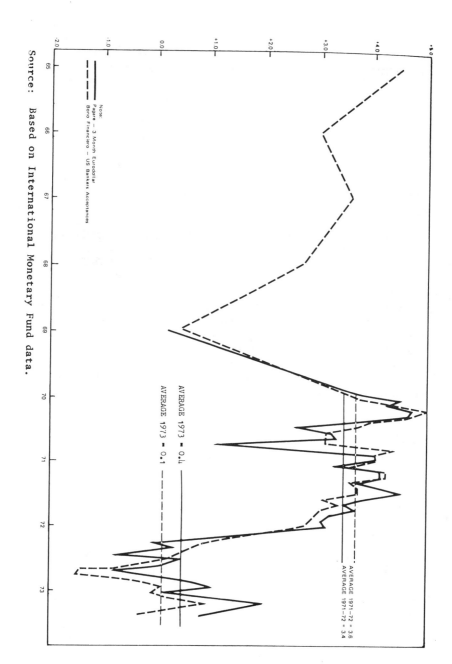

FIGURE 8
INTEREST RATE DIFFERENTIALS

Note:
Pagaré — 3 Month Eurodollar
Bono Financiero — US Bankers Acceptances

AVERAGE 1973 = 0.4
AVERAGE 1973 = 0.1

AVERAGE 1971–72 = 3.6
AVERAGE 1971–72 = 3.4

Source: Based on International Monetary Fund data.

supply of money and changes in prices, the rate of inflation began to accelerate in the fall of 1972.

A further decline in monetary savings during 1973 was reflected in the capital account of the balance of payments. Had these savings maintained the same incremental ratio to GDP in 1973 as in 1972 (itself a poor year), they would have increased by 23 billion pesos more than they did. By the end of 1973 monetary savings were only 9.4 percent higher than they had been a year earlier. This implied a sharp decline in the annual increase in quasi-money as a percentage of GDP.

Causes of the Decline in Financial Savings

The decline in financial savings was obviously not intended by the authorities. Most of the problem lay in: (1) movements in the Mexican-U.S. interest differential; and (2) increased domestic inflation which in turn reduced the real rate of interest on domestic securities and savings.

Decline in the U.S.-Mexican Interest Rate Differential

In the Mexican context, private financial capital flows involve essentially two types of transactions: (1) borrowing abroad by large non-banking concerns, and (2) switching between Mexican and foreign liquid assets by domestic as well as foreign residents. Both are affected to one degree or another by changes in credit conditions in Mexico relative to those prevailing in foreign financial markets (mainly the U.S.). Portfolio investment, in particular, seems to be significantly related to changes in the spread between Mexican and the relevant foreign interest rates.

The behavior of the combined private financial capital and errors and omissions item appears to confirm the existence of this relationship. The US $540 million surplus registered in 1970 by Mexico was associated with a sharp decline in foreign rates coupled with unchanged yields on Mexican assets. Throughout 1971 and 1972, however, the yield differential (Figure 9) exhibited a declining tendency, but on the average remained in favor of Mexico by a substantial margin. During these years, there was a continued inflow of

215

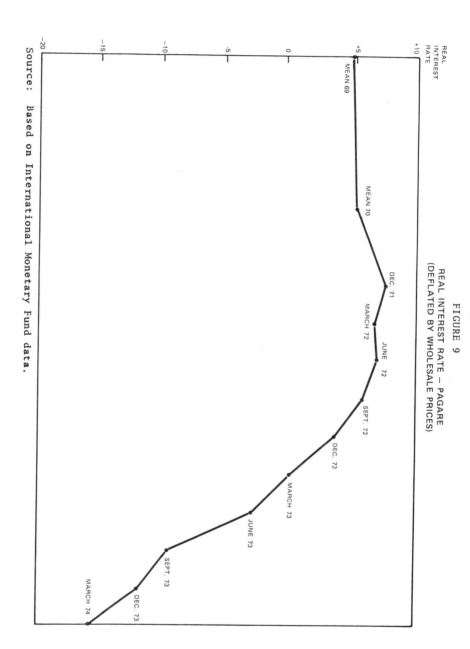

FIGURE 9
REAL INTEREST RATE – PAGARE
(DEFLATED BY WHOLESALE PRICES)

Source: Based on International Monetary Fund data.

216

around US $400 million, of which almost one-half represented net medium and long term borrowing by firms with foreign participation.

In January 1973 the Mexican authorities introduced a new tax schedule applicable to interest earned on fixed income assets. The result was a reduction in the net yields payable by banks on their quasi-monetary liabilities. The most noticeable feature of the new structure was the establishment of a dual tax schedule, designed to stimulate investment in nominal securities. Under the new system, tax rates applicable to nominal assets held by residents were left virtually unchanged, while the rates applicable to bearers' securities (and to all assets held by nonresident foreigners) were increased by 4 to 6 percentage points.

At the same time, foreign interest rates registered a steep increase resulting in a sharp reduction in the yield differential (over the first half of 1973). This reduction was accompanied by a reversal of the private financial capital and errors and omissions item (which registered a deficit of some US $70 million in that period).

Clearly investors are interested in the interest differential between Mexican and U.S. securities. More importantly, however, they are interested in the net yield obtained from each countries' securities.

In June 1973 the Mexican monetary authorities acted to stem the outflow of funds by raising the net interest rates payable by local banks to non-institutional investors (by 1 to 1.5 percentage points). Due however to large increases in foreign rates, the yield spread continued to deteriorate (in July and August before improving somewhat in the last quarter). Partly as a result of these developments, there was a very large capital outflow in the third quarter of 1973. The outflow subsided by the end of the year, but for 1973 as a whole the deficit on private financial capital (including errors and omissions) was around US $300 million.

In addition to the adverse movement in the U.S.-Mexican interest differential, the weak performance of the banking system in 1973 also stemmed from accelerating domestic inflation which eroded the real interest rate structure. In an attempt to adjust for these deficiencies, the monetary authorities authorized investment and mortgage banks (in March 1974) to receive a new, very liquid type of deposit, the certificate of deposit. Authorized denominations varied, as did the maturity period. The net yield depended on both of these factors.

In March 1974, the yield on these assets compared favorably with external interest rates on similar instruments. By May, however, the external rate had increased. This called for an adjustment in the Mexican instruments; the net yield on all certificates of deposit and promissory notes in domestic currency was raised, depending on maturity and denomination, by 0.5 to 1.5 percentage points. For deposit banks, the temporary marginal interest rate introduced in June 1973 to increase the net yield of time deposits was increased from 0.05 to 2.30 percentage points, resulting in a net yield of 9.5 percent.

Toward the middle of 1973, there was some concern that rising external rates would once again outrun Mexican rates. Domestic rates, however, remained fixed, because of the authorities' belief that further increases in yields payable by banks would exert too much pressure on those banks with a large portion of their portfolio tied up in long term loans at fixed, low interest rates. From August, external rates began to decline and the Mexican authorities expected this development to continue. Consequently, no yield change was considered necessary for the remainder of the year.

The emphasis on higher interest rates for longer term time deposits indicated the government's ability and desire to attract foreign savings in the face of rapidly changing and uncertain international investment conditions.

In connection with international investment conditions the central bank in November 1974 authorized several new fixed income investments in U.S. dollars which could be handled by Mexican banks. These were offered only to non-residents of Mexico and Mexican citizens living along the northern border. The time deposits ranged from a minimum of 3 months to a maximum of 24 and carried a net interest rate of 8.5 percent to 9.5 percent.

This brief outline of financial developments in

218

the early 1970s indicates that the authorities had some
control over the domestic interest rate and its spread
vis a vis the U.S. rate.

Capital outflows which reduced financial savings
were not outside of government control but resulted
instead from government inertia in maintaining an adequate differential to attract foreign funds.

Because Mexican securities were fixed income
assets, their desirability decreased with inflation.
Again the government could not adjust the value of new
issues fast enough to maintain their desirability as
inflation accelerated. The government's January 1973
increase in the tax rate paid by holders of securities
was, in retrospect, a colossal blunder.

Increased Domestic Inflation

It is difficult to separate all of the factors
that contributed to Mexico's economic problems. Domestic inflation was caused in part by the lack of financial savings (because the central bank had to extend
credit to the government), but the lack of financial
savings also stemmed from the erosion of the real rate
of interest on Mexican securities caused in part by
that same inflation.

The origins of the inflation are, however, easy to
trace. In 1972, the government initiated an expansionary fiscal policy designed to counter the decline in
the rate of real growth experienced in 1971, and also
to initiate the expansion of public sector involvement
in the economy as a means of attacking some of the
economic and social problems that had built up under
previous administrations. To finance the expansion in
government spending, the central bank was now called
upon to directly provide the necessary funds (since
they were not available in sufficient amounts from
either the private financial sector or from fiscal
revenues). Given the drop in the real savings rate
that began to take place during this period, the
reserve requirement mechanism could not fully finance
the level of expenditures required by the federal
authorities. The inflexibility of the reserve requirement mechanism in 1972 combined with the inelastic
nature of the fiscal revenue system,[21] placed the
responsibility for public finance on the central bank.

To finance government expenditure, the central bank had to increase its holdings of government debt more than two-fold in 1972 and by another 60 percent in 1973. These increases led to a much greater growth in other assets (as other liabilities remained approximately the same) and thus to an expansion in domestic credit.

The new circumstances of 1972--recession and inflation--placed a strain upon the required reserve mechanism. The tool could no longer be depended upon to provide sufficient funds to meet the demands of the Treasury.

A substantial increase in taxes had been proposed within the administration for inclusion in the 1972 budget, but important elements of the package were rejected by the Mexican Congress. The quarterly federal deficit in the second quarter of 1972 was, as a consequence, three times greater than that of the first quarter. The rate of growth in the money supply accelerated throughout 1972 and by December 1972 the level was 21.1 percent above that of December 1971. Correspondingly by December 1972 credit from the Bank of Mexico was 22.4 percent above the level of December 1971.

The inflation which began in latter 1972 accelerated throughout 1973. In no month was the rate of inflation, measured over the year, lower than in the previous month. Rising international interest rates, excess demand, increasing Mexican-U.S. differentials caused by domestic inflation, increased government credit, all contributed to sustain the inflation. It might be argued that much of the acceleration was due to speculation resulting in a decline in the income elasticity of money. The elasticity for 1970-1973 rose, however, to 1.05 from its 1965-1971 average level of 0.98, thus indicating that inflation was lagging monetary changes.

Conclusions on Monetary Autonomy

Monetary policy based on the principal of maintaining a slow growth in the money supply was difficult to maintain in the 1970s. In 1970 and 1971, the policy of tight money was made difficult to implement because the world money supply was growing at a more rapid rate than was the goal of the Mexican authorities.

Later in 1972 and 1973 incipient world recession, slower growth rates in the Mexican real income, and the decline in the Mexican-Euromarket differentials, all acting together, meant that the required reserve mechanism could no longer be relied upon for non-inflationary financing. Savings that were previously channeled through the financial sector were becoming more difficult to capture. Finally the inflexibility of the fiscal revenue structure together with a populist inspired federal government spending binge began to bring greater pressure on the central bank to finance government deficits.

There were, therefore, a number of factors tending to move the money supply at a rate the bank probably felt was too high. One can conclude from these events, however, that the money supply was potentially under the bank's control. The money supply was expanding faster than the bank desired only because the monetary authorities were asked to finance a level of government expenditures that was irresponsible, given the country's fiscal capacity and the authorities ineptitude at maintaining a positive U.S.-Mexican interest differential.

Nothing in the record indicates the authorities did not, given their environment as a semi-dependent country, have the potential to pursue an independent monetary policy.

There is in fact additional evidence that the government can (albeit for a relatively short time) pursue an independent monetary policy. In 1975, for example, public expenditures (including investment) were around 300 billion pesos, an increase from 216 billion pesos in 1974. Stepped-up public expenditure caused the government's deficit to increase from 64 billion pesos in 1974 to approximately 90 billion pesos (or about 10 percent of GNP) in 1975. More than half of this deficit was financed by foreign borrowing, while the remainder came from domestic sources, mainly from the Bank of Mexico through direct monetary creation.

Domestic credit creation times its share of high powered money was 10.74 percent in 1973 and 39.30 percent in 1974. By 1975 it had increased to about 50 percent. On the other hand, in 1975 real income growth had dropped to 4 percent, with inflation at about 15 percent. If in fact the monetary authorities had no

control over the domestic supply of money, there should have been a substantial outflow of foreign reserves. Instead, there was a net inflow.

Conclusions

Analysis of the central bank and government activities between 1955 and 1970 indicates that monetary policy in Mexico has and can be used to direct savings from the private to the public sector. Its effectiveness in mobilizing funds for government expenditure was perhaps responsible for the underdevelopment of the fiscal system. In addition it was shown that the central bank can control domestic credit creation, the money multiplier, and pursue stabilization policy effectively. The central bank cannot, however, completely control foreign reserve levels, and consequently does not have complete control of its money supply or the domestic rate of inflation.

Beginning in 1971, a number of changes in the government's development strategy, expanding the scope of the public sector, gave the economy an inflationary bias. Income redistribution acquired increasing policy importance, and the country's agricultural sector began to stagnate. The latter had, for many years, been the sector from which capital necessary to expand industry had flowed. In addition new government attitudes on financing federal programs emerged. Earlier policies of expanding the money supply in line with GNP were frequently broken, even though the central bank attempted to maintain the standard. The principle requiring that government sale of securities to cover deficits increase at a rate less than or slightly greater than the rate of growth in real income was no longer obeyed. All of these changes sent shocks throughout Mexico's monetary sector.

The rapid real growth of the public sector and the means by which it was financed, not international inflation, was the major cause of the post-1972 Mexican inflation. There can be little doubt that if this expansion had not been attempted within an excessively short period of time, the disequilibrium of 1973-1975 would have been much less severe (although external forces alone would have caused prices to increase somewhat).

223

Large and growing public expenditures, rising from 9.07 to 14.70 percent of GDP between 1971 and 1975, should have been anticipated by fiscal reforms. Instead those tax reforms that did materialize were too little and too late.

Does this mean that the government should not have tried to address Mexico's social and economic problems as vigorously as it did? There is no easy answer; if the government had decided to abandon its commitments, Mexico might well have a more stable economy today and might be facing less severe short run problems. But the authorities hoped that by pressing ahead with the basic tasks, they would be able to initiate the creation of a stronger, less vulnerable, more diversified, and a more equitable economic and social structure. Obviously, this effort has not entirely succeeded because in order to press ahead, Mexico had to incur a heavy external debt, to accept a high rate of inflation, and finally devalue its currency--moves which may have worsened rather than made improvements in the pattern of income distribution.

Notes

1. The model is an adaptation of that originally developed by Arnold Harberger. See his "The Dynamics of Inflation in Chile," in Charles Christ, ed., Measurement in Economics: Studies in Mathematical Economics in Memory of Yehuda Grunfeld (Stanford: Stanford University Press, 1963), pp. 219-250.

2. P. Cagan, "The Monetary Dynamics of Hyperinflation," in Milton Friedman, ed., Studies in the Quantity Theory of Money (Chicago: University of Chicago Press, 1956), pp. 35-69.

3. For a similar derivation see M. S. Kahn, "A Monetary Model of Balance of Payments," Journal of Monetary Economics (July 1976), p. 316.

4. Currency and coin plus time deposits.

5. Milton Friedman, "The Demand for Money: Some Theoretical and Empirical Results," in Milton Friedman, The Optimum Quantity Theory of Money and Other Essays (Chicago: Aldine Publishing Co., 1969), pp. 111-140.

6. The following uses an approach first suggested by John Koehler in his Economic Policy Making with Limited Information: The Process of Macro-Control in Mexico (Santa Monica: The Rand Corporation, 1968).

7. A pattern of expenditures originally discovered by John Koehler. See his Information and Policy Making: Mexico (New Haven: Ph.D. dissertation, Yale University, 1968), pp. 18-21.

8. Cf. the model developed in the next section. The result was also found by Charles Schotta in his "The Money Supply, Exports, and Income in an Open Economy: Mexico 1939-63," Economic Development and Cultural Change (July 1966), pp. 458-70.

9. Results also reported by Gilberto Escobedo in "Formulating a Model of the Mexican Economy," Federal Reserve Bank of St. Louis, Review (July 1973), pp. 8-19; and "Response of the Mexican Economy to Policy Actions," Federal Reserve Bank of St. Louis, Review (June 1973), pp. 15-23.

10. B. Griffiths, Mexican Monetary Policy and Economic Development, op. cit., Ch. 5.

11. A position also taken by D. Sykes Wilford in his Monetary Policy and the Open Economy: Mexico's Experience, op. cit., Ch. 6 & 7. It should be noted many of Wilford's other conclusions as to the effectiveness of Mexican monetary policy are not supported by the analysis contained in the present study.

12. Roger Johnston, "Should the Mexican Government Promote the Country's Stock Exchange?" Inter-American Economic Affairs (1972), pp. 45-60.

13. Padraic Fallon, "The Future for Mexico," Euromoney (April 1978), Supplement, pp. 1-35.

14. As Koehler points out, we really do not know what the intentions of the monetary authorities are or were. There is enough indirect evidence however to support the conclusion given in the text.

15. Cf. J. J. Polak, "Monetary Analysis of Income Formation and Payments Problems," in H. Robert Heller, ed., The Monetary Approach to the Balance of Payments (Washington: International Monetary Fund, 1977),

pp. 15-64. In the same volume see also J. J. Polak and Loretta Boissonneault, "Monetary Analysis of Income and Imports and Its Statistical Application," pp. 133-146; and S. J. Prais, "Some Mathematical Notes on the Quantity Theory of Money in an Open Economy," pp. 147-162.

16. The following description of events is taken from the data contained in various issues of Analisis-- The Mexican Economy (Mexico City: Publicaciones Ejecutivas de Mexico), annual beginning with 1972.

17. Clark Reynolds, The Mexican Economy (New Haven: Yale University Press, 1970).

18. Raymond Goldsmith, The Financial Experience of Mexico, op. cit.

19. Robert Bennett, The Financial Sector and Economic Development (Baltimore: Johns Hopkins, 1965).

20. Cf. D. S. Wilford and W. T. Wilford, "Monetary Approach to Balance of Payments: On World Prices and the Reserve Flow Equation," Weltwirtschaftliches Archiv (No. 1, 1977), pp. 31-39.

21. A fact econometrically verified in Dwaine Sykes Wilford and Walton T. Wilford, "Fiscal Revenues in Mexico: A Measure of Performance, 1950-73," Public Finance (1976), pp. 103-114.

Chapter 13

INFLATION IN SOUTH AFRICA

Introduction

The Mexican economy illustrated a number of problems that semi-dependent countries have encountered in the conduct of their monetary policy during the period of world inflation. The greatest consequence of world inflation on the Mexican economy was undoubtedly the gradual erosion of monetary control. Direct price effects stemming from the increased price of imports, given that imports only account for 12 to 15 percent of GDP, were relatively minor.

South Africa on the other hand illustrates quite vividly the experience of a more open semi-dependent country, where direct price effects appear to be one of the major economic consequences of world inflation.

South Africa has a much more sophisticated tax system than Mexico, hence many of the monetary problems (while potential) encountered by Mexico were not major contributing factors to the South African inflation, a fact that greatly uncomplicates the examination of the direct impact of world inflation on the economy.

Issues in South African Inflation

The nature of South African inflation and its pattern since the late 1950s displays a number of interesting phenomena. The type and source of the inflation experienced seems to have changed over time, raising questions as to: (1) the extent to which recent (post-1970) inflation has been imported rather than domestically induced; (2) the role that wage increases have played in determining the rate of inflation; and (3) the underlying mechanisms that perpetrate the country's inflation. Of particular interest for policy purposes is the manner and degree to which the type of inflation experienced in South Africa in the 1970s is fundamentally different from that taking place in the 1960s.

Characteristics of the South African Economy

Each semi-dependent country possesses certain features in common with other members of the group. Obviously each has certain unique aspects that tend to differentiate it from the other members. The South African economy admittedly possesses several well known social features that make its economy unique. It is very unlikely, however, that these unique aspects are important enough to make it an unrepresentative semi-dependent country. Most of its economic problems are similar to those encountered today in virtually any relatively open semi-dependent country.

Even the importance of gold to the economy does not fundamentally alter the workings of its economy. While gold has a certain mystique, in economic terms its only significance is to place the nation in that group of countries specializing in primary products; it is only another non-oil exporting semi-dependent country. In fact both South Africa and most non-oil semi-dependent countries borrowed heavily during 1974-1975. Similarly both South Africa and these countries reduced their reserves in 1975 (a period of weak export markets for their products) in order to sustain import volume during a period of rising world prices of manufactures, oil, and food. By 1975 the volume of imports into South Africa and these countries was shrinking under the pressure of external financial strains and of restraints on domestic demand (undertaken for the purpose of curbing price increases and protecting their balance of payments positions).

While the South African economy, therefore, does not appear to possess any features that would make it an unrepresentative semi-dependent country, it does as noted possess some features which make it of particular interest to the study of world inflation. By any standard the South African economy[1] is extremely open to international economic influences. From 1970-1973 the ratio of exports and imports (excluding gold) to GDP at market prices was 46 percent, rising to 53 percent in 1974. (Including gold, the ratio increased from 52 percent in 1970 to 55 percent in 1973 and 65.6 percent in 1974.) Several other trade patterns are of particular interest, each tending to reinforce the conclusion that South Africa is a semi-dependent country:

1. By far the country's most important single

228

category of imports is machinery and transport equipment. These items constituted an increasing percentage of total imports during the 1970s, reaching 48.4 percent during 1972.

2. Also in 1972 imports of primary products accounted for only 16.7 percent of the total compared to 73 percent for manufactured articles.

3. An opposite pattern is true for the export trade. In 1972 exports of primary commodities constituted 55 percent of the total compared with 37 percent for manufactured articles.

4. Not only is the country's dependence on foreign trade considerable, but the sorts of commodities exported (especially gold and agricultural products) are particularly subject to price fluctuations.

5. In general the prices of the country's imports, particularly of manufactures (though reflecting world trends) are relatively more stable than export prices.

6. For most traded commodities (other than gold), South Africa's world market share is small, and thus it is reasonable (and customary) to assume that the country's export and import prices (apart from the influence of local tariffs and subsidies) are determined abroad.

7. Until recently the country had adopted a fixed, periodically adjusted exchange rate system which was usually tied to the U.S. dollar. This made the economy extremely vulnerable to short-term capital movements, especially during periods when investors and speculators felt that the South African rand was over or undervalued.

Economic Developments in the 1960s

The South African economy expanded rapidly during the 1960s. The gross domestic product in real terms grew at an average annual rate of 5.8 percent from 1960-1970 (Table 52). During the same period prices rose on the average by 2.9 percent, a rate relatively low by international standards.

TABLE 52

SOUTH AFRICA: AGGREGATE ECONOMIC ACTIVITY, 1960-1976

(Millions of rand)

Year	Gross Domestic Product (Current Prices)	% Change	Gross National Expenditure (Current Prices)	% Change	Gross Domestic Product (1975 Prices)	% Change
1960	5,286	5.9	5,045	6.2	12,173	4.4
1961	5,568	5.3	5,296	5.0	12,665	4.0
1962	5,937	6.6	5,693	7.5	13,347	5.4
1963	6,601	11.2	6,362	11.8	14,371	7.7
1964	7,257	9.9	6,979	9.7	15,341	6.7
1965	7,931	9.3	7,617	9.1	16,280	6.1
1966	8,604	8.5	8,272	8.6	17,009	4.5
1967	9,540	10.9	9,192	10.9	18,269	7.4
1968	10,280	7.8	9,880	7.5	19,047	4.3
1969	11,568	12.5	11,115	12.5	20,293	6.5
1970	12,618	9.1	12,125	9.1	21,285	4.9
1971	13,992	10.9	13,503	11.4	22,177	4.2
1972	15,657	11.9	15,085	11.7	22,901	3.3
1973	19,074	21.8	18,364	21.7	23,712	3.5
1974	23,008	20.6	21,892	19.2	25,388	7.1
1975	25,924	12.7	24,704	12.8	25,924	2.1
1976	29,121	12.3	27,729	12.2	26,258	1.3

Source: International Monetary Fund, International Financial Statistics (May 1978), pp. 344, 345.

While all sectors of the national economy partici-
pated in the country's prosperity, agriculture lagged
somewhat behind due to drought conditions in 1964 and
1965 which resulted in low crop yields for those years.
Gold mining output increased despite rising costs.
There was a tendency for gold production to level off
after 1965, but the expanding output of other minerals
maintained the strong upward trend for mining activities
as a whole. Manufacturing was, however, the leading
sector in the economic expansion; the net value of output rising from R 1,129 million in 1960 to R 2,908 million in 1970--an increase of 158 percent.

Because the early 1960s were characterized by
relatively low rates of inflation, a number of South
African economists, as was the case in Mexico, began
to feel that the economy was capable of sustaining
high rates of growth and with price stability. As one
of South Africa's leading economists, Professor J. Graff,
confidently noted in 1968: "Almost all the textbook
dangers of inflation so confidently listed a generation
ago have proved to be paper tigers,"[2]

Increased Inflationary Pressures

Despite this optimism, by the late 1960s inflationary pressures generated in part by the country's rapid
economic expansion became increasingly present in the
form of: (1) rising prices; (2) pressure on the
balance of payments; (3) capital shortage reflected in
rising interest rates; (4) shortage of skilled labor,
and (5) bottlenecks in transport and shortages of
certain commodities.

Of these, the effect of inflationary pressures on
the balance of payments were perhaps the most important.

The level of exports rose only slightly during the
1960s. Imports, however, increased fairly rapidly,
particularly from 1962 to the middle of 1965. While
imports fell in 1966 by R 110 million, they rose again
in the latter part of 1966 and reached their highest
level ever during the first part of 1967. Imports fell
somewhat in the second half of 1967 but thereafter
resumed their upward course to reach a record high of
R 2,745.1 million in 1970 (Table 53).

Movements in imports and exports during the 1960s,

231

TABLE 53

SOUTH AFRICA: BALANCE OF PAYMENTS INDICATORS, 1960-1977

(Millions of rand)

Year	Total Exports	Gold	Imports (C.I.G.)	Trade Balance (excluding Gold)	Price Exports (1975=100)	Price Imports (1975=100)
1960	1,425.2	530.0	1,163.4	-286.2	51.5	47.2
1961	1,531.0	576.0	1,042.8	-87.8	52.1	46.6
1962	1,588.4	632.0	1,054.6	-98.2	51.5	47.2
1963	1,696.9	688.0	1,265.2	-256.3	52.7	47.2
1964	1,785.2	736.0	1,629.3	-580.1	54.5	47.8
1965	1,846.1	775.0	1,830.7	-759.6	55.7	49.7
1966	1,990.7	769.2	1,710.8	-489.3	56.3	52.2
1967	2,156.0	774.7	1,985.8	-604.5	54.5	50.9
1968	2,293.7	768.9	1,992.3	-467.5	54.5	49.1
1969	2,397.1	846.9	2,278.0	-727.8	56.9	50.9
1970	2,396.2	836.7	2,745.1	-1185.6	57.5	52.2
1971	2,510.6	922.2	3,120.6	-1532.2	55.7	54.0
1972	3,227.3	1,161.0	3,031.2	-964.9	59.9	62.1
1973	4,221.0	1,769.4	3,564.2	-1112.6	72.5	67.7
1974	5,957.2	2,565.2	5,344.3	-1952.3	89.8	80.1
1975	6,573.2	2,540.2	6,083.5	-2050.5	100.0	100.0
1976	6,935.2	2,346.4	6,334.6	-1745.8	118.6	123.0
1977	8,684.5	2,795.1	5,491.4	398.0	-	-

Source: International Monetary Fund, International Financial Statistics (May 1978), pp. 344, 345.

therefore, resulted in a more or less constant increase in the trade deficit. The drought in 1964 and 1965 also aggravated the adverse trade balance causing, on the one hand, a significant fall in the volume of South African agricultural exports, and on the other, increasing imports (as some products normally supplied from domestic sources had to be obtained from abroad).

The main cause of the deterioration in the trade balance was, however, the expansion of national expenditure. The South African economy always exhibited a high propensity to import, and historically there had been a close correlation between increases in individual incomes and the volume of consumer goods imports. High levels of public and private investment in the 1960s served to reinforce this general tendency. The deficit in current account was financed by drawing down the country's foreign exchange reserves. By 1970, the situation became critical. In that year there was a severe contraction in foreign reserves as a result of the mounting trade gap.

Problems in Designing Anti-Inflationary Measures

Being a semi-dependent country dictated that South Africa's anti-inflationary measures initiated in the late 1960s would have to take a somewhat different form from those designed for the large nation group.[4] In many respects the country's task was made easy by the fact that unlike most of the advanced industrial countries, South Africa did not experience any overinvestment in its major industrial sectors, nor was the balance of payments deficit large enough to warrant strong deflationary measures.

Balance of payments deficits,[5] therefore, could be cured simply by keeping the country's inflation below that of its principal trading partners. The policymakers task of maintaining balance of payments stability was, however, made difficult by the fact that gold had a fixed price ($35 per ounce). To prevent a deterioration in the balance of payments, stable costs in the production of gold had to be maintained, a task extremely difficult to achieve in an open economy trading with an increasingly inflationary world.

While the 1960s were thus a period of unbroken prosperity for South Africa, inflationary pressures and

233

associated balance of payments deficits were beginning to appear. Neither the government nor the monetary authorities appeared able to completely stem these trends. As a result, inflation continued to be a problem in the early 1970s.

Economic Developments in the 1970s

The rate of real growth was 6.9 percent in 1969, but this was followed in 1970, 1971, and 1972 by much lower real rates of growth.

While the growth of GDP was only 3.3 percent in 1972, conditions had begun to improve in the fourth quarter of that year, and in the first half of 1973 there was mild recovery. In his 1973 budget speech, the Minister of Finance proposed measures aimed at moderately stimulating the economy but only to the extent consistent with avoiding any additional inflationary pressures. The program was successful. Economic activity increased rapidly in the second half of that year.

The economic expansion continued into 1974, and indeed accelerated during the middle of that year. By the end of 1974, however, there were signs that industrial expansion had reached its limit; little excess capacity remained. Labor and capital markets were also showing signs of strain. Gross domestic expenditure had exceeded gross national product by an increasing margin. From mid-1974 imports rose rapidly, while exports (other than gold) grew slowly. As a result, the balance of payments on current account deficit increased to an all-time high.

Inflationary Problems

The rate of inflation was relatively modest in 1971 and 1972, but the rate was accelerating. By 1973 it had increased to an unprecedented 17.5 percent (Table 54). Various anti-inflationary measures were introduced--interest rates were raised and the return on long term government stock increased to 10 percent. A concerted drive against inflation was initiated by the government. Public corporations and all branches of the private sector were urged to defer capital expenditure, and exercise maximum restraint in price and wage increases. Simultaneously, all groups were extolled to

234

TABLE 54

SOUTH AFRICA: MEASURES OF INFLATION, 1960-1977

(1975 = 100)

Period	Home and Import Goods Price Index	% Change	Home Goods Price Index	% Change	Consumer Price Index	% Change	Implicit GDP Deflator	% Change
1960	45.4	1.3	46.4	2.0	48.8	1.5	43.4	2.1
1961	46.2	1.8	47.2	1.7	49.8	2.0	44.0	1.4
1962	46.5	0.6	47.4	0.4	50.4	1.2	44.5	1.1
1963	47.1	1.3	47.9	1.1	51.1	1.4	45.9	3.1
1964	48.2	2.3	49.0	2.3	52.4	2.5	47.3	3.1
1965	49.7	3.1	50.8	3.7	54.5	4.0	48.7	3.0
1966	51.6	3.8	52.9	4.1	56.5	3.7	50.6	3.9
1967	52.9	2.5	54.3	2.6	58.4	3.4	52.2	3.2
1968	53.5	1.1	55.0	1.3	59.6	2.1	54.0	3.4
1969	54.7	2.2	56.5	2.7	61.5	3.2	52.0	5.6
1970	56.4	3.1	58.4	3.4	64.1	4.2	59.6	4.6
1971	59.1	4.8	61.1	4.6	67.7	5.6	63.1	5.9
1972	63.9	8.1	65.3	6.9	72.1	6.5	68.4	8.4
1973	72.3	13.1	74.3	13.8	78.9	9.4	80.4	17.5
1974	85.3	18.0	86.6	16.6	88.1	11.7	90.6	12.7
1975	100.0	17.2	100.0	15.5	100.0	13.5	100.0	10.4
1976	115.1	15.1	114.4	10.0	111.1	11.1	109.0	9.0
1977	130.1	13.0	130.4	14.0	123.7	11.3	-	-

Source: International Monetary Fund, International Financial Statistics (May 1978), pp. 344, 345.

235

to increase labor productivity.

Despite these efforts, the balance of payments continued to deteriorate (but the consequences were
mitigated by large capital inflow).

By 1975 the economy's growth rate had dropped to
2.1 percent, and there was danger that lack of confidence in its ability to sustain non-inflationary growth
might cause a run on the rand, thus depleting the
country's gold and foreign reserves. By 1976, real
GDP growth had fallen to 1.3 percent.

Exchange Policies

During the 1970s, the government engaged in a fairly
active exchange rate policy, largely in an attempt to
stimulate the economy. From August 1971 to December of
that year, the value of the rand depreciated by 3 percent (while it was allowed to float with the American
dollar). It was devalued in December 1971 by 12.28 percent (8 percent effectively in terms of all other currencies). From June to October 1972 the rand depreciated again by 4 percent (while it floated with ster-
ling). On October 25, 1972, the value of the rand
appreciated by 3 percent, and after this date the value
of the rand was systematically increased to attain its
1967 exchange value in terms of all other currencies.

Between June 1974 and July 1975 a policy of independent managed floating was adopted. Through this
policy the authorities hoped to achieve a relatively
stable weighted average exchange rate. At the same
time, however, the government announced that changes
in the rate might take place if there were fundamental
changes in either the domestic or international economy.
The new rate was fixed at R = $1.40, amounting to a
4.76 devaluation of the rand (against the American
dollar).

By 1975 three fundamental changes seemed to have
occurred: (1) it appeared that the world economic
recession was more serious and long lasting than at
first thought; (2) in September the price of gold fell
suddenly from a peak of slightly over $180 an ounce to
only $135 an ounce; (3) it was becoming clear that
internal unrest and external political developments
would necessitate greatly increased military expenditures.

The rand was thus devalued by 17.9 percent on September 22, 1975. In a statement accompanying the devaluation, the Minister of Finance noted that the decision to devalue the rand took into account not only the need to strengthen the overall balance of payments, but was also intended to halt the gradual slowdown in economic growth. Devaluation was seen by the government as preferrable to deflationary monetary and fiscal measures (since in their view these ran the risk of aggravating the existing recessionary conditions).

The official announcement indicated that the devaluation should:[6]

1. Effectively curb speculation against the rand (which had flared up following the decline in the price of gold).

2. Improve the balance of payments on current account by increasing the value of the net gold output and merchandize exports, and by reducing imports (below what they would otherwise have been).

3. Have an immediate expansionary effect on the export of gold and incomes of workers in the mining sector.

4. Raise the rand prices of imports competing with locally manufactured goods and thus stimulate industrial production and investment.

5. Raise government revenue from taxation on the additional rand income generated and thereby lessen the government's dependence on bank credit as a means of financing its deficits.

The intent to use the devaluation as a means of stimulating growth was somewhat of a break with past policy. All during the 1960s and 1970s South African exchange rate policy had operated in a relatively open economy. As noted there were considerable differences in the types of goods imported and exported, and the country had experienced wide fluctuations in its terms of trade. Given these conditions and the government's announced intention of avoiding dependence on official short term borrowing, it was logical that the exchange rate policy should have given top priority to the balance of payments. The effect alterations in the exchange rate had on economic growth were usually a secondary consideration in policy discussions. Given the structure of the economy in 1975, it is debatable whether or not conditions had changed sufficiently to now justify the use of devaluation as a prime means of stimulating the level of economic activity.

The openness of the economy, however, meant that devaluation was certain to significantly increase the rate of inflation. Given the rate of world inflation by 1975, it is very likely that the country could have experienced a relatively mild inflation (price rise) if the devaluations had not taken place. In addition the existence of a surplus of black laborers (and their legal status) meant that wage-push inflationary forces were not likely to be a major contributor to domestic inflation.[7]

Comparative Patterns of Inflation

An examination of annual data on inflation in South Africa and that of her major trading partners suggests four distinct periods (Tables 55 & 56). During the first period, 1960-1965, South Africa and the U.S. inflated at a lower rate than did the other countries. During this period, the highest rate of inflation occurred in Japan. During 1966-1969, however, South Africa, while still inflating at a lower rate than the U.K. and Japan, was experiencing a slightly higher rate of inflation than in Germany. During this period, South African imports were becoming more expensive in terms of her exports.

During the third period (1970-1973), the South African position changed from that of a relatively low to a relatively high inflation country. Inflation was clearly lower in the U.S. and Germany. The United Kingdom inflated at the highest rate closely followed by Japan and South Africa. For the period covering 1960-1973, South Africa seems to have inflated relatively more in step with her faster inflating trading partners, the United Kingdom and Japan. Her position diverged significantly from that of Germany, while no general pattern seems to exist with the United States. These tendencies generally continued through the final (1974-1977) period.

TABLE 55

RATES OF INFLATION: SOUTH AFRICA AND MAJOR TRADING PARTNERS
1960-1977

(Average annual rate
of change, consumer
price index)

Year	South Africa	Germany	U.K.	United States	Japan
1960	1.5	1.4	1.1	1.5	3.8
1961	2.0	2.4	2.7	1.1	5.4
1962	1.2	2.9	4.0	2.2	6.6
1963	1.4	3.0	2.2	1.2	7.8
1964	2.5	2.2	3.2	1.2	3.7
1965	4.0	3.3	4.6	1.7	6.7
1966	3.7	3.5	3.9	3.1	4.9
1967	3.4	1.6	2.7	2.6	4.1
1968	2.1	1.7	4.8	4.2	5.3
1969	3.2	1.8	5.4	5.4	5.3
1970	4.2	3.3	6.3	5.9	7.6
1971	5.6	5.4	9.4	4.3	6.2
1972	6.5	5.5	7.3	3.3	4.4
1973	9.4	6.9	9.1	6.3	11.8
1974	11.7	7.0	16.0	10.9	24.3
1975	13.5	5.9	24.2	9.2	11.9
1976	11.1	4.5	16.6	5.8	9.3
1977	11.3	3.9	15.8	6.5	8.1

Source: International Monetary Fund, International Financial Statistics
(May 1978).

TABLE 56

ANNUAL AVERAGE PERCENTAGE CHANGE

OF CONSUMER PRICE INDEX

Period	South Africa	Germany	U.K.	United States	Japan
1960-1965	2.1	2.5	3.0	1.5	5.7
1966-1969	3.1	2.2	4.2	3.8	4.9
1970-1973	6.4	5.3	8.0	5.0	7.5
1974-1977	11.9	5.3	18.2	8.1	13.4

Source: Computed from Table 55.

Thus for the period (1960-1977) as a whole, South Africa caught up relatively fast with its high inflation trading partners (particularly after 1966); during this period prices increased relatively more in South Africa than in her trading partners (except for the U.K. between 1974 and 1977). The relative acceleration of inflation in South Africa particularly after 1973 is the main phenomenon that must be explained in any analysis of the country's inflationary process.

In general the pattern of inflation in South Africa, therefore, has been appreciably different from that of her major trading partners. In addition the impact of world inflation on South Africa has deviated somewhat from most of the other semi-dependent countries. Most of these countries experienced a sharp rise in the price of imports (especially after 1973), with export prices rising to a smaller extent (to some extent a result of the import price rise). In contrast, South Africa's position was somewhat different. That country experienced a sharp rise in the price of its principal export (gold) which, in balance of payments terms, offset increases in the prices of its imports. South Africa, therefore, was intermediate between the large and semi-dependent groups and the oil producers (whose situation of course became much more favorable after 1973).

Official Interpretation of Inflation

The government's official position has been that South Africa's recent experience with inflation can be divided into three distinct time periods based on the source of inflation; i.e., demand-pull inflation dominated before 1971, cost-push inflation during 1971-1973, with demand-pull inflation becoming present again toward the end of 1973 and extending into the later years. There is ample evidence supporting the government's position, particularly regarding the 1960s.

The components of aggregate demand, especially consumption and investment, increased during the economic expansion of 1965-1970. During this period, the authorities had some difficulty in controlling the money supply. Ample evidence of the government's concern with excess demand is provided by its ceilings on credit imposed in October 1965. These were so harsh as to cause investment in manufacturing to decline in

241

absolute terms (from 1966 to 1968). Investment in manufacturing recovered to some extent toward the end of the expansionary phase in 1970, but decreased again during the downturn of 1971-1972. High interest rates were also used during this period to discourage investment in marginal activities.

While credit ceilings and high interest rates were successful in restricting investment in plant and capacity, they failed to control funds flowing into real estate, insurance, and services. Investment in these areas actually increased during this period. In general monetary policy was not very successful in controlling aggregate demand.

The monetary impact of fiscal policy during 1970-1972 was also a contributing factor to South Africa's inflation. During the 1970/71 fiscal year, the monetary expansion caused by the budget increased by almost 80 percent over that of the previous year, and by more than 60 percent in the year prior to that. Ironically, the monetary impact of fiscal policy declined substantially in 1972, the year in which the credit restraint measures were eased and credit ceilings abolished.

Clearly, excess demand inflation during this period was associated with increases in the money supply, and thus can be largely explained in terms of conventional aggregate demand analysis. Because monetary policy affected the components of aggregate demand dissimilarly, and was incapable of controlling consumption effectively, it was not capable of stemming the trend toward rising prices. Monetary policy did, however, retard capacity creating investment expenditure. The net effect of policy during this period was to, therefore, reduce aggregate supply vis a vis aggregate demand.

Cost-push inflation was undoubtedly present during the early 1970s. Wage increases took place and began to accelerate from an annual average rate of 10 percent between 1967 and 1970 to 12 percent from 1971 to 1973.

Imported inflation also became a significant factor in South Africa during 1971. The wholesale price index of imported goods increased to an average annual rate of 3 percent from 1965 to 1969, and at 9 percent from 1971 to 1973. This tendency gained momentum after 1973. From January to December 1974, the index increased by 26 percent. During the same period, the

consumer price index for goods and services increased
by 16 percent. It is evident that imported inflation
together with wage increases began to exert great
pressure on the country's price level after 1970.
More detailed analysis of these movements are needed,
however, before the relative contribution of each can
be ascertained.

Sources of South African Inflation

South African inflation can be best analyzed after
deriving four series of data.[8] The first series (Table
57), employment income per unit of output, was obtained
by dividing the current value of such income by an
index of real output. This series reflects movement
in nominal earnings that have been accrued in excess of
changes in physical productivity. The second series
does the same for the gross operation surplus (gross
profits plus other trading and property income).

Indirect taxes (less subsidies) of course contribute
to the final price of a good. The series derived here
reflects changes in the rates of net indirect tax on
domestic inflation (on the assumption that there is no
shift in the tax base between imported and domestically
produced goods, and that there are no net indirect
taxes on goods or services exported). Finally, the
import price index is based on South African customs
figures adjusted for oil imports.

By themselves, the indices do not enable one to
obtain a precise picture as to which costs have been
mainly responsible for the recent upsurge in prices
which has characterized the South African economy. For
analysis of this type, one must multiply the increase
in each series by the weight of that element in aggregate output. The resulting series (Table 58) shows the
percentage rise in overall domestic prices since 1970
attributable to each of the four elements.

Certain trends are apparent. First is the relatively small role (Table 58) played in South Africa's
inflation by increases in wage rates (at least until
mid-1974). The wage restraint in the boom period 1973-
1974 is of particular interest. Second, with regard to
indirect taxation, the tightening of import restrictions in November 1971 is apparent, as also is their
easing in 1972. The progressive reductions in sales

243

TABLE 57

SOUTH AFRICA: PRICE AND COST INDICES

(1970 = 100)

Period	Employment Income per Unit Output	Gross Operating Surplus per Unit Output	Indirect Tax Rates	Imports	GDP + Imports = GDE + Exports	Exports including Gold	Gross Domestic Expenditur
1970 III	103.1	97.5	98.4	100.5	100.7	100	100.8
1970 IV	104.0	99.4	98.9	99.9	101.5	100	101.8
1971 I	106.6	95.5	97.5	98.6	101.8	99	102.3
1971 II	108.1	102.7	97.2	105.1	105.6	100	106.8
1971 III	109.3	103.7	101.8	104.2	106.5	102	107.5
1971 IV	111.4	104.1	103.0	112.6	109.3	106	110.1
1972 I	110.7	108.2	110.5	118.1	111.7	113	111.4
1972 II	116.9	109.2	100.5	114.4	113.9	115	113.6
1972 III	117.9	117.9	101.8	125.6	119.3	123	118.3
1972 IV	118.8	126.2	102.1	125.6	122.6	130	120.6
1973 I	124.6	131.5	99.1	115.3	124.9	144	120.3
1973 II	127.2	135.3	102.7	115.3	127.6	155	121.6
1973 III	128.1	146.6	98.8	120.9	132.6	165	125.8
1973 IV	129.2	152.0	98.8	136.7	138.1	168	132.2
1974 I	128.5	159.2	93.3	151.6	142.6	214	130.2
1974 II	135.8	162.1	91.4	160.6	148.9	229	134.0
1974 III	149.5	160.8	86.9	160.0	154.8	224	142.1
1974 IV	152.1	166.1	78.9	172.1	159.8	246	144.8
1975 I	162.5	165.9	79.8	192.6	168.9	264	153.2
1975 II	163.4	173.5	84.5	195.3	172.2	249	159.3

Source: M. M. Courtney "Exchange Rates Policy and Imported Inflation" in M. L. Truv, Public Policy and the South African Economy (Capetown: Oxford University Press, 1976), p. 182.

TABLE 58

SOUTH AFRICA: COMPONENTS OF PERCENTAGE INCREASE
FROM 1970 III TO 1975 II IN DOMESTIC PRICES

Period	Employment Income per Unit Output	Gross Operating Surplus per Unit Output	Indirect Tax Rates	Imports	Residual	GDE
1970 III	1.5	-0.8	-0.1	0.1	0.1	0.8
1970 IV	2.0	-0.1	-0.1	0.0	0.0	1.8
1971 I	3.4	-0.6	-0.2	-0.2	-0.1	2.3
1971 II	4.4	1.2	-0.2	-1.3	0.1	6.8
1971 III	4.8	1.5	0.1	1.1	0.0	7.5
1971 IV	5.7	1.6	0.2	2.8	-0.2	10.1
1972 I	4.9	2.6	0.7	3.7	-0.5	11.4
1972 II	7.8	2.9	0.0	3.0	-0.1	13.6
1972 III	7.9	5.4	0.1	5.2	-0.3	18.3
1972 IV	7.9	7.8	0.1	5.0	-0.2	20.6
1973 I	9.6	8.7	-0.1	2.4	-0.3	20.3
1973 II	9.9	9.3	0.2	2.1	0.1	21.6
1973 III	10.1	12.6	-0.1	3.1	0.1	25.8
1973 IV	11.1	14.6	-0.1	6.5	0.1	32.2
1974 I	8.1	14.6	-0.5	8.1	-0.1	30.2
1974 II	10.7	15.0	-0.6	9.4	0.2	34.7
1974 III	17.4	15.3	-0.9	9.9	0.4	42.1
1974 IV	17.7	16.3	-1.4	11.8	0.4	44.8
1975 I	22.2	16.2	-1.4	15.7	0.5	53.2
1975 II	24.0	19.5	-1.1	17.0	-0.1	59.3

Source: M. M. Courtney, op. cit., p. 183.

245

duties during 1973 and in the 1974 budget are also significant in this regard. Third, the favorable impact on import prices of the appreciation of the rand in 1972-1973 is evident. As one would expect, the main impact of import price increases came with the 1973 oil price increases. Import prices, however, continued to increase strongly thereafter; from 1973 III to 1975 II, import price increases made up 41 percent of domestic inflation (versus 12 percent from 1970 II to 1973 III). As noted earlier, export prices rose nearly as fast in this second period, and the period as a whole saw an improvement in South Africa's terms of trade. In sum, imported inflation made a significant contribution to the increase in South African domestic prices after 1970, while wage increases were relatively unimportant in this regard.

Imported Inflation Versus Import Prices

The above analysis brings out an important distinction often overlooked in the analysis of inflationary mechanisms; i.e., the difference between inflation that is imported and inflation that stems from higher import prices. These two sources are often associated, but are not necessarily.

Based on inflationary trends in South Africa and those of her principal trading partners, it appears that imported inflation was relatively more substantial during the early rather than the late 1960s. During the latter years South Africa inflated more in step with her trading partners. During the 1970s, however, South Africa began inflating at a higher rate than did her trading partners. In relative terms, therefore, imported inflation accounted for a larger proportion of price increases during the early 1960s than in the early 1970s. This is confirmed by the fact that several South African exports became relatively expensive between 1960 and 1976. The most rapid divergence in the prices of South African exports and those of her trading partners (except for the U.K.) occurred after 1972. (Tables 59 & 60)

There was a conflicting trend however. The wholesale price index of imported goods increased rapidly during the 1970s, and this process gained momentum in later years (1973 was an exception).

TABLE 59

EXPORT PRICE INCREASES: SELECTED COUNTRIES, 1960-1976

(Average annual percent increase)

Year	South Africa	Germany	U.K.	United States	Japan
1960	-2.3	1.8	1.6	0.7	0.4
1961	1.2	0.3	0.5	1.9	-5.8
1962	-1.2	0.7	1.1	-0.6	-5.1
1963	2.3	1.3	2.7	0.2	-4.5
1964	3.4	0.9	1.3	1.1	-0.3
1965	2.2	2.2	2.8	3.2	-0.7
1966	1.1	1.8	3.7	3.1	0.0
1967	-3.2	-0.4	1.7	2.0	3.4
1968	0.0	-0.3	7.8	1.4	-0.5
1969	3.9	2.6	3.3	3.3	4.3
1970	1.6	2.6	6.6	5.6	5.7
1971	-3.1	2.5	5.8	3.4	0.3
1972	7.5	0.8	5.1	2.9	-1.8
1973	21.0	3.4	13.2	16.8	8.5
1974	23.9	14.9	28.4	27.0	37.9
1975	11.4	7.3	22.9	11.9	1.8
1976	18.6	3.8	20.7	3.6	-1.9

Source: International Monetary Fund, International Financial Statistics (May 1978).

247

TABLE 60

COMPARISON EXPORT PRICE INCREASES

SOUTH AFRICA AND MAJOR TRADING PARTNERS

(Average Annual Increase)

Period	South Africa	Germany	U.K.	United States	Japan
1960-1970	0.8	1.2	3.0	2.0	-0.3
1971-1974	12.3	5.4	13.1	12.5	11.2
1975-1976	15.0	5.6	21.8	7.8	-0.1

Source: Computed from Table 59.

To summarize, the price trends outlined above indicate that:

1. Foreign inflation became a less and less important factor in the South African inflation.

2. South African export prices increased vis a vis
those of her major trading partners.

3. The wholesale price of imported goods tended to
increase during the 1970s.

There is an obvious conflict in these trends. Re-
conciliation is possible, however, once the distinction
between imported inflation and rising import prices is
made.[9] It is possible that the increased prices of
imported goods were not exclusively caused by inflationary pressures abroad, but instead were the result of
domestic policies.

Given the fact that domestic inflation gained momentum simultaneously with the sharp increase in the price
of imported goods, it is quite likely that the devaluations of the rand generated cost-push inflation through
increasing the price of imported investment goods. Devaluation could, therefore, account for the three major
trends outlined above.

As noted above, the most important single category
of imports is machinery and transport equipment, while
primary products dominate the export trade. It is
evident that by raising the prices of imported goods,
a broad spectrum of industries would encounter increased
costs, many of which could be passed on to consumers.
This effect can be quantified as follows:

$$P = 6.1 + 0.20y_{-1} + 0.37W_{-2} + 0.37P_m \qquad r^2 = 0.97$$
$$ (1.32) \qquad (6.18) \qquad (14.03)$$

where P is the general price level, and y, W, and P_m
denote the real gross domestic product (lagged for one
year), the money wage rate (lagged for two years), and
import prices, respectively.

The parameter P_m indicates the total effects of the
foreign sector on the domestic price level. Because
its effect on the general price level is more direct
(since it is not lagged) than that of the other variables, its manipulation by the monetary authorities via

the exchange rate would have severe effects on the domestic price level.

The Mechanism of South African Inflation

The above analysis suggests a mechanism that may account for South Africa's recent inflationary patterns:

(1) $\dot{P} = a_1 + a_1 \dot{W}_T + a_2 \dot{P}_m$

(2) $\dot{W}_T = b_o + b_1 V_T^{-1} + b_2 \dot{Q}_T + b_3 \dot{P}$

The dot above each variable indicates the rate of change of the variable with respect to time. $\dot{P}$ denotes the consumer price index; $\dot{P}_m$ is the index of import prices; $\dot{W}_T$ is the average wage rate per unit labor input; $\dot{V}_T$ denotes the rate of unemployment, and $\dot{Q}_T$ is an index of productivity increase.

Equations (1) and (2) determine wages and prices simultaneously. The exogenous factor which affects the price level is import prices. In turn import prices depend on developments in international markets as well as changes in domestic and foreign exchange rates. Any change in imported prices is, therefore, assumed to affect the domestic price level and in turn (via equation 2) the level of wages.[10]

Devaluation means that most capital goods (which are essential for the country's economic growth and are not produced to a great extent locally) become more expensive. Given the country's dependence on imports for investment, their increased prices are easily transmitted throughout the economy. Movements in administrated prices (prices charged by public firms) illustrate the mutual relation between these forces.

Administered prices were very stable until the 1970s, with the weighted index (steel, electricity and railway tariffs) increasing as follows:

1960-1965	0.4 percent per annum
1966-1970	1.6 percent per annum
1971-1976	14.3 percent per annum

Given the monopolistic character of South Africa's public corporations, it appears highly probable that they increased their prices in order to maintain in the face of severe cost increases (the price index of imported goods rose 96.5 percent between 1972 and 1976) an adequate surplus for investment.

In sum, devaluation is of paramount importance in explaining how South Africa's inflation accelerated over that of her major trading partners during the 1970s. Devaluation introduced severe cost-push effects which operated immediately and directly via the investment process to affect most segments of the economy and thus the general price level.

Devaluation and Semi-Dependence

The major conclusion from the above analysis that devaluation of the South African rand led to a vicious cycle is that devaluation raised South Africa's rate of inflation above that of her trading partners. Conventional monetary theory would argue that the devaluation of the rand would lead to a decrease in the real value of the domestic money supply. This in turn would cause a decline in real domestic expenditure, resulting in an excess supply of goods produced domestically (but not traded in international markets). Lack of effective demand for these products would eventually cause a decline in their price relative to other goods.

This sequence of price changes did not take place in South Africa. Why?

Devaluation's failure to achieve balance of payments equilibrium (with a moderate rate of inflation) stemmed largely from a series of offsetting effects, many of which can be traced to policies initiated by the government subsequent to devaluation. According to modern trade theory, successful stabilization policy involves not only expenditure switching (from high priced imports to lower priced domestic products), but expenditure reducing policies as well. To be successful devaluation has to be combined with monetary and fiscal measures not only to support its impact via aggregate demand and the balance of payments, but also to prevent countervailing price changes.

With regard to fiscal policy, the authorities seemed

251

to have moved in the right direction following the 1971 devaluation of the rand. In the March 1972 budget, the Minister of Finance explicitly stated that a restrictive fiscal policy would be implemented. As evidence of his intentions, the rate of increase in government spending was reduced. The deficit and its associated expansion of the money supply declined relative to the previous year.

In 1975, however, fiscal policy was not consistent with that called for subsequent to devaluation. The authorities pursued an expansionary budget. The result was a record deficit as well as an increase in the money supply. The authorities also stimulated aggregate demand by: (1) granting income tax concessions; and (2) reducing sales taxes.

In general South African monetary policy has been even more inconsistent with devaluation than has its fiscal policy. Following the 1972 devaluation, interest rates were lowered and the credit ceilings which had been in operation since 1965 were terminated (in November 1972). Similarly in late 1973 following the devaluations and throughout 1974, stringent monetary policy was introduced even though economic theory recommends expansion.

In sum, the government did not pursue a consistent set of contractionary policies necessary to support the demand switching effects necessary for a successful devaluation. Consequently, the side effects of devaluation, increasing prices, were not duly checked. Devaluation contributed to the acceleration of inflation not only through its direct cost-push effect but also indirectly through the subsequent initiation of monetary and fiscal policies undertaken presumably to prevent increases in unemployment. High levels of aggregate demand and expansive fiscal and monetary policy led to increased investment, but very little switching; i.e., most of the investment was in the form of imports with little switching (because of the underdevelopment of the local capital goods industries) to domestic sources.

Finally, several institutional developments in South African labor markets built an inflationary bias into the price level. Between 1957 and 1975 real earnings per worker had increased at a rate of 3.0 percent per annum, while output per worker increased by only 2.7 percent per annum. Output per worker, of

252

course, is an indication of labor productivity. It is clear, therefore, that labor productivity increased at a fairly constant rate over the whole period. The growth in real earnings per worker were supported by a productivity increase until 1971-1972. Up to that time, therefore, no inflationary cost-push pressures could originate in the labor markets. After 1972 however, earnings per worker increased at a much faster rate than output per worker.

Several factors were responsible for these changing patterns. On the one hand South African companies deliberately tried to reduce the wage differential between the nation's various ethnic groups. Beginning in 1973 foreign companies with subsidaries in South Africa came under international pressure to raise the wages of their black employees. In this case, successive devaluations of the rand apparently induced cost-push effects (since firms were interested in maintaining and even increasing the real incomes of various groups of workers).

Conclusions

The pattern of South Africa's inflation can be easily summarized. During the early 1960s, South Africa inflated at a lower rate than most of her trading partners. From 1966-1969 she inflated more or less in step with her major trading partners. Accelerated inflation occurred during the early 1970s when South Africa tended to inflate at a higher rate than her trading partners.

Successive devaluations of the rand appear to be the most significant factors causing the country's inflation rate to accelerate in the 1970s. Devaluation apparently induced a number of incorrect policy responses on the part of the authorities. The detrimental effects of these factors on the South African economy were unprecedented.

While world inflation was, in the early 1970s, an important contributor to the increase in domestic prices, it was the devaluations of the rand and associated expansionary and fiscal policies pursued by the authorities that brought and maintained this rate above that of her major trading partners.

The experience of South Africa in the 1970s indicates that if the structure of a country's imports is as is the case with all the semi-dependent countries dominated by capital goods, an increase in the relative price of imports can be easily transmitted through the economy via the investment process. As in the case of Mexico, it is critical in these situations that the domestic rate of inflation not be allowed to increase over that being experienced by the country's major trading partners. Otherwise, it is likely that the inflation will get out of hand, and the resulting side effects such as balance of payments deficits will not be amenable to standard policy instruments.

Notes

1. The best source for background information on the South African Economy is L. Hobart Houghton, The South African Economy (Capetown: Oxford University Press, 1976). Much of the data presented below is taken from this source.

2. J. de V. Graaff, "International Inflation and the South African Economy," South African Journal of Economics (1967), pp. 327.

3. Analysis and descriptions of the inflationary patterns during this period are given in: I. M. Hume, "A Study of Inflation in South Africa (1946-66)," Bulletin of the Oxford University Institute of Economics and Statistics (1971), pp. 223-244; and T. Van Waasdijk, "Prices, Profits and Controls. A Study of Price Movements in South Africa 1962-65," mimeo, no date.

4. Some of these issues are discussed in J. J. J. Botha and P. D. F. Strydom, "Recent Policy Issues in the South African Economy," Three Banks Review (1975), pp. 7-31.

5. Desmond Lachman, "A Monetary Approach to the South African Balance of Payments," South African Journal of Economics (September 1975), pp. 271-283.

6. As reported in Botha and Strydom, op. cit.

7. There is some controversy over this point. Cf. M. L. Truu, "Inflation in the South African Economy," South African Journal of Economics (1975), pp. 446-470;

P. D. F. Strydom, "Inflation in South Africa I: Institutional Aspects," South African Journal of Economics (1976), pp. 115-138; and Dudley Kessel, "Non-White Wage Increases and Inflation in South Africa," South African Journal of Economics (1971), pp. 361-376.

8. The following is based largely on M. M. Courtney, "Exchange Rate Policy and Imported Inflation in South Africa," in M. L. Truu, ed., Public Policy and the South African Economy: Essays in Memory of Desmond Hobart Houghton (Capetown: Oxford University Press, 1976), pp. 179-206.

9. P. D. F. Strydom and H. Siehahn, "Cost-Push Inflation and Balance of Payments Theory," South African Journal of Economics (1977), pp. 257-267.

10. Ibid., pp. 259-260.

CHAPTER 14

CONCLUSIONS AND FINAL OBSERVATIONS

Introduction

It is now time to draw the various strands of the analysis together. Implicit in the discussion has been the conviction that an inflation of the magnitude experienced by the semi-dependent countries during the last few years is a serious economic and social problem. Not only do rapidly rising prices create a number of economic inefficiencies, but also an arbitrarily and often politically motivated (undemocratic) transfer of wealth. Ultimately, inflation results in greater worker militancy and tax payer revolts. Left unchecked, unanticipated inflation is likely to destroy most of the institutions crucial to the maintenance of economic and political democracy.

It would be serious enough if the inflationary process took place in stable societies sure of themselves and their values; the seriousness of the present inflation, however, is that it is taking place in societies such as Mexico's and South Africa's, which are either in the process of modifying or are re-examining many of the traditional values which were associated with stability and growth during the 1950s and 1960s.

It might seem obvious that the current inflation should be eliminated as quickly as possible. This is not necessarily the case. In fact there is some doubt as to whether an economy which experiences an inflation that has come to be expected should take steps to reduce the rate of price increase or whether it should simply seek to minimize its disruptive effects. The cost benefit approach[1] to anti-inflationary policy usually leads to the conclusion that in general it will pay a country to validate an on going expected inflation, rather than suffering the temporary recession that is likely to be the cost of eradicating it.

However, the broader set of considerations concerning the costs of inflation itemized above leads us to suspect that this conclusion will require modification when the costs of inflation are adequately allowed for, especially since fully anticipated inflations are analytical devices rather than actual occurrences in the

257

advanced countries let alone the semi-dependent group.

The Problem of Policy Implementation

Although international trade theory is customarily carried out under the assumption that relative goods prices in all countries are equalized through arbitrage, and although much of recent international monetary and macro theory has been developed on the assumption that nominal goods prices (measured in the same currency unit) are likewise equalized between countries, it is clear that monetary and fiscal policy has often been applied by governments on the assumption that the domestic price level is under their complete control. While this assumption might approximately be valid for the United States (an independent country by our classification) in the sense that is is big enough to affect the world price movements, it is not an appropriate one for the large group countries who are integrated into the international financial system (dependent countries) and only partially true for many of the less developed countries (semi-dependent countries).

In view of the potentially costly consequences of decisions based on the wrong premises, and the recent interest in inflation as a worldwide phenomenon, this study was undertaken in order to determine which groupings (independent, dependent, and semi-dependent) individual countries belonged and thus which policy responses to world inflation were appropriate for that country.

A major concern of the study has been the effect of inflation on an open semi-dependent economy and the ability of that economy to maintain, if it wishes, a less inflationary policy than its major trading partners (while maintaining fixed or relatively fixed exchange rates). We do not dispute the proposition that, in the long run, exchange rates reflect prices and, therefore, relative rates of inflation. At issue are the speed and timing of adjustments, the ability of countries to reduce or minimize the effects of foreign inflation, and the effects of the acceleration and deceleration of anti-inflationary policies commonly adopted by semi-dependent countries.

Although there is no logical and necessary relation between money supply, growth, and the size of the government deficit in semi-dependent countries, there usually

258

tends to be a strong relationship in practice. It is no accident that the unprecedented high money supply growth in Mexico during this decade was matched by an equally unprecedented deficit on the government accounts.

But it is not simply the size of the government deficit which is important. What in the long run may turn out to be of even greater importance is the size of the government sector itself. The larger the size of the government sector, the more unwieldy is government expenditure, the greater the proportion of the labor force is in unproductive activities (production of non-consumables), the more likely it is that the public sector prices will be set by political rather than economic criteria, and the easier it is for trade unions to control an industry. By purposely seeking, or un-willingly acquiescing in, an increased role for the government in the economy, countries like Mexico are stacking the cards against being able to readily control the public sector deficit (and thus ·the future growth of the money supply).

While inflation can be controlled only if the rate of growth of the domestic stock of money is brought under control, interest arbitrage means that this is not al-ways possible in developed countries. Semi-dependent countries though should be able to keep their money stock at or near the level consistent with a rate of inflation at or lower than the world rate.

Ultimately, however, those semi-dependent countries that peg their currencies to the dollar will find that their domestic rates of inflation are profoundly in-fluenced if not fully determined by the inflation, or absence of inflation, in the United States. It follows that if the U.S. cannot or will not control its rate of inflation, there is little hope for these semi-dependent countries in completely eradicating their domestic rates of inflation.

While there is widespread agreement on the serious-ness and unsatisfactory nature of the recent trends in inflation, output, capital accumulation, and employment in many of the semi-dependent countries, there is strong disagreement on what should be done. A very popular view, often embraced by the popular press, most govern-ments, and international organizations such as the OECD, is that inflation has become a problem because of a major change in attitudes, especially on the part of

259

organized labor.[2] In particular, a greater concern
with both equity and real income growth has led to
demands for a greater growth rate in money wages. These
in turn, with sluggish productivity growth and (relatively) constant profit margins, have led to a faster
rate of inflation. Growth rates of real output based
on this approach have been low because of a failure of
the market economy to deal adequately with intertemporal
allocation of investment. Uncertainly about the future
has resulted in entrepreneurs investing little and house
holds unwilling to save. On this view, the solution to
the problems of excessive inflation and sluggish growth
are simple and direct. Inflation has to be checked by
direct controls on wages. Prices also need to be controlled directly but only so as to make wage controls
acceptable to organized labor. Growth can only be improved by greater direct intervention. This can be
either in the form of investment subsidies or direct
state involvement in industry. Monetary and fiscal
policy in this view should be continued in an attempt
to achieve full employment, with adjustments in interest
rates, tax rates, and government spending levels the
most effective in this regard.

This essentially Keynesian approach to the causes
and cures of the world's current economic ills stands
in sharp contrast to the theoretical and empirical research outlined in the chapters above. Based on our
findings, it is clear that the acceleration of prices
in nearly all of the world's countries in the late 1960s
and early 1970s was caused (in an approximate sense) by
a rise in the rate of growth of the world money supply.
That money supply growth arose initially as a consequence of United States monetary policy, the centerpiece
of which was the pegging of nominal interest rates and
of a fiscal policy which saw both the scale of public
spending and the size of the country's public sector
deficits rise dramatically.

If, as demonstrated in the preceding chapters,
excessive monetary expansion is a necessary and sufficient condition for sustained inflation, this immediately
raises important problems in the analysis of the control
of inflation. In semi-dependent economies at least the
quantity of money is, to a certain extent, under the
control of government, or would be if the government so
desired. Why then has it not been controlled recently?
How might the governments of these countries be persuaded
to bring monetary expansion under control and to lengthen

the time horizon for their monetary policy decisions? These questions are representative of a large group of unsolved problems in the theory of inflation, problems on which the literature casts only a little light.

The literature that does exist is helpful when it comes to describing, for example, what happened in most economies after 1971, but it does not help us to understand why it happened. Semi-dependent countries which did not like the inflationary impact of world inflation were not forced, for example, to maintain fixed exchange rates or inflate their own economies. Clearly, if we do not know why governments generate (or permit) inflation, it is very difficult to produce arguments that might persuade them to act against continuous increases in the price level.

While there is the potential for successful anti-inflationary policy in the semi-dependent group, most of these countries have experienced inflation rates somewhat above those in the United States. There are two possible types of explanation for the failure of macro policies in semi-dependent countries to contain domestic inflation: (1) policies were not applied in a price stabilizing manner, either because governments and central banks did not care much about price stability or because they made forecasting errors (and other technical miscalculations); or (2) even though world economic conditions had changed, the authorities, even after initial failures, continued to pursue policies that had worked well in the rather low inflationary period of the 1950s and 1960s. These policies were, however, not compatible with the high inflationary world environment of the 1970s.

A third possible explanation for the prevalence of inflation was that many governments believed that there were gains from imperfectly anticipated inflation or losses from reducing the inflation rate in such a way that the change was not anticipated. Along these lines, gains could accrue to the government from the effect of inflation on tax revenues and on the value of government debt outstanding. Moreover, it is always possible that as imperfectly anticipated inflation accelerated there would be a fall in unempoyment. There is little evidence that at least the governments of South Africa and Mexico viewed the inflationary process in this manner. Clearly, however, this does not rule out the possibility that considerations of this type were not influential in structuring policy in each country. For our purposes here the first and second explanations seem to provide more realistic explanations of the developments in both countries after 1970.

Conditions of Growth and Stability

In the 1950s and early 1960s, the international economic system worked well. Most of the semi-dependent economies were linked by a pegged exchange rate to the U.S. dollar. Growth was relatively rapid and by current standards inflation was minor. The price stability of imported inputs and of imported substitutes for domestic finished goods (to say nothing of the goods with which their exports had to compete) put a powerful brake on any tendency for the domestic price level in these countries to deviate much from those in the rest of the world. In effect, economies like Mexico and South Africa imported price stability.

The environment was thus one that placed few demands on governments wishing to maintain price stability. Given this state of affairs, the Keynesian economic policies pursued in Mexico and South Africa during this period appeared extremely successful. At the time, however, it was not widely understood by these same authorities the degree to which that success depended upon a very special combination of circumstances: (1) the co-existence of a fixed exchange rate; and (2) a non-inflationary world economy. Ironically, in the late 1960s and early 1970s, the conventional wisdom among economists in both countries was that this very combination of circumstances, far from being the reason for their economies' successes, stood in the way of an even more successful implementation of Keynesian policies. During the early 1970s, expansionary fiscal policies were undertaken in both countries.

Stabilization Efforts in South Africa

Many South African economists believed that devaluation or the adoption of exchange rate flexibility would alleviate the balance of payments problem created by their fiscal policies. Clearly, they had not anticipated that their actions would lead to world price increases and eventually to an accelerating rate of inflation. The 1970s, therefore, saw inflation taking the place of

262

balance of payments deficits whenever domestic policy was over-expansionary.

The rationale for these expansionary policies was largely based on the assumption that the new exchange rate regime after 1971 would permit greater flexibility in their exchange rates. It was felt, at least in the case of South Africa, that as real income and employment increased following expansionary fiscal policy, any tendency for imports to rise would set in motion an exchange rate depreciation. If domestic wages (due to surplus non-white labor) and prices were relatively insensitive to aggregate demand, the result would be higher income. The deficit on the balance of payments could in turn be offset by a once and for all fall in the exchange rate. Hence, according to this line of thought, greater flexibility in exchange rates actually made it easier to carry out an efficient full employment policy (by removing the balance of payments constraint that so often in the past had caused expansions to terminate).

The analysis in the preceding chapters, however, has shown the weakness of this argument. As noted, if the money supply begins to grow more rapidly than the economy's willingness to absorb it (at going rates of inflation and real expansion), attempts of firms and households to rid themselves of unwanted cash will lead to an increase in their expenditure. To the extent that this increased expenditure is for domestic goods and services, domestic output will rise--and in doing so will put indirect upward pressure on prices. To the extent, however, that it is spent on imports, on the acquisition of foreign assets, or on domestically produced goods that would otherwise be exported, it puts immediate pressure on the exchange rate, and hence (if devaluation occurred) on domestic wages and prices.

The relevant argument for South Africa developed here is straightforward. When, as was often the case, prices were sluggish in responding to variations in supply and demand, changes in the rate of monetary expansion affected output (with fixed exchange rates) rather than prices. Because there was a pool of surplus labor, wages were slow to increase with greater aggregate demand. In this case the impact of expansionary policies fell mainly on the labor market. Because wages and prices responded slowly to increases in demand, output increased instead.

263

Given increased flexibility in exchange rates that characterized South Africa after 1971, pressures induced by expansionary policy fell directly on the foreign exchange market. The nature of that market, however, is very different from that of the labor market. It is dominated by specialist dealers whose function is to vary the prices of currencies on a continuous basis in response to changing supply and demand conditions.[3]

Such dealers make a living by being able to read such conditions better than the importers and exporters of particular goods with whom they deal. It, therefore, pays them to invest a great deal of time and resources in forming expectations about how market conditions are going to evolve over time. Since the rate of increase in the money supply is an important determinant of the behavior of the exchange rate, then the foreign exchange market is going to monitor it carefully and respond rapidly to its behavior. When the South African authorities increased aggregate demand too rapidly in the 1970s downward pressure was placed on the rand. Exchange markets began to mark down the rand in anticipation of increased inflation.

As inflation accelerated due to higher import prices (following devaluation), monetary expansion did not yield beneficial effects on real output or employment. The (limited) wage and price controls that were adopted did not offer any way around these problems. Nor would they have even if they were effective in controlling every price and wage bargain to which they could conceivably have been applied. Because the so-called domestic component of the price level was prevented from rising to absorb monetary expansion, a monetary disequilibrium was created which in turn exerted extra downward pressure on the exchange rate. The foreign component of prices rose in turn. Its rise, however, was more rapid than it otherwise would have been to compensate for the failure of the domestic component to rise as much as it should have.

The stabilization policies undertaken by South Africa in the early 1970s collapsed in the face of what was then widely termed imported inflation. Closer examination of the facts indicates, however, that inflation was the result of an excessively expansionary monetary policy (simultaneously with a set of controls which did, at least initially, succeed in holding back domestic components of the price index). In general,

South Africa's experience during the 1970s tends to confirm that income policies will work in semi-dependent
countries only if the conduct of monetary policy is such
as to make them unnecessary.

The Erosion of Monetary Autonomy in Mexico

The 1976 devaluation of the peso illustrates the
new problems faced by semi-dependent countries in the
1970s--the increased difficulty in pursuing stabilizing
monetary policy where the exchange rate, not the wage
rate, is the variable that will ultimately determine the
new level of prices and income.

Before the August 31, 1976, devaluation of the
Mexican peso, many economists argued that if the central
bank pursued a policy of steady increase in the country's
monetary base, the domestic rate of inflation would be
independent of resulting exchange rate changes.

Their claim was too strong. The exchange rate
collapse was a symptom of a decreased demand for the
peso. The fall in the demand for the peso and its devaluation were in themselves highly inflationary. The peso
depreciated by an amount far below what was justified
by differential Mexican-U.S. inflation differentials.
In the case of Mexico, the new depreciation of the peso
(undervaluation relative to what would be expected based
on its purchasing parity) can be explained by international capital flows.

Fears of political disorder and inconvertibility
were all responsible for a large capital outflow, beginning about a year before devaluation. In theory, depreciation of the peso need not have been inflationary--
the outcome depended on the supply of money remaining
constant and not affected by developments in the foreign
exchange market. In reality, however, external developments are always present and largely out of the authorities' control.

The Mexican peso crisis before and after the August
31 devaluation was (due to capital outflow) characterized
by the currency's external purchasing power declining
more than its internal.

The authorities were faced with the possibility
that tight monetary policy would set off a major

recession (caused by bankruptcies) or further inflation caused by the external depreciation of the peso. The central bank responded by injecting more money to relieve the credit and cost squeeze facing firms (brought about by rising import prices following the devaluation).

The Mexican devaluation and attempts at stabilization illustrates a problem faced by most semi-dependent countries. While the country has some degree of monetary autonomy (again due to the lack of capital market development), it may still be impossible once inflation is underway for the central bank to pursue a specific target expansion of the monetary base.

Movements in the ratio of non-resident to resident deposits make the desired target unattainable; i.e., the central bank cannot ignore the performance of its currency in the foreign exchange market. Even if the reserve money target is being strictly observed by the bank, external depreciation of the currency brought about by non-residents switching out of the currency may, in light of increased inflation, force the bank to expand the monetary base at a rate faster than desired, thus perpetuating the period of price increase and under certain circumstances even accelerating the rate of inflation.

Policy Implications

There are several implications stemming from the analysis in the preceding chapters. In terms of the conduct of demand management policy, the change in world economic conditions beginning in the late 1960s need not mean that the semi-dependent countries have less control over their economies. Nor must they accept higher rates of unemployment and lower rates of growth than were previously attained. The changing world environment does mean that these countries must gear the conduct of macro policy in general, and monetary policy in particular, toward achieving a target for the inflation rate. They can no longer rely on a fixed exchange rate and a stable world economy to contain their rate of domestic price increase. In accepting this situation, the semi-dependent countries must also recognize that expansionary monetary policy cannot be used to reduce unemployment.

The analysis above is consistent with the monetarist prediction that at a more or less constant inflation rate, semi-dependent countries can, by allowing some flexibility in their exchange rates, reduce unemployment to the natural unemployment rate. These countries must also give up expecting fiscal policy to have anything other than transitory reductions in unemployment. This does not mean that fiscal policies have no role in the economy. On the contrary, the less they are relied on for macro demand management, the more attention can be given to using them to influence resource allocation and the income distribution. Low unemployment need not be given up as a policy goal. The implication of the analysis is, however, that micro policies must bear the main burgen of achieving that goal.

To sum up, semi-dependent countries must use macro policies for attacking inflation. Monetary policy is the most effective tool in this regard. A gradual but steady reduction in the growth of the money supply is a necessary and sufficient condition for reducing the rate of inflation.

Notes

`   1.   The cost benefit approach was developed by E. S. Phelps. See his "Money Wage Dynamics and Labor Market Equilibrium," Journal of Political Economy (1968), pp. 678-711; and Inflation Policy and Unemployment Theory: The Cost Benefit Approach to Monetary Planning (New York: W. W. Norton & Co., 1972).

    2.   In particular see OECD, Inflation: The Present Problem (Paris: OECD, 1970); and Gardner Means et. al., The Roots of Inflation: The International Crisis (New York: Burt Franklin & Co., 1975).   The dust cover of this volume notes that "...prices rise not by levitation but by human action--usually action by those who profit from the change."

    3.   Cf. David Laidler, "How to Maintain Stability-- A Monetarist View," The Banker (April 1978), pp. 37-40, for a detailed analysis of these points.

BIBLIOGRAPHY

Achwartz, Anna J. "Secular Price Change in Historical Perspective," Journal of Money Credit and Banking (February 1973), p. 264.

Ally, Asgar. "The Potential for Autonomous Monetary Policy in Small Developing Countries," in Percy Selwin, ed., Development Policy in Small Countries. New York: Holmes & Meier Publishers, 1975, pp. 191-207.

Analisis--: The Mexican Economy. Mexico City: Publicaciones Ejecutivas de Mexico, 1972-1977 (annual).

Argy, Victor. "Structural Inflation in Developing Countries," Oxford Economic Papers (March 1970), pp. 73-85.

Aukrust, Odd. "Inflation in the Open Economy: A Norweigian Model," in Lawrence Krause and Walter Salant, eds., Worldwide Inflation: Theory and Recent Experience. Washington: Brookings Institution, 1977, pp. 107-176.

_____. "Prim I: A Model of the Price and Income Distribution Mechanism of an Open Economy," Review of Income and Wealth (March 1970).

Bardarich, Michael. "Inflation and Monetary Accommodation in the Pacific Basin," Federal Reserve Bank of San Francisco, Economic Review (Summer 1978), pp. 23-36.

Bennett, Robert. The Financial Sector and Economic Development. Baltimore: Johns Hopkins, 1965.

Bicanic R. "The Threshold of Economic Growth," Kyklos (No. 1, 1972), pp. 7-28.

Bisignano, Joseph. "The Interdependence of National Monetary Policies," Federal Reserve Bank of San Francisco, Business Review (Spring 1975), pp. 41-48.

Blain, Calvin. "Echeverria's Economic Policy," Current History (March 1977), pp. 124-127.

Blinder, Alan and Robert Solow. "Analytical Foundations of Fiscal Policy," in Alan Blinder et. al., The Economics of Public Finance. Washington: The Brookings Institution, 1974, pp. 3-115.

Botha, J. J. J. and P. D. F. Strydom. "Recent Policy Issues in the South African Economy," Three Banks Review (1975), pp. 7-31.

Branson, William. "A Keynesian Approach to Worldwide Inflation," in Lawrence Krause and Walter Salant, eds., Worldwide Inflation: Theory and Rcent Experience. Washington: The Brookings Institution, 1977, pp. 65-81.

Brewster, Havelock. "Economic Dependence: A Quantitative Interpretation," Social and Economic Studies (March 1973), pp. 90-95.

Brothers, Dwight and Leopoldo Solis. Mexican Financial Development. Austin: University of Texas Press, 1966.

Cagan, P. "The Monetary Dynamics of Hyper-Inflation," in Milton Friedman, ed., Studies in the Quantity Theory of Money. Chicago: University of Chicago Press, 1956, pp. 35-69.

Cardozo, Ovidio. "Flexible Exchange Rates, Inflation and Economic Development," World Development (No. 7, 1976), pp. 613-626.

Chenery, Hollis. "Targets for Development," in B. Ward, The Widening Gap. New York: Columbia University Press, 1971.

Cheng, Hang-Sheng and Nicholas P. Sargen. "Central Bank Policy Towards Inflation," Federal Reserve Bank of San Francisco, Business Review (Spring 1975), pp. 31-41.

Cochrane, Susan. "Structural Inflation and the Two-Gap Model of Economic Development," Oxford Economic Papers, 1973.

Conlisk, John. "Cross-Country Inflation Evidence on the Moneyness of Time Deposits," Economic Record (June 1970), pp. 222-229.

Courtney, M. M. "Exchange Rate Policy and Imported In-
flation in South Africa," in M. L. Truu, ed., Public
Policy and the South African Economy: Essays in
Memory of Desmond Hobart Houghton (Capetown: Oxford
University Press, 1976), pp. 178-206.

Davis, Tom E., ed., Mexico's Recent Economic Growth:
The Mexican View. Austin: University of Texas
Press, 1967.

Demas, William. "Economic Independence: Conceptual and
Policy Issues in the Commonwealth Caribbean," in
Percy Selwin, ed., Development Policy in Small Countries. New York: Holmes & Meier Publishers, 1975,
pp. 191-207.

Edgren, G., K. O. Flaxen and C. E. Odhner. Wage Formulation and the Economy. London: George Allen &
Unwin, 1973.

Emminger, Otmar. "The D-Mark in the Conflict Between
Internal and External Equilibrium, 1948-75," Princeton Essays in International Finance (June 1977).

Escobedo, Gilberto. "Formulating a Model of the Mexican
Economy," Federal Reserve Bank of St. Louis, Review
(July 1973), pp. 8-19.

_____. "Response of the Mexican Economy to Policy Ac-
tions," Federal Reserve Bank of St. Louis, Review
(June 1973), pp. 15-23.

Eshag, Eprime. "The Relative Efficacy of Monetary
Policy in Selected Industrial and Less-Developed
Countries," Economic Journal (June 1971), pp. 294-
305.

Fallon, Padraic. "The Future for Mexico," Euromoney
(April 1978), Supplement, pp. 1-35.

Felix, David. "Income Inequality in Mexico," Current
History (March 1977), pp. 111-114.

Frank, Charles and William Cline. "Measurement of Debt
Servicing Capacity: An Application of Discriminant
Analysis," Journal of International Economics (Aug-
ust 1971), pp. 327-344.

271

Frenkel, Jacob and Harry Johnson. "The Monetary Approach to the Balance of Payments: Essential Concepts and Historical Origins," in Jacob Frenkel and Harry Johnson, The Monetary Approach to the Balance of Payments Toronto: University of Toronto Press, 1976, pp. 21-45.

Friedman, Irving S. Inflation: A World-Wide Disaster. Boston: Houghton Mifflin, 1973.

Friedman, Milton. The Optimum Quantity of Money and Other Essays. Chicago: Aldine Publishing Company, 1969.

_____. "The Role of Monetary Policy," American Economic Review (March 1968), pp. 1-17.

Frisch, Helmut. "Inflation Theory 1963-1975: A Second Generation Survey," Journal of Economic Literature (December 1977), pp. 1289-1317.

Giersch, Herbert. "On the Desirable Degree of Flexibility of Exchange Rates," Weltwirtschaftliches Archiv (No. 2, 1973), pp. 191-213.

Girvan, Norman. "The Development of Dependency Economics in the Caribbean and Latin America: Review and Comparison," Social and Economic Studies (March 1973), pp. 1-33.

Goldsmith, Raymond. The Financial Experience of Mexico. Paris: OECD, 1966.

Gordon, Robert. "Recent Developments in the Theory of Inflation and Unemployment," Journal of Monetary Economics (April 1976), pp. 185-219.

Graaff, J. de V. "International Inflation and the South African Economy," South African Journal of Economics (1967), p. 327.

Griffiths, B. Mexican Monetary Policy and Economic Development. New York: Praeger Publishers, 1972.

Grubel, H. G. "Domestic Origins of the Monetary Approach to the Balance of Payments," Princeton Essays in International Finance (June 1976).

272

_____. "International Monetarism and the Expansion of World Inflation," Weltwirtschaftliches Archiv (No. 1, 1978).

Hansen, Roger D. Mexican Economic Development: The Roots of Rapid Growth. Washington: National Planning Association, 1971.

Harberger, Arnold. "The Dynamics of Inflation in Chile," in Charles Christ, ed., Measurement in Economics: Studies in Mathematical Economics in Memory of Yehuda Grunfeld. Stanford: Stanford University Press, 1963, pp. 219-250.

Herring, Richard and Richard Marston. National Monetary Policies and International Financial Markets. Amsterdam: North Holland Publishing Company, 1977.

Hinshaw, Randall, ed., Inflation as a Global Problem. Baltimore: Johns Hopkins Press, 1972.

Holtem, F. C. "A Model of Estimating the Consequences of an Income Settlement," Economics of Planning (No. 1-2, 1968).

Holtrop, M. W. Money in an Open Economy. Leiden: H. E. Stenfert Kroese, 1972.

Horvat, Branko. "The Relation Between Rate of Growth and Level of Development," The Journal of Development Studies (April/July 1974), pp. 382-394.

Houghton, D. Hobart. The South African Economy. Capetown: Oxford University Press, 1976.

Hume, I. M. "A Study of Inflation in South Africa (1946-66)," Bulletin of the Oxford University Institute of Economics and Statistics (1971), pp. 223-244.

Ingram, James C. Regional Payments Mechanisms: The Case of Puerto Rico. Chapel Hill: University of North Carolina Press, 1962.

_____. "The Case for European Monetary Integration," Princeton Essays in International Finance (1973).

International Monetary Fund. International Financial Statistics.

Iyoha, Milton Ame. "Inflation and Openness in Less Developed Economies: A Cross-Country Analysis," Economic Development and Cultural Change (October 1973), pp. 31-37.

Johnson, Harry. Inflation and the Monetarist Controversy. Amsterdam: North Holland Publishing Company, 1972.

____. "Secular Inflation and the International Monetary System," Journal of Money Credit and Banking (February 1973, Part II), p. 513.

____ and A. R. Nobay, eds., The Current Inflation. London: Macmillan, 1971.

Johnston, Roger. "Should the Mexican Government Promote the Country's Stock Exchange?" Inter-American Economic Affairs, 1972, pp. 45-60.

Kahn, M. S. "A Monetary Model of Balance of Payments," Journal of Monetary Economics (July 1976), p. 316.

Kessel, Dudley. "Non-White Wage Increases and Inflation in South Africa," South African Journal of Economics (1971), pp. 361-376.

Keynes, J. M. The General Theory of Employment, Interest and Money. London: Macmillan, 1936.

Kierzkowski, Henryk. "Theoretical Foundations of the Scandinavian Model of Inflation," The Manchester School (September 1976).

Kitamura, Hiroshi. "Trade and Capital Needs of Developing Countries and Foreign Assistance," Weltwirtschaftliches Archiv, (1966).

Koehler, John. Economic Policy Making with Limited Information: The Process of Macro-Control in Mexico. Santa Monica: The Rand Corporation, 1968.

Krause, Lawrence and Walter Salant, eds., World Wide Inflation: Theory and Recent Experience. Washington: The Brookings Institution, 1977.

Kwack, Sung. "Price Responses to Exchange Rate and Activity Changes," Paper Presented for the National Bureau of Economic Research Conference on Research in Income and Wealth, Price Behavior: 1965-1974, November 21-23, Washington, D.C.

Lackman, Desmond. "A Monetary Approach to the South African Balance of Payments," South African Journal of Economics (September 1975), pp. 271-283.

Laidler, David. "How to Maintain Stability--A Monetarist View," The Banker (April 1978).

_____ and J. M. Parkin. "Inflation: A Survey," The Economic Journal (December 1975), pp. 741-809.

Lall, Sanjaya. "Is Dependence a Useful Concept in Analyzing Underdevelopment?" World Development (Nos. 11 & 12, 1975), p. 799.

Lewis, W. A. The Theory of Economic Growth. London: Allan & Unwin, 1955.

Lundberg, Erik. Inflation Theory and Anti-Inflation Policy. Boulder, Colorado: Westview Press, 1977.

Magnifico, G. European Monetary Unification. New York: John Wiley Publishers, 1973,

Maris, Robin. "Can We Measure the Need for Development Assistance?" Economic Journal (September 1970).

Mayer, Tom. "The Relative Efficacy of Monetary Policy in Selected Industrial and Less-Developed Countries: A Comment," Economic Journal (December 1972), pp. 1368-1371.

Maynard, Geoffrey and W. van Ryckeghem. A World of Inflation. New York: Barnes and Nobel, 1975.

_____. "Argentina 1967-70: A Stabilization Attempt that Failed," Banca Nazionale del Lavoro, Quarterly Review (December 1972).

Means, Gardiner et. al. The Roots of Inflation: The International Crisis. New York: Burt Franklin & Co., 1975.

Meiselman, David. "Worldwide Inflation: A Monetarist View," in Patrick Boarman and David Tuerck, eds., World Monetary Disorder: National Policies Vs. International Imperatives. New York: Praeger Publishers, 1976, pp. 21-65.

275

_____ and Arthur Laffer, eds., The Problem of Worldwide Inflation. Washington: American Enterprise Institute for Public Policy Research, 1975.

Muller, Marine. "Structural Inflation and the Mexican Experience," Yale Economic Essays (Spring 1965).

Newlyn, W. T. "Monetary Analysis and Policy in Financially Dependent Economies," in I. G. Stewart, ed., Economic Development and Structural Change. Edinburg: Edinburg University Press, 1969, pp. 71-82.

Nunnally, Jum. Psychometric Theory. New York: McGraw Hill, 1978.

Opie, Redvers. "The Last Informe of President Echeverria: Inflation and Devaluation," American Chamber of Commerce of Mexico, Economic Report (September 10, 1976).

Organization for Economic Cooperation and Development. "The International Transmission of Inflation," OECD Economic Outlook, Special Section (July 1973), pp. 81-96.

_____. Inflation: The Present Problem. Paris: OECD, 1970.

Overall, John and C. James Klett. Applied Multivariat Analysis. New York: McGraw Hill, 1972.

Parkin, Michael and Alexander Swoboda. "Inflation: A Review of the Issues," The Graduate Institute of International Studies, Discussion Paper No. 10, Geneva (June 1976).

_____. "Inflation: A Review of the Issues," in Erik Lundberg, Inflation Theory and Anti-Inflation Policy, Boulder, Colorado: Westview Press, 1977, pp. 7-10.

Parkin, Michael and George Zis, eds., Inflation in the World Economy. Manchester: Manchester University Press, 1976.

_____, eds., Inflation in Open Economies. Toronto: University of Toronto Press, 1976.

Phelps, E. S. Inflation Policy and Unemployment Theory: The Cost Benefit Approach to Monetary Planning. New York: W. W. Norton & Co., 1972.

_____. "Money Wage Dynamics and Labor Market Equilibrium,"
Journal of Political Economy (1968), pp. 678-711.

Polak, J. J. "Monetary Analysis of Income Formation and
Payments Problems," in H. Robert Heller, ed., The
Monetary Approach to the Balance of Payments. Wash-
ington: International Monetary Fund, 19771.

_____ and Loretta Boissonneault. "Monetary Analysis of
Income and Imports and Its Statistical Application,"
in H. Robert Heller, ed., The Monetary Approach to
the Balance of Payments. Washington: International
Monetary Fund, 1977, pp. 133-146.

Prais, S. J. "Some Mathematical Notes on the Quantity
Theory of Money in an Open Economy," pp. 147-162, in
H. Robert Heller, ed., The Monetary Approach to the
Balance of Payments. Washington: International
Monetary Fund, 1977, pp. 147-162.

Rao, V. V. Bhanoji, ed., Inflation and Growth. Singapore:
Samford College Press, 1974.

Reynolds, Clark. The Mexican Economy. New Haven: Yale
University Press, 1970.

_____. "Why Mexico's Stabilizing Development was Actually
Destabilizing," Paper presented to the Joint Economic
Committee, Subcommittee on Inter-American Relation-
ships Hearing on Recent Developments in Mexico and
Their Economic Implications for the United States.
Washington, D.C.: January 17, 1977, p. 8.

Robinson, Austin. The Economic Consequences of the Size
of Nations. London: Macmillan, 1963.

Santos, T. dos. "The Structure of Dependence," American
Economic Review (May 1970), pp. 231-236.

Schotta, Charles. "The Money Supply, Exports, and Income
in an Open Economy: Mexico 1939-63," Economic Development and Cultural Change (July 1966), pp. 458-70.

Schwartz, A. J. "Secular Price Changes in Historical
Perspective," Journal of Money Credit and Banking
(February 1973).

Sears, D. "A Theory of Inflation and Growth Based on Latin American Experience," *Oxford Economic Papers* (June 1962).

Selden, Richard. "Monetary Growth and the Long-Run Rate of Inflation," *American Economic Review* (May 1975), p. 125.

Shaw, Edward. "International Money and International Inflation: 1958-1973," Federal Reserve Bank of San Francisco, *Business Review* (Spring 1975), pp. 5-17.

Shinkai, Yoichi. "A Model of Imported Inflation," *Journal of Political Economy* (July-August 1973).

Sims, Christopher. "Money, Income, and Causality," *American Economic Review* (September 1972).

Stevens, Willy J. *Capital Absorptive Capacity in Developing Countries.* Leiden: A. W. Sijthoff, 1971.

Strydom, P. D. F. "Inflation in South Africa I: Institutional Aspects," *South African Journal of Economics* (1976), pp. 115-138.

_____ and H. Siehahn. "Cost-Push Inflation and Balance of Payments Theory," *South African Journal of Economics* (1977), pp. 257-267.

Sunkel, O. "Big Business and Dependencia," *Foreign Affairs* (April 1972), pp. 517-534.

_____. "National Development Policy and External Dependence in Latin America," *Journal of Development Studies* (October 1969), pp. 23-48.

_____. "Translation Capitalism and National Disintegratio in Latin America," *Social and Economic Studies* (March 1973), pp. 132-176.

Swamy, Subramanian. *Indian Economic Planning.* New York: Barnes and Nobel, 1971.

Swoboda, Alexander K. "Causes and Origins of the Current Worldwide Inflation," in Erik Jundberg, ed., *Inflation Theory and Anti-Inflation Policy.* Boulder, Colorado: Westview Press, 1977.

Takayama, Akira. International Trade: An approach To The Theory. New York: Holt, Rinehart, and Winston, 1972.

Taylor, Lance. "Short-Term Policy in Open Semi-Industrialized Economics--The Narrow Limits of the Possible," Journal of Development Economics (September 1974), pp. 85-104.

Thomas, Clive. Monetary and Financial Arrangements in a Dependent Monetary Economy: A Study of British Guiana 1945-1962. Kingston, Jamaica: Institute of Social and Economic Research, 1965.

_____. The Structure Performance and Prospects of Central Banking in the Caribbean. Kingston, Jamaica: Institute of Social and Economic Research, 1972.

Triffin, R. and H. Grubel. "The Adjustment Mechanism to Differential Rates of Monetary Expansion Among the Countries of the European Economic Community," Review of Economics and Statistics (November 1969), pp. 486-491.

Truu, M. L. "Inflation in the South African Economy," South African Journal of Economics (1975), pp. 446-470.

Turnovsky, S. J. and Andre Kaspura. "An Analysis of Imported Inflation in a Short-Run Macroeconomic Model," Canadian Journal of Economics (August 1974), pp. 355-380.

Van de Geer, John. Introduction to Multivariate Analysis for Social Sciences. San Francisco: W. H. Freeman, 1971.

Waasdijk, T. Van. "Prices, Profits and Controls: A Study of Price Movements in South Africa 1962-65," Mimeo, no date.

Weintraub, Sidney. "The Price Level in the Open Economy," Kyklos (No. 1, 1977), pp. 22-37.

Whitman, Marina V. N. "Economic Openness and International Financial Flows," Journal of Money, Credit and Banking (November 1969), pp. 727-749.

Wilford, D. Sykes. Monetary Policy and the Open Economy: Mexico's Experience. New York: Praeger Publishers, 1977.

_____ and W. T. Wilford. "Fiscal Revenues in Mexico: A Measure of Performance, 1950-73," Public Finance (1976), pp. 103-114.

_____. "Monetary Approach to Balance of Payments: On World Prices and the Reserve Flow Equation," Weltwirtschaftliches Archiv (No. 1, 1977), pp. 31-39.

Willms, Manfred. "Comment on Laidler and Nobay," in E. Claassen and P. Salin, eds., Recent Issues in International Monetary Economics. Amsterdam: North Holland Publishing Company, 1976, pp. 309-310.

World Bank. World Bank Tables 1976. Baltimore: The Johns Hopkins University Press, 1976.

ABOUT THE AUTHOR

ROBERT E. LOONEY is Associate Professor of International Economics at the Monetery Institute of Foreign Studies. He has been a faculty member of the University of California at Davis, the University of Santa Clara, and is Adjunct Professor of National Security Affairs at the U.S. Naval Postgraduate School.

He was a development economist at the Stanford Research Institute and senior economist at Louis Berger International. Currently he is a senior associate at Systan, Inc.

Dr. Looney has served as an economic adviser to the governments of Iran, Panama, Mexico, and Saudi Arabia. His publications include The Economic Development of Iran (Praeger, 1973), Income Distribution in Semiindustrialized Countries (Praeger, 1975), The Economic Development of Panama (Praeger, 1976), Iran at the End of the Century: A Hegelian Forecast (Lexington, 1977), A Development Strategy for Iran Through the 1980s (Praeger, 1977), and The Mexican Economy: A Policy Analysis (Westview, 1978).

Dr. Looney received his B.S. degree in Chemistry and Geography and Ph.D. degree in Economics from the University of California at Davis.